Ninety Feet

from

Fame

Ninety Feet

from

Fame

*Close Calls with
Baseball Immortality*

MIKE ROBBINS

CARROLL & GRAF PUBLISHERS
NEW YORK

NINETY FEET FROM FAME: *Close Calls with Baseball Immortality*

Carroll & Graf Publishers
An Imprint of Avalon Publishing Group Inc.
245 West 17th Street, 11th floor
New York, NY 10011

Copyright © 2004 by Mike Robbins

First Carroll & Graf edition 2004

Library of Congress Cataloging-in-Publication Data is available.

ISBN: 0-7867-1335-6

All interior art Copyright © Transcendental Graphics/ruckerarchive.com

Printed in the United States of America
Interior design by Paul Paddock
Distributed by Publishers Group West

For my parents, Stephen and Mary Robbins, whose research and proofreading assistance was very much appreciated. I'm told they also played some part in my birth and upbringing.

ACKNOWLEDGMENTS

The author would like to thank all those who provided assistance with this project. That list begins with Clint Willis, my editor, followed by Claudette Burke, Gabriel Schechter, Tim Wiles, and Freddy Berowski in the research department at the Baseball Hall of Fame Library in Cooperstown, New York. Also deserving special note are author John Holway, for his valuable insight into the forgotten stars of the Negro Leagues; Frank Russo, creator of the www.thedeadballera.com web site, for his help tracking down players' cause of death; and Cappy Gagnon, who always has been willing to share his ample files on Lou Sockalexis and other matters related to college baseball.

Among the many other baseball researchers and friends who offered support or suggestions are Paul Adomites, Richard Beverage, Clem Comly, Bill Deane, Rob Edelman, Ron Henry, Bill Hickman, Father John Hissrich, Tom Hufford, Rodney Johnson, Maxwell Kates, Herm Krabbenhoft, Bill Maisannes, Wayne McElreavy, Barry Mednick, Dorothy Mills, Cyril Morong, Rod Nelson, Michael Olenick, John Pastier, David Paulson, Eric Sallee, Jim Sandoval, Matt Scease, Steve Steinberg, Richard Thurston, Jules Tygiel, and Mark Wernick.

Special thanks go to Brett Wickard, owner of Bull Moose Music, for providing the greatest gift one person can give another: the emergency loan of a used, 15-inch color computer monitor. Finally, and most of all, the author would like to thank Shondra Guilbault, who for the duration of this project voiced only mild complaint when the author spent an evening in front of a ballgame and referred to it as "research."

NOTE ON STATISTICS

Old baseball statistics occasionally are revised when researchers discover errors in the historical record. In situations where a long-standing stat is in conflict with an amended figure, I've used the number that seems more likely to be correct, rather than the number that might be more familiar. Statistics on current players are updated through the 2003 season.

For all sad words of tongue or pen,
The saddest are these: 'It might have been!'
                    —John Greenleaf Whittier, Quaker poet

It's hard to win a pennant . . .
but it's harder to lose one.
                    —Chuck Tanner, Pirate manager

★ CONTENTS ★

INTRODUCTION

The trouble with fame is we've heard it all before.

We've heard about DiMaggio's streak and Mays' catch. We've heard about Buckner's error and Brooksie's glove and Aaron's 755. We've heard about Ted Williams and Jackie Robinson and Babe Ruth and Sandy Koufax and all the other celebrated players and celebrated plays that make up baseball's mythology. There's a reason Bobby Thomson's Shot Heard 'Round the World is called the Shot Heard 'Round the World—everybody heard about it.

This book is about none of those men, and none of those moments. Rather, it's about the players who fell just short of a place in baseball lore. They're the men who got big hits in big games, only to see their efforts eclipsed by even bigger hits an inning later. They're the men who had great careers in leagues that have long since been forgotten. They're the men who came up inches short of setting records . . . who suffered injuries . . . who were called off to war . . . who never played for a contender. There are, it seems, many more ways to fall short of fame than there are to achieve it.

It is possible to fail in one's pursuit of a notable accomplishment yet still become famous. Pirates pitcher Harvey Haddix remains well known for *not* throwing a perfect game in 1959. As most baseball fans are aware, his teammates couldn't get him a run and he lost the perfect game in the 13th inning. But such examples are rare. Usually when a player misses out on glory, his story fades from collective memory. As Hall-of-Fame outfielder Frank Robinson once noted, "close don't count in baseball."

Eleanor Gehrig, widow of Yankee first baseman Lou Gehrig, wrote in her autobiography, *My Luke and I*, that she once asked her husband what the difference was between a player in the high minors and one in the major leagues. "One step," Lou answered. In baseball the difference between famous and forgotten can be just as fine as that line between the majors and the minors: one step, one hit, one base.

—Mike Robbins

Hal W. Smith

PART I

THE POSTSEASON

Baseball provides players with two paths to fame. The first is to have a long and successful career. Rack up enough hits, homers, wins, or what-have-you and you'll get that plaque in Cooperstown and the lifetime of lucrative endorsement deals that comes with it. But for those who lack the talent or patience for this long-term approach, there is an alternative. All it takes is one swing of the bat . . . and some exceptional timing. In the moments required for a baseball to travel 300 feet, Bobby Thomson becomes BOBBY THOMSON, Bucky Dent becomes BUCKY DENT (BUCKY F———ING DENT in Boston). For these men, fame rests not so much on what they did as when they did it—with the leaves changing color and a season on the line.

Unfortunately for a wretched few, sudden fame works in reverse as well. Our autumn fields are full of goats. Many of these goats once were considered skilled ballplayers and, no doubt, fine human beings. But these players each made mistakes so poorly timed that a single failure trumped a lifetime of success. Such was the fate of Fred Merkle in 1908, Bill Buckner in 1986, and an assortment of unfortunates in between. October baseball has produced more instant goats than instant heroes, an endless procession of Vinko Bogatajs in flip-down sunglasses, forever missing that ski jump and tumbling down the side of the mountain while we hum the theme from Wide World of Sports.

Thomson and Dent, Merkle and Buckner—their stories are well known to baseball fans. Lost in the shuffle are those ballplayers who seemed to have done everything necessary to become instant heroes, only to come up short . . . and those players who appeared destined to live with scarlet "E"s pinned to their uniforms, only to make narrow escapes with their reputations more or less unscathed. Also forgotten are those who found themselves at the plate in a hero-making situation, but failed to deliver.

These are the players who might have been October legends . . . if only.

1
OCTOBER'S NEAR-HEROES

They delivered the key hits when they were most needed. They pitched the best games of their lives in the biggest games of their lives. But somehow, something went wrong. These men did all that is required of a baseball hero. It simply wasn't meant to be.

THE OTHER HAL SMITH

The perfect fame-generating hit is easy to imagine. It's a home run, of course. Legends aren't built on singles. It comes in the seventh game of the World Series. It comes with two outs in the bottom of the 9th. And it takes a team—preferably an underdog—straight from impending defeat to instant victory. (Ideally, one also might ask to have the bases loaded, a three-run deficit, and a full count, but there's no point getting greedy.)

Such homers convey instant immortality on their authors—or they would, if anyone had ever taken the trouble to hit one. In the long history of the World Series, no one has ever hit this perfect home run. Who's come the closest? That's open to debate, but two hits seem particularly strong contenders. One was a bottom-of-the-9th, *no*-out, *solo* homer in a *tied* game seven that sent an underdog to victory. The other was a bottom-of-the-*8th*, two-out, three-run homer that took an underdog from within spitting distance of defeat and left it a mere three outs from the win. Which hit was more dramatic? More important? More deserving of instant fame? History has selected the former. That homer belongs to Bill Mazeroski, who in 1960 used it to elevate himself from "promising defensive second baseman" to "instant legend." As for the other near-perfect hit—the 8th-inning, three-run homer—both the hit itself and the man who produced it are today footnotes in baseball history.

In 1960, baseball fans knew Hal Smith as the two-time All-Star catcher of the St. Louis Cardinals. Those who followed the game closely also might have been aware of another Hal Smith, a journeyman catcher and sometimes third baseman who in 1960 found himself with the Pittsburgh Pirates.

In the long history of major league baseball, there have been three men known by the name Hal Smith. One was a pitcher who made 51 appearances for the Pirates in the early 1930s. The other two played the same position (catcher) at the same time (the late 1950s and early 1960s). Being the one of this matched pair of Hal Smiths who'd played exclusively on what might charitably be described as mediocre teams was not a great way to garner lasting fame, or even to ensure oneself good tables at popular restaurants. But such was the fate of Harold Wayne Smith five years into his major league career.

Once a rising prospect in the farm system of the powerful New York Yankees, Smith hit .370 in spring training in 1954 and appeared poised to take the Yankees backup catching job behind Yogi Berra. "I had made the club," Smith would later tell the *St. Louis Post-Dispatch*. "Then I contracted glandular fever. I was in the hospital for ten days, off my feet for nine days. I lost 13 pounds and had a 107 temperature five days. When I got out of the hospital, I had to take spring training all over."

Smith returned to the minors, and late that year was sent to the Baltimore Orioles in an 18-player trade. The Yankees netted Bob Turley in the deal (not to mention Don Larsen, a man who found his own instant October fame with a World Series perfect game in 1956). The Orioles netted next to nothing, as was the franchise's long-standing custom in trades dating back to its pre-relocation days as the St. Louis Browns.

The Orioles struggled in 1955 despite generally solid play from Smith. When the team finally started to show some signs of life in 1956, the young catcher promptly was dealt to an even worse club, the Kansas

City Athletics. It is difficult to express just how unlikely it would have been for a Kansas City Athletic of the mid-1950s to become a post-season hero. The Athletics of that era were a club that, in a good year, had a fighting chance to be better than the Washington Senators. The Senators were a club fortunate to play in an era when there was little talk of contraction. Kansas City was not going to the World Series.

Meanwhile, baseball's better-known Hal Smith, Harold *Raymond* Smith, had twice been named an All-Star. And he played for the popular and generally competitive St. Louis Cardinals just across the state from Kansas City. The Athletics' Hal Smith was stuck in another player's shadow. So it was hardly front-page news when the Pirates acquired Kansas City's Hal Smith as a possible backup for their All-Star backstop, Smoky Burgess, in December of 1959. The Pittsburgh media made light of the deal, noting that Smith increased the number of receivers the Pirates had under contract to five. "Pirate officials," wrote the *Pittsburgh Press,* "are in the process of cornering the market on catchers."

For Smith the trade must have felt like a demotion. He was moving from a team where he knew he'd get his at-bats to one with an All-Star at catcher and four men fighting him for the second-string job. Pittsburgh also had a former All-Star, Don Hoak, at Smith's other position, third base.

The Pirates weren't even a glamorous club. While a trade anywhere this side of Washington represented a step up the baseball food chain from Kansas City, Smith had little reason to believe he was joining a pennant contender. Great things had been expected of the Pirates in 1959, following a strong second-place finish in 1958. But the team had skidded to a solidly mediocre 78-76 mark. Incidentally, much of the blame for the failure of the 1959 Pirates was heaped upon a young infielder named Bill Mazeroski. Maz had let his weight balloon in '59 and his skills seemed to deflate as a result. Pittsburgh's expectations were low for 1960.

If Smith did harbor concerns about his new baseball home, they would turn out to be partly justified. The trade would cost him playing time—Smith got into only 77 regular-season games in 1960, easily the lowest total to that point in his career. But everything else went Smith's way. He easily outdistanced the competition for the number two catching job and soon was in a virtual platoon with Burgess. Better yet, the Pirates were considerably better than expected. When the regular season ended, Pittsburgh had won 95 games and the National League pennant. The Other Hal Smith was going to the World Series. As was traditional at the time, the American League would be represented by the New York Yankees, the juggernaut that had traded Smith away six years before.

No one figured Pittsburgh would offer much of a challenge to the mighty Yankees, but the 1960 World Series turned out to be one of the most compelling in the sport's history. While the Yankees pounded Pittsburgh by a combined 38–3 score in games two, three, and six, Pittsburgh eked out close victories in games one, four, and five, sending the Series to a deciding game seven.

FAME'S A GAME OF INCHES

On September 20, 1973, Pirate outfielder Dave Augustine missed by a matter of inches, becoming perhaps the most obscure ballplayer ever to deliver a key pennant-race home run. The Pirates started the day in first, a game and a half ahead of the Mets, in a tight five-way battle for the National League East title. Pittsburgh seemed poised to increase their lead over New York to two and a half when pinch runner Augustine, a rarely used rookie called up earlier in the month when the rosters expanded, scored the go-ahead run in the top of the 9th in a crucial game against the Mets. But New York tied the game in the bottom of the 9th on a two-out pinch double from backup catcher Duffy Dyer. The game remained tied into the 13th, when with two outs and Richie Zisk on first, Augustine hit what by many accounts appeared to be a certain home run to left. Only the ball struck the very top of the outfield wall and stayed in the park. A fine Met relay cut down Zisk at the plate, and New York won the game in the bottom of the 13th. When the season ended, New York was two games ahead of Pittsburgh—the difference between winning and losing that September 20 contest.

Augustine had missed his chance at glory. Even his close call didn't get much play in the papers, since there was a bigger story from Shea that day. Willie Mays had announced his retirement before the game. "Maybe I'll cry tomorrow," said Mays when he spoke with the press. It was a sentiment Dave Augustine no doubt shared after his home run bid fell just short. Augustine would get just 29 at-bats in his major league career. He never homered; he never drove in a run.

Smith had caught in two of the first six games—both Yankee blowouts—and managed a pair of meaningless singles in seven at-bats. But he wasn't scheduled to catch game seven, not with Bob Turley throwing for the Yanks. Turley was the key figure in the trade that had sent Smith to a baseball wasteland in 1954. He was also a right-hander. Left-handed-hitting All-Star catcher Smoky Burgess would be behind the plate for the Pirates. Smith had had a fine season, but he looked likely to watch its final game from a seat in the bullpen. Smith watched as Pittsburgh built an early 4–0 advantage, and he watched as New York stormed back to reclaim the lead in the 6th. The Yankees added a pair of runs in the top of the 8th to push their advantage to 7–4 with just six outs to go.

The 36,000 fans packed into Pittsburgh's Forbes Field were "enveloped in a deep and profound silence," wrote *The New York Times* the next day. The Pirates hadn't won a World Series since 1925, and it didn't look likely they'd do so this year. Instead, the Yankees were about to win their 15th title in the past 25 seasons. Pirate fans might have been depressed, but few could have been surprised.

What happened next *was* surprising. Down three runs, the Pirates opened the bottom of the 8th with three straight singles. After a pitching change, a sacrifice, and a fly out, Pittsburgh trailed by two with runners on second and third, two out, and future Hall-of-Famer Roberto Clemente at the plate. Clemente grounded to first, and for a moment it seemed the Yankees had escaped the 8th with their lead intact. But pitcher Jim Coates was slow in covering the bag, and the speedy Clemente legged out an infield hit. New York's lead was down to one. Pittsburgh was inching closer, but the Yankees were just four outs from victory.

Due up after Clemente was the hot-hitting Smokey Burgess' spot in the order. Burgess had six hits in 18 at-bats so far in the Series, a .333 average that was tops among Pirate regulars. With a runner at third, even a single would tie the game up. There was just one problem: The hot-hitting Smoky Burgess no longer was in the hot-hitting Smokey Burgess' spot in the order. Burgess had led off the bottom of the 7th with a single and been pulled from the game for a pinch runner. (It would be a mistake to infer from the man's nickname that "Smokey" Burgess had anything approaching smoking speed. The aging catcher ran like an aging catcher.)

So with the season on the line, Hal Smith, *this* Hal Smith—a man seemingly destined to be remembered as *The Other* Hal Smith by those few who chose to remember him at all . . . a man in the game by circumstance, not design . . . a man who'd never hit for much power . . . a man the Yankees had cast off from their rich farm system a few years before—stepped to the plate.

Naturally, he homered. Smith crushed a Jim Coates pitch over the left field wall, turning the Pirates' impending defeat into a probable victory with just three Yankee outs to go. This secondary Hal Smith was on the verge of baseball stardom. Conversely, Jim Coates, the Yankee pitcher who had failed to cover first then coughed up a gopher ball, was on the verge of infamy. *The New York Times* would write of Coates' defensive mistake, "It was a rock . . . that was to grow bigger than Gibraltar." It was also a rock that was destined to be all but forgotten over the years, because of what happened in the 9th.

Bob Friend, who'd started and lost game two of the Series for the Pirates, then started and lost game six just the day before this game seven showdown, was summoned from the bullpen to preserve Pittsburgh's 9–7 lead. Friend was perhaps Pittsburgh's best starter, but he'd appeared in relief exactly once in the past three seasons. That is, not counting his relief appearance in the 1958 All-Star game—in which he'd taken the loss.

Friend would last exactly two batters, and both would single. With the tying runs on base, Pirate manager Bill Virdon went back to the bullpen for another starter, Harvey Haddix, a man who'd achieved lasting fame the year before by proving that perfection isn't always enough—he'd thrown a 12-inning perfect game, only to lose in the 13th. Haddix managed to get 1960 American League MVP Roger Maris— a man who would find his own fame in the coming season with 61 home runs—to foul out to Smith. With one out, Mickey Mantle singled to right-center, tightening the score to 9–8 and sending the tying run to third. Yogi Berra followed with a hard grounder to first. Had the Pirates regular first baseman, the notoriously poor-fielding Dick Stuart, been in the game, an error hardly would have been a surprise. But the Pirates had sure-handed veteran Rocky Nelson at first. Nelson fielded the ball cleanly, and with the slow-footed Berra plodding toward first, appeared in excellent position to start a Series-ending double play.

Only rather than throw to second, Nelson headed to first, apparently intending to retire Berra and then throw to second to double up Mantle. If this was his plan, it was a poor one. Stepping on first would have eliminated the force on Mantle. The Pirates might have turned the double play, but if Mantle could elude the tag until the runner on third crossed the plate, the tying run would count. As it happened, Mantle had an unusual idea of his own. Rather than run to second, he dove back into first. Trouble was, Mantle wasn't entitled to first. According to the rules, he was forced to try for second. All Nelson had to do was tag Mantle before touching first base and the Series would be over.

He didn't.

Nelson stepped on first before tagging Mantle, negating the force. Mantle was safe, and the tying run scored. Numerous explanations have been offered for this play over the years, some concluding that Mantle thought the ball was caught on the fly, some that Nelson hadn't seen Mantle diving back in until it was too late. Whatever the reason, the odd play cost Pittsburgh their lead, and Hal Smith his status as World Series hero. It didn't, however, cost Pittsburgh the game. Bill Mazeroski led off the bottom of the 9th with the game tied and hit his famous homer.

For one night, Pittsburgh was a better party town than New York. The man everyone thanked for the party, then and now, was Bill Mazeroski.

Hal Smith isn't a World Series hero because Bob Friend and Harvey Haddix couldn't get three outs before they'd given up

> **EVERYONE'S A VICTIM**
> Dick Stuart, on deck when Mazeroski hit his game-ending homer, later complained that Maz had cost him *his* shot at fame.

two runs. He isn't a hero because Rocky Nelson couldn't make a tag before he stepped on first base. At least the homer earned him a few dollars. Smith and teammate Roy Face spent the off-season touring as a musical act. According to Smith, the name recognition he garnered from the homer was worth as much as $10,000 in additional bookings. But even on the winter singing circuit, Smith couldn't grab the headlines. Roy Face sang lead.

By the following February, the Pittsburgh media thought it necessary to remind its readers of Smith's role in the Pirates' victory. "The heavy contributions Hal Smith made to the fabulous Pirates in 1960 really never have been fully appreciated," *The Pittsburgh Press* wrote. "Even his dramatic and timely three-run homer in the vital seventh game was drowned out by Bill Mazeroski's shot an inning later."

Smith would never get another opportunity for fame. Though only 30, his skills went into sharp decline after the fleeting moment of glory. A career .282 hitter through 1960, Smith hit only .223 in 1961, a showing poor enough to send him packing to the expansion Houston Colt .45s. Smith was Houston's regular catcher in 1962, but hit just .235. The following spring Smith broke a finger and landed back in the minors. He worked his way back to the Houston roster, but appeared in just 31 games, then was given his unconditional release.

Smith knew his playing career was nearing its end, but decided to try to hang on for one more season, as the backup catcher in Cincinnati. "I need the money," he explained. Smith hit just .121 in limited action, and was released in late July. The Reds needed to make room on the roster for a promising young first baseman named Tony Perez. "[The World Series home run was] the greatest thrill of my baseball career," Smith said that year. "But since then my baseball luck has all been bad."

In 1965, Smith became a sales rep for the Houston, Texas office of the Jessop Steel Company.

Bill Mazeroski was famous; Hal Smith was selling steel. It hardly seems fair, since Smith's homer scored more runs and came with the Pirates trailing. But that's the way baseball portions out fame in October. Only the final blow is remembered; only one man gets to be a legend.

Years later Pirate pitcher Tom Cheney would tell baseball historian Danny Peary that he still remembered something he'd heard Smith say after that game seven. "Hell, yes, I'm jealous," Smith reportedly complained. "I was supposed to be the hero."

A PAIR OF SOX MISS MAJOR FEATS

Baseball fans tend to remember Bill Lee for two things: for being a unique and free-spirited individual (that is to say, for being a flake) and for giving up a two-run homer to Tony Perez in game seven of the

1975 World Series—a hit that put Cincinnati on the path to its comeback win. There's no question Lee deserves the former rap—he was a Hall-of-Fame flake—but it's worth noting how close the man they called Spaceman came to taking a completely different reputation from that '75 World Series.

By the end of the 1975 regular season, Bill Lee appeared on the verge of stardom. Though not blessed with a blazing fastball, the University of Southern California grad had won 17 games each season for three years running. Winning 17 every year isn't like winning 20—it won't make you famous. But 17 wins from a young pitcher is enough to get people thinking he might win 20 someday.

Lee started two games in the 1975 World Series. In game two, on a rainy day in Boston, he exited having allowed just one run in eight-plus innings of work. Unfortunately, he also left with the tying run on base—Johnny Bench had doubled to right on a sinker low and away to lead off the final frame for Cinncinnati. Lee would later learn that Bench had told a television audience during a seventh-inning rain delay that he intended to look for an outside pitch in his next trip to the plate. "Bench was now telling sixty-five million Americans that he was going to take the ball to right," wrote Lee in his autobiography, "and not one of them thought to call me with a warning."

Cincinnati rallied to win game two, leaving Lee without his win.

Lee would get his second Series start on the biggest stage of all: game seven, Fenway Park. For five innings Lee made the Big Red Machine sputter, as Boston built a 3–0 lead.

The Red Sox hadn't won a World Series since 1918, but they'd been close before. Boston had reached the seventh game of the World Series in both 1946 and 1967. Yet neither of those close calls had created as much optimism for a Fenway crowd as Lee's left arm delivered in 1975. Game seven in 1946 had been played in St. Louis. Game seven in 1967 had been a blowout, as the Sox trailed 7–1 after six innings. In game seven of 1975, buoyed by the relative ease of Lee's success and convinced by Carlton Fisk's famous extra-inning homer in game six that this was Boston's year, the Fenway fans grew increasingly confident as the contest rolled into the middle innings.

Cincinnati had threatened only once, and that hadn't even been Lee's fault. In the 5th, an infield hit and Sox second baseman Denny Doyle's error might have opened the door for the Reds. But Lee struck out Cesar Geronimo and got pinch hitter Merv Rettenmund to ground into a double play, ending the danger. Lee seemed totally in control.

Then came the 6th. Pete Rose led off with a single, but Lee again fought back, getting one future Hall-of-Famer—Joe Morgan—to fly out and a second future Hall-of-Famer—Johnny Bench—to hit an apparent inning-ending double-play grounder. Only the double play didn't happen. Denny Doyle threw the relay over Carl Yastrzemski's head at first, and the inning continued, with dangerous Tony Perez due up. "I let it bother me," Lee later told sportswriter Peter Golenbock of the botched double play. "And out of the stretch I threw a curveball too hard and hung it, and he hit it about 40 miles."

The Perez homer trimmed Boston's lead to 3–2. Two hitters into the 7th, a burst blister on Lee's thumb forced him from the game. "I just wish I could have thrown strikes after my thumb went," Lee said. "But I couldn't."

For the second time in a week, Boston's bullpen lost Lee's lead and then the game, this time on a Ken Griffey walk and a Joe Morgan bloop in the 9th. By the time Yastrzemski flied out to end the 4–3 Boston loss, the Fenway crowd, tense since the Perez home run in the 6th inning, was all but silent.

Lee was left without a decision in the Series and a pedestrian 3.14 ERA, numbers that failed to show how close he'd come to delivering Boston a long-awaited World Series victory with a game seven masterpiece.

TWO DOYLES, TWO TEAMS, TWO FATES

Oddly, Boston fans chose not to tar and feather Denny Doyle for his costly miscue. Doyle remained with Boston for two more seasons, and retired as a career .250 hitter in 3,290 at-bats. It was an average major league career, no better. Doyle's younger brother could only dream of such mediocrity. Brian Doyle, also a second baseman, hit just .161 in 199 major league at-bats during parts of four seasons with the Yankees and A's—atrocious numbers. Like Denny, the younger Doyle was a regular in a World Series. The difference? Brian hit a team-leading .438 in *his* series, filling in for an injured Willie Randolph in the Yankees' 1978 defeat of the Dodgers.

The Doyle family thus provides some valuable insight into a deep truth concerning two of the American League's most storied franchises. Two men were taken from the same gene pool and sent to the World Series. The one with the greater talent was assigned a Red Sox uniform, the one with lesser abilities the Yankee pinstripes. The Red Sox player committed a key error; the Yankee hit .438 and fielded flawlessly. Perhaps Bill Lee never really had a chance.

Would Lee have become a legend if he'd won game seven? It isn't easy for a pitcher to be a World Series hero. Generally speaking, pitchers are paid to prevent thrilling moments, not to produce them. But had Lee shut down the Big Red Machine and won a Series for a city as starved for baseball success as Boston, it just might have been enough.

Instead, Lee's career started a downhill slide. Though he'd won 17 games each year from 1973 through 1975, Lee didn't win more than 10 games in any of the next three seasons. To the Red Sox front office, that meant the free-spirited Lee was more trouble than he was worth. The near-hero was banished to Montreal. There Lee would have one more notable season—16–10 with a 3.04 ERA—followed by three mediocre years. Always at odds with management, Lee finally was released by the Expos after skipping part of a game to protest the release of infielder Rodney Scott. Lee pitched semi-pro ball after his release in hopes of making a major league comeback. He never did.

Lee would be remembered as the flake who threw the pitch that Tony Perez clubbed in one of Boston's many disastrous World Series moments. If not for an infield misplay and a burst blister, his legacy might have been very different.

The Red Sox returned to the World Series 11 years later, but things wouldn't go any better for Boston that October. The 1986 Series is remembered for the Bill Buckner error that capped a three-run, two-out Met rally in the bottom of the 10th inning of game six. There's little question who would have been the hero for Boston if the Sox hadn't blown that seemingly unblowable lead. Dave Henderson had led off the top of the 10th with a home run to put Boston just three outs from victory. He'd hit .435 with a pair of homers to that point in the Series. And if not for Henderson's two-out, two-run, 9th-inning, game-tying homer in the final game of the American League Championship Series, and his tie-breaking sac fly two innings later, Boston wouldn't have been in the 1986 World Series in the first place. It had been a heroic performance, but Henderson had made the crucial mistake of producing it for the Red Sox, a team with a history of wasting such efforts.

> ## BUCKNER'S OTHER SERIES
> Bill Buckner's error in the 1986 Series is well known. Less remembered is the only other trip to the postseason of Buckner's 22-year career. In 1974, Buckner's Dodgers took on Oakland in the World Series. Los Angeles was down one run in game five when Buckner led off the 8th with a hit to right center. It was a crucial single for the Dodgers—or it would have been, except the ball got away from A's center fielder Billy North, and Buckner kept running. The ball was retrieved by right fielder Reggie Jackson, a man who would one day enjoy an October reputation as good as Buckner's was bad. Jackson made a perfect throw to the cut-off man, and Buckner was out at third. The Series ended an inning later when the Dodgers lost the game by a single run.

Unlike most Red Sox, Henderson would get a second shot at fame. He managed this by taking the rather sensible precaution of getting traded away from Boston. In 1988, Henderson landed with the Oakland A's just in time for their three-year World Series run. The A's were upset by the Dodgers and Reds in 1988 and 1990, respectively, but they did manage a win in 1989, thanks in no small part to Henderson, who led or shared the team lead in homers, RBIs, runs, walks, and doubles in the Series. Unfortunately, no one much remembers this performance

FISK'S FOLLOWERS

No one has ever gained more fame for hitting a home run in what was ultimately a losing cause than Carlton Fisk. His game-winning, game-six shot in 1975 only delayed the inevitable, as Boston lost the Series in game seven. Might Fisk's World Series fame be based purely on a fortuitous spot in the batting order? Reds catcher Johnny Bench maintains that Cincinnati pitcher Pat Darcy could barely get the ball over the plate in the 12th. Indeed, Fisk needed just two Darcy pitches to end the contest. It's not as though there was help on the way, either. Darcy was the eighth Reds pitcher of the game—among the pitchers used by the Reds in the series, only the next day's starter, Don Gullett, remained.

If Fisk hadn't delivered, someone behind him in the batting order very well might have. Following Fisk in Boston's lineup were Fred Lynn, Rico Petrocelli, and Dwight Evans. All three hit well in the 1975 Series; none would be much remembered for it. In 2000, Carlton Fisk was elected to the Hall of Fame in his second year on the ballot. An 11-time All-Star, Fisk might very well have made the Hall anyway. Then again, he might not have; Ted Simmons, a catcher with offensive skills comparable to Fisk's and a career nearly as long, hardly received any Hall votes when he was on the ballot in the mid-1990s. For that matter, neither did Dwight Evans, due up three hitters after Fisk in that 12th inning. Despite his 385 career home runs, Evans never has come close to landing a place in the Hall.

either, since the one and only story of the one-sided 1989 Series was the deadly earthquake that interrupted the proceedings.

THE CUBS' CLOSEST CALL

Like the Boston Red Sox, the Chicago Cubs have spent generations waiting for a World Series hero. Unlike the Red Sox, they haven't even reached the Series since 1945, leaving precious few opportunities for herohood. Hank Borowy had perhaps the best shot. The Cubs' ace was designated to start game seven of that '45 Series, and did his part. When Borowy was handed the ball with the Series on the line, he pitched masterfully and earned the win. The only trouble was, it wasn't yet game seven.

The Cubs' relief corps had frittered away a big Chicago lead in game six. With the Cubs trailing in the Series three games to two, manager Charlie Grimm saw no other option but to bring his intended game seven starter in just to ensure there would *be* a game seven. Borowy came through with four innings of shutout relief in game six—even though he'd started game five only the day before.

Japan had surrendered in September, and Americans were in a mood to enjoy themselves. For the first time in years, October baseball seemed like big news, not merely a momentary diversion from more important events. The baseball world was in the process of returning to normal, like the rest of American society. But it wasn't an instant transition. In October 1945, many of the game's stars still hadn't traded in their military uniforms for baseball flannels. That meant the 1945 season offered one last chance for a perennial also-ran outfit like the Cubs to compete for the title before better clubs got their better players back. This game seven would be the Cubs' last, best hope. And it all hinged on the performance of a very tired Hank Borowy, a man who'd only been a Cub for a little over two months.

Borowy had been a college star, compiling a 23–1 record for New York's Fordham University, just miles from his New Jersey hometown. The pitcher kept right on winning in the majors. Heading into the 1945 Series, his major league record was 67–32. Borowy even had started the 1944 All-Star Game. But only 11 of Borowy's wins had come with the Cubs. He'd spent the first three and a half seasons of his big-league career with the New York Yankees, a team that symbolized winning as much as the Cubs symbolized losing. Not until late July 1945 did Borowy reach Chicago, sold to the Cubs for close to $100,000. Given his choice, Borowy would have remained in New York. "I hate to leave the Yankees," he told the press. "But that's baseball."

Grimm sent Borowy back to the mound to start game seven two days after his lengthy game-six relief outing, but the pitcher had nothing left. Borowy surrendered three runs without recording an out. The man who might have been a game seven star instead was a game seven goat. "Pitching for the third time in four days was an assignment that would have taxed even the most rubber armed of pitchers," wrote *Baseball Magazine* that winter. "The none too robust Borowy never had a chance. . . . They belted him out in the first inning and with that went Hank's last chance to win the hero's rank."

The '45 Series would be the turning point of Borowy's career. Plagued by a sore arm and blister problems and faced with stiffer competition as players returned from World War II, Borowy would win only 41 of his 91 decisions after 1945. "There are only so many pitches in your arm before it wears out," Borowy would later say. He was speaking of his career, but could just as easily have been talking about that 1945 World Series.

CHICAGO FANS BLAME ONE OF THEIR OWN

With a few exceptions, players tend not to become famous for producing key hits in League Championship Series. Their heroics typically are overshadowed by whatever follows in the World Series. But you can become infamous for making the misplay that costs your team a league playoff series—particularly if your team is one that doesn't reach the postseason often.

Cubs shortstop Alex Gonzalez nearly found this out the hard way when he made a crucial error in Chicago's disastrous 8th-inning meltdown in game six of the 2003 National League Championship Series. Ordinarily, Cub fans would have burned Gonzalez in effigy—in effigy, if he was lucky—for costing them their first trip to the World Series in nearly 60 years. But Gonzalez seems to have caught a break. Chicago instead appears to have focused its blame on the Wrigley fan who failed to give Cub left fielder Moises Alou a chance to catch a foul ball earlier that inning.

It's somewhat reminiscent of Jack Clark's escape from the 1985 World Series with his reputation still largely intact. History remembers the mistake of a non-player—first-base ump Don Denkinger's blown call on Jorge Orta's 9th-inning squib—in St. Louis' dramatic game six loss, rather than the foul pop Clark let drop or any of the other Cardinal miscues that followed.

By 1951 Borowy was out of the majors and soon on to a new career as a New Jersey real estate agent. Borowy never appeared in another World Series after 1945. For that matter, neither have the Cubs.

YOU'RE NOT A HERO IF NO ONE'S WATCHING

Perhaps no World Series in history has been more overshadowed by world events than that of 1918. The Great War was raging in Europe, and a worldwide influenza epidemic recently had reached American shores. The baseball season was cut short, the Series was pushed up to early September and played before sparse crowds. Only 15,238 fans showed up at Fenway to see the Red Sox topple the Cubs in game six. It remains, to date, Boston's last Series-clinching win. Good tickets are still available.

The poor attendance cost the players money—the size of their post-season bonus depended on gate receipts. It also cost the stars of the Series their rightful fame. The biggest star of the 1918 Series was, arguably, Carl Mays, the ornery but effective submarine pitcher who'd won 22 games in 1917, then 21 in 1918 to lead the Sox to the pennant. Mays threw a three-hit, one-run masterpiece to win the final game 2–1. He'd already delivered a 2–1 win in game three. Mays' picture graced the front page of *The Sporting News* after the Red Sox claimed the Series.

With a bit more fan interest, Mays might have become a popular player in Boston sporting circles. If nothing else, he might be remembered by history as the Red Sox' last true World Series hero. Instead his career took a very different turn. In 1919, Mays got off to a 5–11 start. He blamed his teammates for the losses, accusing them of playing half-hearted defense behind him because they didn't like him. Mays further sullied his reputation by firing a baseball at a heckler in the stands. Then in July, Mays deserted the Sox between innings of a game, reportedly telling manager Ed Barrow, "I'm through with this ball club."

Mays was sold to the Yankees for $40,000. Given a fresh start in New York, he immediately regained his winning form, going 9-3 for his new team to even his 1919 record at 14-14. Mays won 26 games for the Yanks in 1920, then led the league with 27 wins in 1921 as the Yankees won their first pennant. But just as Mays wasn't destined to be remembered as the pitching star of the last Red Sox World Champions, neither was he destined to be remembered as the pitching star of the first

Yankee pennant winner. He would be remembered instead for a single pitch he delivered in a game against the Indians on August 17, 1920. That pitch, a fastball, struck popular Indians shortstop Ray Chapman in the head, killing him. It remains the only fatal pitch in major league history.

Despite an excellent pitching career, Mays is thought of as one of the game's villains. There even have been rumors, never substantiated, that Mays intentionally lost a game in the 1921 World Series. The Yankees used Mays less frequently in 1922 and 1923, either because of their suspicions about that 1921 World Series, or because the fractious pitcher was so intensely disliked by manager Miller Huggins and most of his Yankee teammates. Sold to Cincinnati in 1924, Mays showed he was still one of the most effective pitchers in baseball, finishing tied for third in the National League with 20 wins. After suffering from a sore arm in 1925, Mays ended the year one off the league lead with 19 wins in 1926. He'd pitch in the majors for three more seasons, but never again start regularly. His career record was 207–126. That's a career winning percentage of .622, which places Mays right between Hall-of-Famers Carl Hubbell and Bob Feller in the all-time rankings.

The widely disliked pitcher seemed a good candidate to leave baseball forever after his pitching skills deserted him. But Mays became a scout in the late 1950s and early 1960s. One of the clubs that employed him was the Cleveland Indians, the team whose star shortstop he'd killed so many years earlier. Mays died in 1971, more than half a century after throwing his famous fatal pitch. "I won over two hundred big league games, but no one today remembers that," sportswriter Fred Lieb would quote Mays as saying. "When they think of me, I'm the guy who killed Chapman with a fastball."

OCTOBER'S GREATEST LOSER

Virtually all of baseball's greatest players have appeared in the postseason at least once—19th-century players, Negro Leaguers, and Chicago Cubs aside. But for all of those stellar players, one could make a decent case that the very best October career totals were produced by a man whose name is only mentioned in association with the game's greats because he happens to be named after one of them. A relatively obscure ballplayer named Willie Mays Aikens delivered like none before on baseball's October stage, a fact that more fans might remember if Aikens' team hadn't lost the only Series in which he appeared. In fact, Aikens' Royals did something no team before or since has managed: They lost a World Series to the Philadelphia Phillies.

If baseball is a game of inches, it also is a game of numbers. If something happens on a baseball field, somewhere out there there's a baseball fan with too much time on his hands and a statistic to track it. Batting average and home runs are the most-cited offensive statistics. They're not the most useful stats, mind you. They've simply been around so long that we've all grown used to them. It's the same thinking that keeps Andy Rooney employed. The truth is, there are statistics that provide a much better barometer of hitting ability. High on this list of meaningful stats is something called OPS, a number calculated by combining a player's on-base percentage with his slugging average. OPS, it turns out, correlates very strongly with run production. That is to say, if a player has a high OPS, he's probably helped his team score a lot of runs—and scoring runs is more or less the reason batters step to the plate in the first place.

OPS and a passel of other newfangled stats are getting some press these days, as a new generation of general managers including Billy Beane and Theo Epstein exploit their potential in player evaluation. But this recent attention doesn't seem to have led to any increased acclaim for the large, defensively challenged Aikens. Perhaps it should. Back in the early 1980s, Aikens set the standard for October OPS, even if few had even heard of the stat at the time.

Remove players with fewer than 40 postseason plate appearances and those still active whose numbers might come down in future years, and you'll find all-time greats Babe Ruth, Lou Gehrig, and Hank Aaron among the top five in career postseason OPS. Also in the top five is Bobby Brown, not a great perhaps, but a well-remembered contributor to the great Yankee teams of the late 1940s and early 1950s. But none of these men owns the top spot in the rankings. That honor belongs to none other than Willie Mays Aikens.

Virtually all of Aikens' postseason plate appearances came in 1980, the year Kansas City finally beat the Yankees in the ALCS to reach the

World Series . . . only to lose to Philadelphia in six. Had Dan Quisenberry not blown a pair of saves in that Series, Aikens' efforts might be remembered as one of the greatest postseason performances in history. He went eight for twenty in that Series with four homers, a triple, six walks, eight RBIs, and five runs scored. But the Royals lost, so when Aikens' career is remembered, it tends to be for everything that came later.

THREE WINS, NO GLORY
Thirteen pitchers have won three games in a single World Series, but only one has done so in a losing cause: Pittsburgh's Deacon Phillippe in 1903, the very first modern Series. Playing in a day when pitchers worked more frequently— and with the benefit of a best-of-nine Series that went eight games— Phillippe also lost two games as Pittsburgh fell to Boston and *its* three-game winner Bill Dinneen.

Aikens' career didn't immediately fall apart after the 1980 World Series. He was one of the few bright spots in the Royals' brief playoff run in the strike-shortened 1981 season. Then after a fine 1982, Aikens put up the best regular-season numbers of his career in 1983, hitting .302 with 23 homers. He was just 28 years old, and should have been in his prime. But for Aikens, 1983 was virtually the end of the road. That winter, Aikens and teammates Willie Wilson and Jerry Martin were suspended for cocaine use. Aikens eventually spent three months in jail, prompting the Royals to trade him to Toronto for Jorge Orta.

Perhaps it was the toll taken by the drugs, perhaps it was the glare of negative attention brought on by his conviction. Whatever the reason, Aikens was a shell of his former self in 1984, hitting just .205 for the Jays. His new team failed to reach the playoffs that year, but his old team, Kansas City, returned without him. Steve Balboni, the Royal starting at first in place of the jettisoned Aikens, proved a poor postseason replacement. Balboni managed just one hit in ten playoff at-bats as K.C. was swept by Detroit in the American League Championship Series.

The following March gave the Blue Jays reason to hope for an Aikens rebound, as the one-time slugger hit .345 in spring training. Then the Blue Jays faced four straight left-handed starters to open the regular season, and the left-handed-hitting Aikens didn't get to start for the better part of a week. (The first three of those lefties were thrown at Toronto by Aikens' old club, Kansas City.) By the time he finally got a chance to play regularly, Aikens' sweet spring swing had vanished. On April 27, Aikens pinch hit a two-run, game-tying, 9th-inning home run off Tommy Boggs of the Rangers. It was his first home run of the season. It would be his last at-bat. Aikens was released by the Jays. "There's no doubt in my mind I can still hit," he told the press. "I don't think it is over yet."

It was over. Though just 30 years old, Aikens never returned to the majors. That October Toronto and Kansas City—the two teams that had recently dumped Aikens—met in the ALCS without him. Toronto's first baseman, Willie Upshaw, managed only a .231 post-season average. Balboni followed his .100 average in the 1984 postseason by hitting .120 in the '85 ALCS. Neither man hit a homer. Kansas City won four games to three. (In fairness, Balboni's numbers improved in the 1985 World Series.)

> **MAYS' MARK**
> Willie Mays' famous back-to-the-infield catch off Vic Wertz in game one of the 1954 World Series wasn't the only way Wertz was denied glory that October. Despite being robbed on that play, the Cleveland first baseman produced a .500 average in the Series, including four extra-base hits. Ordinarily such a performance might have been enough to build a reputation as an October star. But no other Indian receiving regular playing time hit better than .250 and Cleveland lost in four straight. Despite his stellar play, Wertz would be remembered by baseball history as Mays' victim.

In a roundabout way, Aikens did contribute to Kansas City's 1985 World Series victory. Jorge Orta, the man the Royals received when they traded Aikens, produced just one hit in the entire 1985 postseason, a little infield dribbler in the bottom of the 9th inning of the sixth game of the World Series. But that little dribbler helped turn the tide of the Series, as Orta was called safe at first by umpire Don Denkinger and the Royals rallied to win. Replays showed that Orta actually had been out by a considerable margin. The Royals won the Series the next day. Jorge Orta got a World Series ring and even a small dose of glory for his lucky squib. Aikens' Herculean efforts in 1980 are forgotten.

Although Major League Baseball had given up on Aikens, it would be some time before Aikens gave up on baseball. The first baseman continued to play wherever he could find a job in the minors, and he often played very well. One year for Puebla in the Mexican League, he hit .454 with 46 homers, enough to finally make Aikens a household name, assuming your household is in Puebla, Mexico. It didn't earn him another shot at the majors.

By the early 1990s, Aikens was back in the U.S. His baseball career was over, but that was the least of Aikens' problems. The former star athlete weighed well over 300 pounds and was addicted to crack cocaine. Aikens was still in his 30s, an age when many power hitters are still productive, but the majors must have seemed a different life.

There was still farther to slide. In 1992 Aikens met a woman who asked him to buy her some drugs. Aikens complied, only to discover his new friend was an undercover narcotics officer. Aikens was arrested for drug trafficking. When a gun was found in his apartment, a weapons charge was added to the indictment. Aikens was sentenced to 20 years and eight months. He remains in jail. It's certainly the furthest any near-Series hero has fallen.

HARPER'S FORGOTTEN HIT

If Don Denkinger hadn't blown the call on Jorge Orta's dribbler in the 9th inning of game six of the 1985 World Series, or Jack Clark hadn't let that foul ball drop later in the inning, Cardinal journeyman backup catcher Brian Harper might have been remembered as a hero. Harper's pinch-hit single with two out in the top of the 8th scored game six's first run and seemed to put St. Louis in a position to win the Series. Robbed of this fame, Harper continued to kick around baseball, playing in a total of 207 career regular-season games spread over five teams and eight years and never hitting much . . . until 1988, when he landed with his sixth team, the Twins. Harper would play six years for Minnesota, the last five of them as the starting catcher. The former mediocrity posted season averages between .294 and .325.

In the 1991 World Series, Harper led all Minnesota regulars with a .381 average, as the Twins beat the Braves in seven. Harper wouldn't get to play hero in this Series either, since pinch-hitter Gene Larkin got the big hit, and pitcher Jack Morris threw ten shutout innings in the final game. But he finally had his ring.

A GLIMPSE OF REDEMPTION

We remember the heroes. We remember the goats. But what if the game's most infamous goat later delivered the hit that won a classic World Series? Surely such a story would become legend. Surely the goat would be redeemed. Surely he one day would be portrayed by Kevin Costner to mixed reviews but strong box office receipts. It's the perfect baseball story . . . and for a few minutes in 1912 it seemed to be coming true.

On September 23, 1908, Fred Merkle, a teenager with fewer than 100 major league at-bats, made the most famous baseball blunder of the first decade of the 20th century. Merkle's New York Giants were locked in a tight pennant race against, among other teams, the Chicago Cubs, that day's opponent. Young Merkle wouldn't ordinarily have started such a crucial game, but Giants' regular first baseman Fred Tenney was out that day with a strained back.

For a brief moment in the bottom of the 9th, it appeared that Merkle's presence in the lineup would work in New York's favor. The raw teenager singled sharply to right with two down in the bottom of the 9th, moving teammate Moose McCormick to third with the potential winning run. Shortstop Al Bridwell followed with an apparent single of his own, and McCormick trotted home from third. New York fans rushed the field to celebrate the victory, while Merkle, wary of the fans, rushed for the safety of the clubhouse.

Unfortunately for Merkle, the umpires concluded that he had neglected to touch second base before departing. The Cubs had retrieved the ball and stepped on second, turning the hit into a force out and negating the run. After considerable controversy, the game was replayed, and the Giants lost the rematch and the pennant to the Cubs. The "Merkle boner" went down in history as perhaps the stupidest mistake in baseball history.

It was not a just fate. What Merkle had done was not unheard of at the time—with stadium security nonexistent, ballplayers tended to sprint for the clubhouse as soon as important games ended to avoid the onrush of fans. "I think that under the circumstances any player on any ball club would have done the same thing Merkle did," Bridwell later told baseball historian Lawrence Ritter. "They did it all the time in those days."

It's not even as though the Merkle game was the last game of the season. It was just the most memorable of a handful of New York losses down the stretch that cost the team the pennant. But mostly the "Bonehead" rap was unfair because by all accounts, Merkle had one of the sharpest minds in baseball. He even played a mean game of chess. But when it comes to placing blame in baseball, perception is more important than reality. Merkle was branded a bonehead and the biggest goat in the history of the sport. "I wish I'd never gotten that hit that set off the whole Merkle incident," said Bridwell a half century later. "I wish I'd struck out instead. If I'd done that, then it would have spared Fred a whole lot of unfair humiliation. . . . The fans ragged him unmercifully all the rest of his life."

Merkle persevered in baseball despite the taunts that followed him wherever the Giants played. For a time, he even prospered. By 1912, Fred Merkle was one of the best players in the game. He hit .309 that year, was fifth in the league in steals, and tied for third in homers. Thanks in part to Merkle's mistake, the Giants had blown their shot at the pennant in 1908. In 1912, thanks in part to Merkle's marvelous play, they won the pennant and faced the Red Sox in the World Series. The 1912 Series would be a classic.

The words "game seven" carry a certain weight with the modern baseball fan. It's safe to say this was not the case prior to the mid-1920s. For starters, in 1903 and from 1919 through 1921, the World Series was a best-of-nine affair. During those years, "game seven" would have meant nothing more than "game five" does today. (Neither, incidentally, did the words "game nine" carry any special meaning—none of those best-of-nines reached a decisive ninth game.) And even when the Series used a best-of-seven format, "game seven" drama was in decidedly short supply early in the century. Only two pre-1924 best-of-seven modern World Series reached a seventh game. The first was 1909, when Babe Adams pitched Pittsburgh to an 8–0 rout over Detroit. Pittsburgh led that game seven 7–0 after six innings, so if fans were on the edge of their seats, it must have been to keep themselves awake. The only other early-20th-century Series to go the distance was that of 1912. Unlike 1909, the 1912 game seven was one to remember, stretching into extra innings. (Technically, the 1912 Series required not only a game seven, but also a game eight, since game two had ended in a tie. But that's semantics.) It was, arguably, the tensest drama 20th-century baseball had yet produced.

Such a World Series seems certain to produce a hero. Instead, 1912 produced a goat. That goat was, of course, another Giant named Fred—this time outfielder Fred Snodgrass, perpetrator of the "$30,000 muff." It was an error so famous that even today, more than 90 years later, most baseball fans could tell you that someone named Snodgrass once screwed something up quite badly, even if many can't recall specifically what that might have been. In short, what Snodgrass screwed up was an easy fly ball off the bat of Clyde Engle to lead off the bottom of the 10th inning in the deciding game of that first photo-finish World Series. The Giants had taken a one-run lead in the top of the 10th and needed just three outs for a Series victory. They wouldn't get them. Thanks in part to Snodgrass, Boston put two across for the win. It was one of those errors you're stuck with for the rest of your life.

"For over half a century I've had to live with the fact that I dropped a ball in a World Series," Snodgrass said in the 1960s. "Whenever I'd be introduced to somebody, they'd start to say something and then stop, you know, afraid of hurting my feelings." When Snodgrass died in 1974, 62 years after the drop, his obituary in *The New York Times* mentioned the miscue in the headline.

Under most circumstances, it might be tempting to wonder if Fred Merkle wasn't secretly glad that Snodgrass, a fellow Giant, had taken over the club's goat horns. It's been reported that after Boston's Bill Buckner's famed error in 1986, Mike Torrez, the Red Sox pitcher who had allowed Bucky Dent's equally famed homer run in 1978, was heard to exalt, "I'm off the hook!" As it happens, we can safely assume that Snodgrass' error was the last thing Merkle wished to see. For when the Giants lost that lead in 1912, Merkle lost his chance at becoming baseball's greatest ever story of redemption.

The odds against Merkle's second chance were astronomical. Merkle's 1908 blunder was the most memorable moment in the *only* National League pennant race decided by less than two games during a stretch of more than a quarter century. Now 1912 offered the *only* down-to-the-wire World Series until the mid-1920s. Yet when the rare career-making moment came, it fell into the lap of the man who needed it most.

A half-inning prior to Snodgrass' error, the score had been tied in the top of the 10th. New York's Red Murray was on second with one out. The batter was none other than the infamous Fred Merkle. Bonehead Merkle delivered a single to right, bringing Murray home with what seemed extremely likely to be the winning run. After four years of living in shame, all Merkle needed to become the hero of the best Series to date was for the Giants to hold their lead in the bottom of the 10th. It must have seemed a pretty safe bet: The Giants had Christy Mathewson on the mound. Matty had thrown 28 innings in the 1912 World Series and had given up just three earned runs.

KLEINOW MISSES BALL, BUT CATCHES BREAK

The Merkle boner's only real competition for the title of most-famous pre-Snodgrass 20th-century baseball screw-up was Jack Chesbro's 1904 9th-inning wild pitch on the final day of the regular season. The pitch ended New York's hopes of taking the American League pennant and ended Chesbro's famous 41-win season with a dramatic loss. (It probably didn't cost the team a shot at the World Series, however, since none was played that year.)

Narrowly escaping those first 20th-century goat horns was Chesbro's catcher, Red Kleinow, who—Chesbro's wife would later argue to anyone who would listen—might have caught the ball. But most in attendance agreed with the official scorer that the pitch was so high it couldn't be handled. It was certainly higher, one would imagine, than Mr. Kleinow's opinion of Mrs. Chesbro.

Mathewson might have been a good bet, but the Giants defense wasn't. Snodgrass dropped the ball, and Engle wound up on second. Now Snodgrass was the Giant in need of redemption. And against all odds, he, like Merkle, seemed to find it—at least for a moment. With Engle leading off second, Harry Hooper lined what appeared to be a game-tying hit to center. But Snodgrass, a goat one moment, played the hero the next, making a fabulous over-the-shoulder catch for the first out of the inning. "I made one of the greatest plays of my life," Snodgrass would later say. "They always forget about that play when they write about that inning. In fact, I almost doubled up Engle at second base."

The next hitter walked, and the Boston crowd was in a frenzy. But Mathewson got future Hall of Famer Tris Speaker to loft a foul pop-up near first base, and the crowd instantly fell silent. It appeared Merkle would be one out away from redemption, Snodgrass one out away from avoiding infamy entirely—errors aren't remembered if they don't lead to runs. Only Speaker's foul pop wasn't caught. Catcher Chief Meyers, pitcher Mathewson, and the first baseman—none other than Fred Merkle—let the ball drop among them. It probably was Merkle's catch to make. According to some accounts, Mathewson called him off, yelling "Chief, Chief," signaling Meyers to make the play. Others allege it was Speaker, the Boston baserunner, who yelled for Meyers to make the play, in a successful attempt to confuse the Giant defense.

Given new life, Speaker singled home the tying run. One batter later, a sac fly by Boston third baseman Larry Gardner scored the game winner. Many things had happened in the bottom of the 10th after Snodgrass dropped Engle's fly ball. Foul pops were dropped, great catches were made, and clutch hits were delivered. None of these things would be remembered. As far as history was concerned, Fred Snodgrass was the extent of the inning. "I did drop that fly ball and that did put what turned out to be the tying run on base, but that's a long way from 'losing a World Series,'" Snodgrass would argue years later. "However, the facts don't seem to matter."

One fact mattered for Merkle: He would not be remembered as the goat who would be king. He was just a goat, and always would be.

Fred Merkle played ten more years after the 1912 World Series, but he never matched his 1912 performance. He appeared in three more World Series with three different clubs after 1912, but was never on the winning side. In his career, Merkle appeared in five World Series—and was on the losing team each time. His last appearance came in 1918 with the Chicago Cubs, the club that had started his problems to begin with.

Merkle's RBI single wasn't the only seemingly vital, yet eventually forgotten, moment in that 1912 World Series game. Boston's Larry Gardner drove home the winning run in that first truly dramatic World Series without receiving much lasting fame for the feat. Unfortunately for Gardner, it's tough to get excited about a sac fly; they seem more workmanlike than wonderful. Maybe he would be remembered as a hero if his long fly ball had fallen in for a hit. But the Giants right fielder was a fine defensive player named Josh Devore. Devore already had made a memorable catch to save game three for the Giants. Though he couldn't prevent the winning run from tagging and scoring in the final game, he did make the futile catch, thereby depriving Larry Gardner of a measure of glory.

Larry Gardner would play in three more World Series and be on the winning side of all three. But none of the Series were particularly close, and Gardner never had another opportunity for lasting fame after his mostly forgotten sac fly. The third baseman retired in 1924 after 17 years in the majors and later became baseball coach and athletic director at the University of Vermont. The University of Vermont has never exactly been a hot-bed of athletic excellence, but like hitting sac flies, it was good, honest work.

Fred Snodgrass would be remembered for his failure in baseball, but his post-baseball life was a success. The former outfielder capped a long and prosperous career in banking and retailing with a term as mayor of Oxnard, California. Apparently there aren't many Giants fans among the voting populace of Oxnard. "Well, life has been good to me since I left baseball," Snodgrass said in the 1960s. "In contrast, my years in baseball had their ups and downs, their strife and torment. But the years I look back at most fondly, and those I'd like most to live over, are the years when I played center field for the New York Giants." Snodgrass died in 1974.

As for Fred Merkle, he spent a season coaching for the Yanks after retiring as a player in 1926, then did a bit of managing in the low minors. But by the 1930s, Merkle had completely cut himself off from his former life in baseball. He lost his savings in the depression, worked for the WPA, and later started a small business making fishing

THOSE GREAT RED SOX PITCHERS

No Boston player earned more recognition in the team's 1912 Series victory than pitcher Smoky Joe Wood. Wood's star had been climbing all year. The 22-year-old flame-thrower posted a 34–5 record in 1912 with a 1.91 ERA, and followed that with a 3–0 record in the World Series, including the win in the clincher.

Wood's brilliance that year obscured the work of another young Boston pitcher, rookie Hugh Bedient. Bedient had compiled a 20–9 record with a 2.92 ERA in 1912, a terrific first season—though not one likely to attract much attention next to Wood's 34 victories. In the Series it was Wood's three wins that got the glory, but Bedient might well have been the more effective pitcher.

Bedient's first appearance in the Series came in the 11th inning of game two. With no margin for error, he pitched one inning of scoreless baseball before the game was called for darkness. It's tough to gain fame by playing in a tie. The next day Bedient threw again, this time working a scoreless 9th inning. Unfortunately, Boston couldn't rally, and New York won 2–1. After a single day's rest, Bedient started game five . . . against Christy Mathewson. Bedient held the Giants to three hits and one unearned run, out-dueling one of history's great pitchers 2–1. That performance earned Bedient the start in the Series' decisive game. Again Bedient was matched up with Mathewson, again he limited New York to one run. But this time Bedient was lifted for a pinch hitter, and Wood took over in the 8th inning of a 1–1 tie. Wood allowed a run in the top of the 10th, but with a bit of help from Snodgrass and company, Boston scored twice in the bottom of the 10th, and Wood had his third win. Overall, Bedient had pitched in four games, including two starts lures. In 1950, after nearly a quarter century of refusing to have anything to do with the sport that made his name synonymous with stupidity, Merkle attended an old-timers game in the Polo Grounds. The Giants fans greeted him with cheers. Merkle died six years later in Florida.

against the famed Matty. His ERA for the series was 0.50, his record 1–0. Wood was 3–1, with an ERA of 3.68.

Bedient must have expected his future to hold other chances at fame. He was just 22 years old—Bedient and Wood were born two days apart in October, 1889—and his career was off to a great start. Instead, Bedient's record would slip to 15–14 in 1913 then 8–12 in 1914. After a single year in the Federal League, Bedient's major league days would be over. He was just 25. By the late 1930s, Bedient reportedly was running a gas station in his hometown of Falconer, New York. The name Hugh Bedient would briefly return to the newspapers in 1940. Bedient's only son, Hugh Bedient, Jr., was killed when his army bomber collided with another military plane over a residential neighborhood in Queens, New York.

Wood would fare no better. He hurt his arm the year after his 34-win seaseon, and was never again a star. Wood had slipped on wet grass that spring and injured his thumb. It's been speculated that attempting to pitch with the bad thumb altered Wood's delivery and led to the arm problem. Wood would later say he never was sure if the two mishaps were related. Whatever the cause, the man who'd produced a 34–5 record at age 22 was destined to win only 35 more games over parts of six more seasons. Neither Bedient nor Wood would appear in another World Series. The Red Sox returned in 1915, when they added a promising young pitcher named Babe Ruth.

2
A TRIP OF
NEAR-GOATS

A group of lions is known as a pride, a group of fish, a school. A group of goats can be referred to as a trip. This seems particularly appropriate for baseball's goats, whose trips, falls, and other assorted October errors have altered the course of seasons. Yet not all of these missteps have doomed players to infamy.

There is an inherent inequity to how baseball history selects new goats for its trip. It isn't the biggest blunders that are remembered. In 1918, *The Sporting News* awarded former Reds catcher Larry McLean the informal honor of having committed the "greatest, grandest bone play ever pulled upon the diamond." In a close game several years before, a Cincinnati shortstop had fielded a ground ball and thrown home to cut down a run. McLean stepped on the plate and threw to first to complete the double play. Trouble was, the bases hadn't been loaded—first was unoccupied. With no force in effect, the run scored while McLean's throw was on its way to first. But Larry McLean wasn't destined to become one of baseball's great goats, and he knew the reason: it wasn't October. "If that play had only been made in a World's Series [sic] game, or some game that decided a pennant, I'd have made Merkle and Snodgrass look like little pikers," admitted McLean later. "But it came off in just an ordinary, mid-season affair—just one game out of 154— and so the world has long since forgotten."

As McLean understood, baseball's biggest goats aren't so much guilty of bad plays as they are of bad timing. "The world's series [sic] throws so strong a light on a player's record that it completely distorts his work," noted 1910s pitcher Ray Fisher. "I say it is unfair, and yet it is human nature I suppose."

It's easy for Fisher to dismiss such things as human nature. He appeared in just one World Series, with the Cincinnati Reds in 1919. Fisher committed a glaring error that arguably cost the Reds a game. But Cincinnati's opponent in the 1919 World Series were the so-called Chicago Black Sox, many of whom had conspired with gamblers to help the Reds win. Thanks to the Cincy victory, Fisher's flub was destined to be forgotten. He isn't the only apparent goat who received a reprieve. Throughout the sport's history, players have narrowly avoided joining the likes of Merkle, Snodgrass, and Buckner in baseball's informal Hall of Infamy.

> **MCLEAN'S MISADVENTURES**
> Larry McLean had a penchant for unusual trouble. In 1919, the former catcher was reported to be in critical condition in a Newark hospital. He'd received severe burns after passing out in a Turkish bath. In 1921, McLean—a loveable bear of a man when sober, but a 6'5" menace when drunk—got into an argument with a bartender. He was shot dead at age 39.

THE GIANT GOAT WHO ESCAPED

Heinie Zimmerman would never live down the fourth inning of the sixth game of the 1917 World Series. For some reason Dave Robertson would.

Robertson, a quiet, sensitive man, had never quite fit in with his fellow ballplayers. He certainly didn't get along with often-overbearing Giant manager John McGraw. McGraw was quick to criticize; Robertson didn't take criticism well. "Several times Robertson had his bag all packed to return to his Virginia home," reported *Baseball Magazine*, "but he was always persuaded to stay."

On one occasion, McGraw fined the outfielder $500 for hitting a home run. McGraw said he'd given the signal to bunt.

Robertson seemed the least of McGraw's problems through the first five games of the 1917 World Series. The right fielder was one of the few Giants hitting. Heading into game six, the Giants were fighting for survival, trailing the White Sox three games to two. World Series history was not on New York's side. No team to that point had ever trailed three games to two in a seven-game Series and come back to take the title. Besides, McGraw's vaunted Giants hadn't won the big prize since 1905, long enough that the vaunted Giants had become a bit less vaunted in the interim. The team had represented the National League in three prior World Series that decade . . . and lost them all. The mood in the sold-out Polo Grounds that day was tense.

Chicago pitcher Red Faber and Giants pitcher Rube Benton matched zeros for the first three innings in game six. But in the 4th everything went wrong for New York. Chicago star Eddie Collins led off with a simple groundball to third—which Giants third baseman Zimmerman threw over first baseman Walter Holke's head for an error. Benton got Shoeless Joe Jackson to loft an easy flyball to right—which Giants outfielder Dave Robertson dropped, an error every bit as blatant as Snodgrass' of 1912.

That brought White Sox center fielder Happy Felsch to the plate with runners on the corners. Felsch tapped a comebacker to the mound, and Benton threw to Zimmerman at third, catching Collins in a rundown. Zimmerman threw to catcher Rariden, who threw back to Zimmerman guarding third. The play was going better than most for the Giants that inning, in that no one had dropped the ball or thrown it away. Instead the Giant defense found a whole new way to screw up: Neither pitcher Benton nor first baseman Holke were covering home. The speedy Collins raced across the unmanned plate for the run, Zimmerman trailing helplessly behind. Chicago would add two more runs that inning and hold on to win both game and series 4–2.

There was plenty of blame to go around for that disastrous 4th inning. But somehow Zimmerman took nearly all of the abuse—not for the throwing error that opened the inning, but for chasing Collins across the plate. "Who did you expect me to throw to?" he would later be widely quoted as asking. "[Umpire Bill] Klem?"

There's some question whether Zimmerman really spoke these words. They might have been put in his mouth by a reporter. But the point was valid. Pitcher Benton and first baseman Holke somehow escaped blame for failing to cover home plate. Catcher Bill Rariden was not held responsible for his part in a poorly executed rundown. True, chasing Collins was wasted effort—Zimmerman might have instead tried to prevent the other runners from advancing to second and third—but since Chicago followed with a pair of singles and a walk that inning, those runs might have been destined to score either way.

Whoever was to blame for the blown rundown, it wasn't just the White Sox who benefited. Dave Robertson had done exactly what another Giant outfielder had done five years before—dropped an easy fly ball that led to the key run in a World Series—yet thanks to the fielding follies that followed, he escaped with his reputation largely intact.

GOAT SELECTION

Why is one error remembered over another? Perhaps Heinie Zimmerman's miscues were simply more distinctive than Dave Robertson's. Or maybe poor offense opens one up to blame for defensive lapses . . .

- In the 1912 Series, Fred Snodgrass hit only .212. First baseman Fred Merkle and catcher Chief Meyers, who fouled up that foul pop fall, hit .273 and .357, respectively. Snodgrass took the blame. (See page 24)
- In the 1917 Series, Heinie Zimmerman's .120 average fell far short of Walter Holke's .286, Rariden's .385, and Robertson's .500. Though all of these men had a part in the Giant's game-six 4th-inning debacle, Zimmerman was held responsible for the loss.
- In 1939, Ernie Lombardi and Ival Goodman each contributed to a bungled play. (See page 39). But Lombardi's .214 average in the Series was unimpressive compared to Goodman's .333. Lombardi was blamed.
- In 1946, Boston's Johnny Pesky was accused of hesitating as Enos Slaughter scored the winning run for the Cardinals (See page 44). More fault likely rested with Leon Culberson for his bobble and weak throw in from the outfield. Neither player hit for much of an average in the Series— Pesky hit .233, Culberson .222. But Culberson's low batting average is deceptive. He had just nine at-bats, yet hit a relatively important homer in game five. Pesky, a starter expected to help carry Boston, didn't have an extra base hit in 30 at-bats. Pesky took the heat for the defensive misplay.
- In 1986, Bill Buckner hit a powerless .188 in the Series and of course committed a famous error (See page 29). The other contender for the goat horns that year were pitchers Bob Stanley and Calvin Schiraldi. The former didn't allow an earned run in the Series (at least not one of his own), and the latter had appeared just once before in the Series heading into the eventful game six, picking up the save in the Sox' 1–0 game one win.

The future would not be kind to many of the players involved in that pivotal 4th inning. Dave Robertson, a power hitter who had somehow escaped ignominy, couldn't escape World War I, and spent 1918 in the military. Robertson returned to baseball in 1919, but drifted around the National League, playing regularly in only one more season. By the time he retired in 1922, Robertson's once-impressive power stats had joined Robertson himself on baseball's scrap heap. In 1916 and 1917 he'd led the National League in home runs . . . with 12 a season. In 1919, Babe Ruth hit 29. In 1920, Ruth hit 54. No one would ever again be impressed by back-to-back dozen-dinger years. The quiet man spent many of his post-baseball years alone in the woods, employed for nearly three decades as a Virginia state game warden. He died in 1970 at the age of 81.

The years after 1917 would be even worse for Zimmerman. The Giants third baseman was banned from baseball in 1919 for encouraging team-mates to throw games. After baseball, Zimmerman turned to the relatively unglamorous life of a professional steamfitter. He died in 1969.

In 1920, many members of the White Sox—the Giants' opponents in that 1917 Series—followed Zimmerman onto baseball's black list. Eight Chicago White Sox were famously thrown out of the game for involvement in or knowledge of a plot to throw the 1919 World Series. Zimmerman must have wondered why they couldn't have gone in the tank two years sooner and saved him a lot of grief.

Only Eddie Collins, the man who outran Zimmerman for the plate for that key 4th-inning run, would prosper. One of the "Clean Sox" not involved in the Black Sox scandal, Collins put together a Hall of Fame playing career. He later become general manager and part owner of the Boston Red Sox . . . not that owning the Red Sox is everyone's definition of prosperity. Collins died of a heart attack in 1951.

SHUFFLIN' OUT OF BASEBALL

Heinie Zimmerman isn't the only pre-Black Sox player to commit an error that contributed to a World Series loss, then later be thrown out of baseball for involvement in game fixing. The winning run in game four of the 1918 Series scored when Cubs pitcher Shufflin' Phil Douglas misplayed a bunt. Chicago lost the Series in six. Four years later, Douglas was banned for a half-baked and apparently alcohol-induced attempt to throw games during the pennant race.

LOST IN RUTH'S SHADOW—FOR BETTER AND FOR WORSE

It's difficult to get noticed when you play in the shadow of a star, and no ballplayer ever has cast a larger shadow than Babe Ruth. Even the great Lou Gehrig spent much of his career playing a very faint second fiddle to the Babe. So what chance did Aaron Ward have? Ward was an unexceptional second baseman who would never have a fatal malady named after him. He was by all accounts an infielder of modest talents who made up for his athletic shortcomings with hustle and desire. "I never met a more ambitious kid than Aaron," said Yankee manager Miller Huggins. "That boy wants to play so badly that he actually suffers when he has to sit on the bench."

Aaron Ward might have been the least gifted starter on the Yanks of the early 1920s. Yet in two separate World Series, the name Aaron Ward seemed destined to be remembered. On neither of these occasions would this come to pass. When all was said and done, everyone was left talking about Ruth, same as always.

The aggressive, hard-nosed Ward missed his first shot at World Series notoriety in 1921, his second year as a regular in the majors. He probably was happy to have missed it. With Ruth in the lineup, the Yanks led their Polo Grounds landlords, the New York Giants, three games to two in the best-of-nine format then in place. But an injured knee and an infected arm kept Ruth out of games six, seven, and eight, aside from a failed pinch hitting attempt in the 9th inning of game eight. The Giants won all three, and everyone walked away talking about Ruth, the man cheered wildly for playing through his pain in games four and five, then conspicuous in his absence the rest of the way.

Had the Series been in need of a story line, Ward might have been it. In game seven, Ward's 7th-inning error had allowed the Giants to score the winning run and take a 4–3 lead in the series. "Weakness in a club anywhere is bound to show," Ward later told *Baseball Magazine*, "but weakness around second base is likely to be fatal."

In game eight, with the Yanks down 1–0 in the bottom of the 9th, and the crowd still buzzing from Ruth's failed pinch-hit attempt, Ward worked a walk. But his aggressive nature cost him. Frank Baker followed with a sharp groundball to the right side that Giant second baseman Johnny Rawlings somehow managed to turn into an out at first. Ward tried to advance all the way to third on the infield groundout. He was tagged out, ending the Series.

In modern baseball, it's considered not just a gaff but a mortal sin to make the first or third out of an inning at third base. Back in 1921 that rule of thumb might not have been as strict, but getting nabbed on the bases to end a Series is still no way to build membership in one's fan club. Yet Ward was not vilified for the mistake. The enduring story line was Ruth's absence, just as the story in 1922 would be Ruth's lack of production in the Series, and the story in 1923 would be Ruth's success and October vindication.

Ruth hit .368 with three home runs in that 1923 Series and was widely credited with winning the Yankees their first World Series title. Ward hit a team-leading .417 with one home run and was more or less forgotten. "Babe Ruth was great, but then we expect Babe Ruth to be great," said Yankee owner Col. Jacob Ruppert after the Series. "Let us give credit where credit is due, and give most of the credit to Wardie [and manager Miller Huggins]."

It was a nice thought, but Ward's significant contributions in 1923 are no more remembered than his baserunning blunder in 1921. The story in '23 was Ruth. "Ward is still plain Ward to most people," wrote *Baseball Magazine* of the infielder, "and doubtless he will so remain to the end of the chapter."

Ward's career began to decline after 1923, and he was out of the majors for good in 1928 at age 31. Aaron Ward's father had been involved in Arkansas politics, and Aaron himself had been a page and later sergeant-at-arms in the Arkansas State Legislature before joining the Yanks. With a

PECKINPAUGH ESCAPES THE SHADOWS

It's interesting to contrast Aaron Ward's World Series experiences with those of Roger Peckinpaugh. In the 1921 World Series, Yankee shortstop Peckinpaugh let a ball roll through his legs, leading to the only run in a decisive 1–0 game eight. Since the error took place in the first inning—and since Ruth was destined to be the story—Peckinpaugh's error, like Ward's later baserunning misadventure, largely escaped notice.

While Ward stayed with Ruth's Yankees and in Ruth's shadow, Peckinpaugh was traded to the Senators after the 1921 season. Given a chance to become a star in his own right, Peckinpaugh led Washington to the American League flag in 1925, earning the American League MVP award in the process. Then Peckinpaugh committed eight errors in the World Series, including one in the 8th inning of game seven that gift-wrapped the victory for Pittsburgh. This time, with no Babe to hide behind, people took notice. Who would have been the hero if Peckinpaugh's 8th inning error hadn't doomed the Senator's chances? Most likely Peckinpaugh himself, who had hit the homer in the top the 8th to give the club the lead.

little World Series fame on his side, Ward might have become a big wheel in Arkansas politics. Instead Ward ran a tire company in New Orleans and worked for the telephone company. It was not a failed life, but neither was it a famous one. Aaron Ward died in 1961 at age 64.

MORE SUBTEXT THAN YOUR AVERAGE SWEEP

Yankee pitcher Don Larsen joined the baseball pantheon with his 1956 World Series perfect game. Yankee pitcher Bill Bevens is remembered for his near-no-hitter in the 1947 Series. But Yankee Monte Pearson's near no-hitter in game two of the 1939 Series has been all but forgotten. Granted, Pearson didn't lose his with two out in the 9th and the game on the line as Bevens later would, but taking a no-hitter to the 8th in the World Series still seems to deserve some recognition.

Instead catcher Ernie Lombardi would supply the lasting image for the last Series of the 1930s. The plodding future Hall of Famer was the man who broke up Pearson's no-hit bid with a clean single to right, but Lombardi would enter collective memory as a goat. Of all the World Series goats, Lombardi's horns might be the least deserved. If fingers needed to be pointed, they really should have been directed at Reds right fielder Ival Goodman.

The name doesn't ring many bells these days, but for two years in the late 1930s, Goodman seemed on his way to becoming a star. His 30 home runs in 1938 shattered the previous Reds club record of 19. It was a display of power made all the more impressive by the fact the outfielder weighed in at just 170 pounds. Pitchers stopped challenging Goodman inside in 1939, but the outfielder was savvy enough to adjust and hit the ball the other way. Goodman's home runs declined that year, but his batting average soared to .323. He made the National League All-Star team in both 1938 and 1939. In June 1939, Tom Swope of the *Cincinnati Post* wrote that between his hot hitting and his fine fielding, Goodman was well on his way to becoming best all-around right fielder in Reds history.

That 1939 season was a heady time for the Reds. The club had won just one World Series in their history—the tainted 1919 World Series that the White Sox essentially had handed to them. Now 20 years later, Cincinnati breezed to their second National League pennant of the century, taking it by four and a half games and earning a chance to take on the Yankees in the Series.

The World Series opened with two games in New York. By the time the Reds returned to Cincy, they were down two games to none. Cincinnati had scored a grand total of one run on six hits in those first two games, and a season's worth of optimism had been torn to pieces in the space of 18 innings. Crosley Field would offer little refuge, as the Yanks won game three in Cincinnati. No team had ever come back from a 0–3 deficit in a World Series, and up against the powerful Yankees, the '39 Reds didn't seem likely to be the first.

Through eight innings of game four, it seemed that Cincinnati would at least avoid the sweep. The Reds led 4–2 with three outs to go. But the Yankees scored two in the 9th to tie the game up, and were poised for the kill in the top of the 10th. New York had runners on the corners, just one out, and Joe DiMaggio—that year's American League batting champ—at the plate.

True to form, DiMaggio singled to right, bringing Frankie Crosetti home from third with the run that seemed all but certain to wrap up a one-sided Series. If that wasn't enough, usually sure-handed outfielder Ival Goodman bobbled DiMaggio's single, opening the door for Charlie Keller to charge all the way around from first. Keller and

Goodman's throw arrived at the plate at roughly the same time, but Keller saved umpire Babe Pinelli the trouble of making a tough call by steamrolling catcher Lombardi. When the ball rolled free, Keller was safe. But Lombardi was out—or out of it, anyway. He lay dazed by the plate, the ball nearby. The Yankees were now up three games to none in the Series *and* six runs to four in the fourth game. New York needed just three outs to wrap up the title. They were, in other words, in pretty good shape.

The World Series was as good as over, but its defining moment was still moments

THE MAN IN THE ERRANT MASK

Washington's Joe Judge and Ossie Bluege committed errors to hand the Giants a 3–1 lead in the 6th inning of game seven, 1924. Fortunately for them, the Senators rallied to tie the game, providing New York's Hank Gowdy with an opportunity to trip over his catcher's mask in pursuit of a foul ball, leading to the Senators' winning run in the 12th.

It has been nearly eight decades since that Series. Lives have been lived. Nations have risen and fallen. And in those eight decades, no catcher has come within five feet of stepping on his mask without some coach, fan, or broadcaster mentioning Gowdy. If you're going to commit a key error in the World Series, it's probably best not to make it a distinctive one.

away. As Lombardi lay on the ground, knocked into a fog by his collision with Keller, DiMaggio dashed all the way around to score the third Yankee run of the inning. It wasn't Lombardi's fault he'd been run over. And it wasn't as though the third run made much difference anyway.

Yet, oddly, media and fans chose to make a scapegoat of Lombardi, the slow-running, heavy-hitting, big-nosed catcher whose only sin was to get knocked silly by Keller, a man whose nickname was, after all, "King Kong." If anyone deserved to be blamed, it was probably Goodman, whose outfield bobble had created the problem. Goodman seemed particularly lucky to have escaped, considering that an earlier misplay by the right fielder had resulted in Keller's game-winning triple in the 9th inning of game one, costing Cincy its only other legitimate shot at avoiding a sweep.

Perhaps Lombardi's perceived gaff was easier to capture in a photo.

Images of the catcher lying prone as DiMaggio raced home were more compelling than an outfield error. The press dubbed it "Lombardi's swoon," and a goat was born.

Lombardi nearly got a shot at redemption the very next year. The Reds returned to the World Series, and this time beat the Tigers 2–1 in game seven to capture their only title between the Black Sox scandal and the Big Red Machine. But the catcher had sprained an ankle in mid-September, certainly a surprise to those unaware that the lumbering Lombardi had jointed legs. He was limited to one start in the series, and that, as it turned out, was in one of the Reds' losses. Lombardi *was* sent up to pinch-hit late in game seven, with the score tied 1–1 and a runner on third. It was the perfect opportunity for redemption . . . until the Tigers walked him intentionally, leaving it to shortstop Billy Myers to deliver the key sac fly.

> ### THE WORSE YOU LOSE, THE LESS YOUR DANGER
> The Philadelphia A's lost game two of the 1914 World Series 1–0 when Amos Strunk lost a fly ball in the sun in the 9th. They lost game three 5–4 when Joe Bush threw the ball away after fielding a bunt in the 12th. Presumably because the series ended in a four-game sweep, neither man was forced to live with any great shame over his error.

Lombardi's 1940 injury made for a particularly compelling story because only a month earlier the Reds had lost their other catcher. Talented backup Willard Hershberger had slit his own throat in a Boston hotel room after an early-August game, for reasons that have never been fully explained. Scrambling for a replacement, the Reds activated 40-year-old coach Jimmie Wilson. Wilson had caught a grand total of two games in 1938 and 1939, but he would get behind the plate for 16 big games down the stretch for the Reds, then six of the seven World Series games. Remarkably, Wilson managed a .353 average in the Series, and even stole a base. Wilson is remembered for his fountain-of-youth performance in the 1940 Series. But somehow his unexpected success fails to receive mention among the top World Series accomplishments of all time, odd considering his team won a dramatic seven-game showdown.

Perhaps he had the wrong venue. The 1940 World Series matched

Cincinnati and Detroit. With less than half a million residents, Cincinnati was the smallest city in the majors. Detroit was larger, but hardly on par with the likes of New York, Chicago, or Philadelphia. That 1940 World Series was in fact only the third Series since 1910 that didn't feature at least one team from those big-three population centers. (The other two were Pittsburgh/Washington in 1925 and St. Louis/Detroit in 1934.) And of course television wasn't yet beaming Series games to the rest of the country. Maybe Wilson's efforts are written in small print in baseball history because not many fans cared about them.

All of the principal players in the story remained in baseball after their playing careers. Jimmie Wilson never played in another major league game after that 1940 Series, but he coached and managed for Cincinnati for another six seasons. Wilson finally left baseball after the 1946 campaign and moved to Florida. He died there of a heart attack a few months later, at the age of 46.

Lombardi stayed in the majors through 1947, winning his second batting title in 1942. The man they called Schnozz wasn't considered coaching material, but he would later spend seven more years in baseball as press box attendant in San Francisco. The former star also worked at a gas station. Lombardi died in 1977 at age 69, nine years too soon to attend his own induction into the Hall of Fame.

Ival Goodman escaped ignominy in 1939, but he didn't escape injury. It happened in Yankee Stadium, though not during the World Series. In the 1939 All-Star Game in New York, Goodman hurt his shoulder in a failed attempt to make a shoestring catch. (One year earlier, in the 1938 All-Star Game in Cincinnati, his sterling grab had robbed Lou Gehrig of a hit and helped secure the National League's victory.) Goodman played through the discomfort in the second half of 1939, but the shoulder only got worse in 1940, and Goodman's average dropped to .258. The outfielder complained that his swing hadn't been right since the injury. Goodman hung on for four more years as a platoon player, but would never again star. When he injured himself once more crashing into an outfield wall in 1944, his playing days were over. Goodman remained in baseball as a scout and minor league manager until the late 1950s, eventually leaving baseball for a career in sales. He died in Cincinnati in 1984, at the age of 76.

OPPORTUNITY LOST

O nly very rarely in baseball history has a player been presented with the perfect fame-making moment. When such opportunities do occur, they don't always land in the laps of the top talents. Baseball isn't basketball. You can't just pass the ball to Michael Jordan as the clock ticks down. In baseball, opportunity falls to whoever's next in the batting order. Often the Michael Jordans of the sport have to sit and watch with the rest of us while the Bill Wenningtons take the big swings. More often than not, the Wenningtons of the world fail to deliver.

The following men all had their shots to abruptly alter the outcome of a World Series game seven, either in the top or the bottom of the 9th. For some it would be their only chance to be remembered.

THREE SHOTS AT GLORY

Heading into the 1946 season, only two ballplayers in the history of the World Series had come to the plate in the 9th inning of a deciding game seven with their team trailing and the tying run on base—in other words with a chance to take a team from Series defeat to victory (or near victory, if in the *top* of the 9th) with a single swing of the bat.

The first was Bob Meusel, who got his chance with two men out in the bottom of the 9th in game seven, 1926, down one run with Babe Ruth on first. The Series ended before Meusel could take his shot at glory though, as Ruth was cut down trying to steal. Then in game seven, 1931, Philadelphia A's leadoff hitter Max Bishop came to the plate with two out and runners on the corners in the 9th, his team trailing by two. Bishop, known as Camera Eye for his ability to draw a walk, faced Cardinals pitcher Bill Hallahan, known as Wild Bill for his sometimes erratic acquaintance with the strike zone. With heavy hitters like Mule Haas, Mickey Cochrane, Al Simmons, and Jimmie Foxx due up after Bishop, a walk to load the bases wouldn't have been a bad outcome for the A's. But Camera Eye flew out to center.

(Completists will note that a comparable opportunity for glory occurred in 1912, when Harry Hooper, Steve Yerkes, and Tris Speaker came to the plate in the bottom of the *10th* with a chance to turn defeat into victory.)

In 1946, four men would find themselves in such an everything-on-the-line, instant-glory, 9th inning at-bat—twice as many as had in the entire previous history of the World Series. One of these four managed a hit, albeit not a run-generating or fame-producing hit. As for the other three . . .

The Red Sox and Cardinals had traded punches through the first six games of the 1946 Series, with Boston grabbing games one, three, and five; St. Louis games two, four, and six. It was the first baseball season played after the end of World War II, and fans reveled in the return of star players like Stan Musial of the Cardinals and Ted Williams of the Red Sox. Each man had captured the MVP of his league in 1946 and led his club to a pennant. But neither would excel in the Series. Musial hit just .222 without a home run. Williams hit a powerless .200 in what would be the only World Series of his career. (Boston's star was hampered by a bad right elbow. He'd been hit by a pitch thrown by Washington's Mickey Haefner in a meaningless postseason practice game, possibly the last time a Washington Senator ever affected the outcome of a World Series.)

With the big stars failing to grab the spotlight, other players had opportunities to become heroes or goats. Game seven of the 1946 Series would create one of each. With two outs in the 8th and game and series each tied at three, Enos Slaughter earned his place in baseball lore by scoring from first on Harry Walker's "single" to left center. Officially Walker would be credited with a double, but no matter,

Slaughter became one of the few players in history to gain more fame for scoring a run than his teammate did for driving him in. Combined with his .320 batting average in the Series, the mad dash around the bases would be enough to make Slaughter a hero.

Sox shortstop Johnny Pesky landed on the other side of the ledger. According to baseball legend, Pesky hesitated at the crucial moment, "holding the ball" as Slaughter raced home.

IN CELEBRATION OF ROUND NUMBERS

Bob Watson, like Enos Slaughter, once received more attention for crossing the plate than did the teammate who delivered the RBI. On May 4, 1975, Watson earned a modicum of fame for scoring baseball's one millionth run. His spikes were put on exhibit in the Hall of Fame. He was given a $1,000 watch. Teammate Milt May, who'd driven in that millionth run with a three-run homer, for some reason received far less notice, not to mention no watch.

Scoring the millionth run was considered a notable achievement at the time. Ballplayers all across the country had been alerted when run number 999,999 crossed the plate. When Reds shortstop Dave Concepcion hit a home run with no one on in a game against Atlanta, he sprinted around the bases in hopes of writing his own name in the record books. He lost the race to Watson by just seconds. When Concepcion was alerted of this loss in the top of the following inning, he raised his arms above his head in dismay. Others fared worse in the race for one million. Twins star second baseman Rod Carew tried to score from third on a short fly to right with baseball's run counter at 999,999. He not only was thrown out, he hurt his right leg in the play.

Over the years some have questioned how much Pesky really was to blame. His hesitation was not a long one. Certainly outfielder Leon Culberson's momentary bobble and weak throw to Pesky was the greater problem. (Culberson was only in the game because regular Sox center fielder Dom DiMaggio had hurt his leg the inning before. Slaughter later said he wouldn't have tried for home if DiMaggio had been in center.) Yet Culberson's role in the play has been forgotten.

Often overlooked is that Slaughter scored his run in the bottom of the 8th. The Red Sox had one more chance to bat against tiring St. Louis left hander Harry Brecheen. Had the Cardinals lost, the game would have been reminiscent of the Cubs' loss in game seven the year before. In 1945, Chicago had asked Hank Borowy, a pitcher not known for his endurance, to start game seven after finishing game six. Borowy was hit hard, and the Cubs lost. One year later, the Cards were asking Brecheen, at 160 pounds one of the smallest pitchers in baseball, to finish game seven after throwing nine innings in game six. The Cards had called on Brecheen when game seven starter Murry Dickson tired in the 8th, and Brecheen allowed a two-run double before escaping the inning. He later would admit he had very little left in his tank for the 9th.

Red Sox first baseman Rudy York opened the top of the 9th with a single. With Boston down 4–3 and one on, that made future Hall of Famer Bobby Doerr the first man since 1931 to bat in the 9th inning of a game seven with a chance to take his team from a deficit to a lead with one swing. Doerr managed a single. You don't get remembered for singles in these situations, of course, but neither can you be blamed. Doerr had done his job; the tying run was now in scoring position, the winning run at first. The fate of the 1946 Red Sox would fall to three men: Pinky Higgins, Roy Partee, and Tom McBride.

Higgins was the best of the bunch. The third baseman was a three-time All Star who'd produced a .292 average during a 14-year career and twice had driven in one hundred runs in a season. With Detroit in 1940, Higgins had helped Hank Greenberg carry the Tigers in the World Series, hitting .333 in seven games. Higgins' six RBIs in that Series had tied Greenberg for the club lead. Unfortunately, those 1940 heroics had gone for naught. With Detroit down 2–1 in game seven, Higgins had led off the 9th . . . and grounded out to third. Detroit lost the Series to Cincinnati.

Now Higgins had a second chance. A home run, even a double, and he'd be a World Series hero. Instead he was asked to bunt. There was little chance for glory in a bunt, but there was the potential for disaster. Higgins' bunt was too hard and too close to charging Cardinal third baseman Whitey Kurowski. Pinch-runner Paul Campbell, in for York, reached third with the potential tying run—but the potential winning run was cut down at second, and the aging Higgins barely beat the relay throw to first, narrowly avoiding the double play. Higgins efforts would go down as a ground out to third, the same result as his crucial at-bat in game seven of the 1940 World Series. Boston was left with runners on the corners and two outs left in their season, still down one run.

The bunt would be Higgins' last major league plate appearance, as he retired after the Series. While Higgins had failed in two separate opportunities for World Series glory, he was destined to be remembered—and not just for his record 12 consecutive hits in 1938. The hard-drinking Higgins would later become manager and then general manager of the Red Sox. Under Higgins' guidance, the Red Sox were the last team in the major leagues to integrate their roster, not doing so until 1959. By some accounts, Higgins' reportedly racist views were a major factor in this delay.

In 1968, an intoxicated Higgins plowed his car into a Louisiana highway department road crew. One man was killed. Higgins pleaded guilty to negligent homicide and was sentenced to four years of hard labor. He was paroled after two months for health reasons and died of a heart attack two days after his release.

Of course Sox fans weren't thinking about Pinky Higgins' future after his 1946 game-seven bunt. Their eyes were on Roy Partee, the man heading to the plate. Partee was a backup catcher who'd entered the game just an inning before. Years earlier, Partee had nearly blown his career before it began when he showed up for spring training overweight. The pounds, he explained, were a result of his new bride's delicious lemon meringue pie. Partee slimmed down enough to hit a competent .262 against war-depleted pitching staffs during his first two seasons in the majors, 1943 and 1944, albeit without much power. By 1945 Partee himself was in the war, coming under fire during the invasion of the Philippines. He returned to the majors in time to get into 40 games in 1946 and took full advantage of his limited at-bats, hitting a career-high .315. Still, he was a player kept around more for his glove than his bat.

Partee certainly wasn't much of a candidate for a fame-generating, game-winning home run—he'd hit only two round trippers in his major league career—but even a double would have won the game. A simple sac fly could have tied things up, robbing Slaughter of his fame and Pesky of his infamy in the process. As a man just back from fighting the war, Partee would have made a particularly appealing hero.

Only Partee fouled out to Musial at first base. He'd survived both his wife's meringue and the war in the Pacific, but he'd survive only two more seasons in the majors, hitting .231, then .203. Partee never did hit another home run. He managed in the minors after his career and later had some success as a scout for the Mets, signing Bud Harrelson and Tug McGraw.

The pitcher's spot was due up next, which meant Boston manager Joe Cronin had to make a decision. With the season on the line, Cronin sent a man named Tom McBride to the plate. McBride had surfaced as a spare outfielder with Boston during the war years, a 28-year-old rookie in 1943. Never a power hitter—he'd produced just one homer in 1,186 career at-bats—McBride did manage to push his batting average over .300 in 1945. The slap-hitting outfielder had seemed a likely candidate to disappear from the majors when the real players returned after the war. But McBride had unexpectedly held his own, posting an average just above .300 in 1946. He'd even been one of the heroes of game one of the World Series, delivering a clutch 9th-inning, game-tying single.

Tom McBride might not have been the first player you'd want at the plate with the season at stake, but considering Cronin's other options off the bench, he likely was the best choice. The other non-pitchers available were Don Gutteridge, Johnny Lazor, Eddie Pellagrini, and Ed McGah. Only Gutteridge, a powerless infielder at the tail end of his career, had even appeared in the Series. McGah was a backup catcher who would accumulate all of eight hits in his big league career. Lazor was a wartime backup outfielder who'd hit .138 in 1946, and Pellagrini was a rookie infielder who'd hit .211 that year in limited action. It was one of the most dramatic situations in the sport's history to that point—World Series, game seven, 9th inning, two out, team behind with the tying and winning runs on base—and these were the men Cronin had at his disposal.

McBride hit a chopper to the right of the mound. Card pitcher Brecheen, known as The Cat for his nimble fielding, couldn't reach it. That left it up to St. Louis second baseman Red Schoendienst. To most in the stands, the play appeared routine. They didn't know that McBride's hit had taken a bad hop before reaching the charging fielder. The ball bounced high into Schoendienst's shoulder, then rolled up his arm. With the tying run heading home from third, Schoendienst finally corralled the ball and backhanded it to shortstop Marty Marion just ahead of Higgins' slide. Schoendienst would later refer to the play as the toughest he had to make in the Series.

Had the Cardinals second baseman not been one of the best fielders in the business, had the Red Sox runner on first been a little faster, or had Higgins successfully bunted both runners up, negating the force, the tying run might have scored on McBride's chopper. Instead the Series was over, and McBride was forgotten. Would tying the game up have made him famous? Not to the degree that driving home a winning run would have. But when he passed away half a century later, at least his hometown paper wouldn't have written, "Tom McBride was never a big-name star."

MORE MEN JUST ONE SWING FROM GREATNESS

Tom McBride wouldn't be the last player to hit with the tying run on base in the 9th inning of a World Series game seven, but he would be one of the last obscure players to do so. In the half century stretching from 1947—the year after McBride—through 1996, nine players had similar opportunities.

Most of these nine men didn't need one big moment to become a star. They already were stars—or were well on their way to stardom—big hit or no. While the 1946 Sox' fortunes rode on the likes of McBride, Partee, and the aging Higgins, four of the nine who followed would become Hall of Famers: Mickey Mantle had his shot in the 1960 Series, Willie Mays and Willie McCovey had theirs in 1962. Yogi Berra managed to hit in the Hollywood dream situation twice, in 1957 and again in 1960, which perhaps explains one of Yogi's many famous lines: "It was a once-in-a-lifetime opportunity, and I've had a couple of those."

True to their talents, most of these future Hall of Fame players came through with productive at-bats, even if none of them ended up as an instant hero (just as future Hall of Famer Bobby Doerr had managed a single in 1946). Mantle singled. Berra brought the tying run home with a grounder in 1960 (he did make a non-productive out in his 1957 chance). Mays doubled, though the tying run held at third. McCovey hit the ball about as hard as a ball can be hit . . . right at Bobby Richardson.

Another four of these nine could-have-been heroes are not in the

Hall of Fame (though one, Pete Rose, is Hall of Fame caliber), but they were All Stars and in some cases even MVPs. This list includes Roger Maris and Bill Skowron for the Yanks in 1960, Felipe Alou in 1962, and Rose in 1972. All of these players made outs, but only Alou failed to make contact.

That leaves just one remaining player who had a dream shot at fame: Chuck Hiller, a largely forgettable second baseman who came to the plate for the Giants in game seven of the 1962 Series with one out and one on in the bottom of the 9th, and the Giants down 1–0. In game four, Hiller had become the first National Leaguer to hit a grand slam in the Series. But that, the well-earned nickname Iron Hands, and the fact he wore a hairpiece as a coach in the 1970s and 1980s, were about the only things Hiller would be remembered for in baseball history. With the 1962 series on the line, he struck out.

There was, then, a relatively reliable rule of thumb for predicting the results of at-bats in the 9th inning of World Series game sevens with the tying run on base. The future Hall of Famers would manage a productive at-bat, though they wouldn't produce a hit sufficient to score both the tying and winning runs. The very-good players tended to make contact, but be retired. Chuck Hiller would strike out. But from Hall of Famer to Chuck Hiller, they all had two things in common—none came through with the hit that put their team in the lead, and every team that trailed going into the 9th inning of game seven eventually lost.

Then a funny thing happened. In 1997 and 2001 two different clubs found themselves trailing in the 9th inning of a Series seventh game. Against the run of history, both teams came out winners.

In 1997, the Florida Marlins came back to stun the Indians. Florida trailed 2–1 heading to the bottom of the 9th, when Moises Alou opened the inning with a single to center. (Alou's uncle, Matty Alou, had opened the bottom of the 9th inning of the seventh game of the 1962 World Series with a bunt single for the Giants. Moises' father Felipe, up next, struck out.) That gave Bobby Bonilla the first shot at a Series-ending dream homer. Bonilla struck out on a 3–2 pitch. Charles Johnson followed with a single, putting runners on the corners. Second baseman Craig Counsell took his shot at glory, lifting a fly ball deep to right. He came up short of the miracle home run, but at least delivered a game-tying sac fly. Jim Eisenreich was up next. Eisenreich suffered from Tourette's Syndrome, a malady that had once forced him to abandon professional baseball (see page 164). He would have made an appealing hero . . . had he not grounded out to second.

The Marlins won it in the 11th. Cleveland second baseman Tony Fernandez became the goat of the Series when he let a Counsell grounder roll through his legs, putting runners on the corners with one out. That gave Eisenreich a second shot at fame . . . or it would have, had Eisenreich not been intentionally walked. Devon White then grounded into a fielder's choice, Fernandez making a nice play to cut down the runner at the plate (shades of Fred Snodgrass' great catch in the 1912 Series that seemed for a moment to make up for his error). So it fell to Edgar Renteria to hit a seeing-eye ground ball single up the middle. No Marlin had come through with the one hit that took the team straight from deficit to victory, but for the first time, a club had come back to win after trailing heading to the 9th inning of a game seven.

Four years later, in 2001, another team rallied for the win after trailing heading into the 9th inning of a game seven. This time it was the Arizona Diamondbacks scoring twice in the 9th to beat the Yankees 3–2. Mark Grace opened the inning with a single to center, leaving the Diamondbacks who followed with a chance play the hero. The first two—Damian Miller and Jay Bell—were asked to bunt, precluding any real chance for heroism. The third batter, Tony Womack, came through with a game-tying double. But Womack lost his shot at lasting fame when the winning run was held at third. That gave former Marlin Craig Counsell, now a Diamondback, a second shot at glory. Yankee pitcher Mariano Rivera hit him with a pitch. All of this set things up nicely for Luis Gonzalez, a one-time minor league teammate of Edgar Renteria's brother Edinson. Gonzalez lofted a soft fly ball over a drawn-in infield for the win. Neither Edgar Renteria nor Gonzalez had hit the ball particularly well, but both came away with a measure of fame.

SOMETIMES A WALK ISN'T AS GOOD AS A HIT

These days it's taken for granted that endless rounds of playoffs come between the end of the regular season and the start of the World Series.

But prior to 1969, league playoffs only occurred when two teams ended the season in a tie. That didn't happen in the modern era until 1946. But beginning that year, playoffs occurred with some regularity. Between 1946 and 1962, there were four best-of-three playoffs in the National League—1946, 1951, 1959, and 1962—and one single-game playoff in the American League, in 1948. The very first league playoff game was lost in 1946 by Dodgers pitcher Ralph Branca, who would lose again in the first game of the 1951 playoff, then once more, famously, two days later.

The Dodgers appeared in all five National League tie-breaking playoffs during the pre-Wild-Card era—the four best-of-threes, and a one-game playoff in 1980.

AFTER THE SHOT

The acclaim heaped upon Bobby Thomson for his homer in the final game of the 1951 National League playoff has come to overshadow the Giants' loss in the subsequent World Series. The Yankees took the subway Series in six . . . but only after the Giants missed a pair of golden opportunities to push it to a seventh game. Trailing 4–1 with two out in the bottom of the 8th inning of game six, the Giants sent weak-hitting Cuban backup catcher Ray Noble to the plate to pinch-hit with the bases loaded. He was called out on strikes. Still down three runs in the 9th, the Giants again loaded the bases, this time with no one out. Monte Irvin made a bid for glory, but his deep fly to left stayed in the park. All three runners tagged and advanced, and the Giants were down to their final two outs.

Either of the next New York batters *could* have tied the game with a single or won it with a three-run homer. Instead, each flew out. One of those final two batters was backup catcher Sal Yvars, taking his first swings of the postseason. The other was none other than Bobby Thomson. Apparently he had just so much magic in him.

That should have provided the Boys of Summer with plenty of opportunities to become playoff heroes or goats. But most of those five playoff series didn't provide enough down-to-the-wire drama to create a hero. The 1946 playoff was a two-game sweep by the Cardinals. The 1959 playoff was taken in two straight by the Dodgers. Even single-game playoffs are no guarantees of drama. The Dodgers'

1980 one-game playoff against the Astros was never much of a contest, as Houston scored seven runs in the first four innings and cruised to a 7–1 win.

Only twice did National League tie-breaking playoffs create great drama. The 1951 playoff provided the gold standard of legend-making moments, the Thomson/Branca matchup. That leaves just the 1962 playoff, a three-game set that doesn't get the recognition it deserves.

The first thing one notices about the 1962 playoff is how much it resembles the far more famous 1951 three-game series. In both cases, The Dodgers faced their long-time rival, the Giants. In both cases, the series went the full three games, the only two times that ever happened. In both cases the Giants rallied in the 9th inning of the third game for a dramatic come-from-behind win. But that's where the similarities end.

By 1962, Dodgers/Giants meant L.A./San Francisco, a rivalry to be sure, but not one to match the intensity of a New York subway series. The players had changed as well. Only Willie Mays and Duke Snider played in both third games. But the most important difference was the nature of the final blow. Thomson's game-winning homer in 1951 raised the bar on baseball drama. In 1962 the winning hit was . . . a walk.

The Dodgers entered the top of the 9th in that 1962 third game with a two-run lead, but pitcher Ed Roebuck was tiring. He was starting his 4th inning of work . . . after pitching two-thirds of an inning the day before . . . after pitching four innings the day before that. Matty Alou opened the inning with a single (just as he would open the 9th inning of game seven of that year's World Series with a single). Roebuck retired Harvey Kuenn, but walks to both Willie McCovey and Felipe Alou followed. That brought Willie Mays to the plate with the bases loaded, one out, and the Giants down two. Mays hit Roebuck hard—literally. His comebacker deflected off the pitcher, and everyone was safe before the ball could be retrieved. L.A.'s lead was down to one. That was it for Roebuck, as Dodger manager Walter Alston went to his pen. New pitcher Stan Williams gave up a game-tying sac fly to Orlando Cepeda. A wild pitch and intentional walk re-loaded the bases with two out. Jim Davenport was due up next.

Davenport might not have been Willie Mays or Orlando Cepeda, but he was a San Francisco Giant through and through. Davenport's first game in the majors had been the Giants' first game in San Francisco, and he'd been the team's regular third baseman ever since. No one questioned Davenport's abilities . . . as a fielder. As a hitter, Davenport had been merely adequate. In his first four seasons he'd hit .261 with an average of nine home runs a season, a decent showing, not a great one.

Then in 1962, Davenport's offensive numbers dramatically improved. His average leapt to .297; his home run total climbed to a career high 14. Davenport made his first All-Star appearance that year, and added his first Gold Glove for good measure. He'd sparkled in the NL playoff series, with two hits in each of the first two games and one already in game three. One more hit would make him a hero. Despite his hot bat, Davenport didn't even expect to get the chance. "I was kind of surprised they didn't pinch-hit for me," Davenport would tell *USA Today* decades later. "I guess we didn't have any left-handed pinch-hitters left. In that situation [manager Alvin Dark] had hit for me before."

Davenport didn't get a hit. But what he did was just as effective. Davenport worked a five-pitch walk to force the winning run home from third. The Giants added an insurance run on an error by Dodger second baseman Larry Burright, and retired the Dodgers in order in the bottom of the inning. Eleven years later and a continent away, the Giants had done it to the Dodgers again. Only a walk lacks the drama of a home run, or even of a single, so Jim Davenport wouldn't go down in history as the new Bobby Thomson. Perhaps Camera Eye Max Bishop was smart to swing away in his big at-bat in the 1931 Series. You don't get famous walking to first.

The Giants took on the Yankees in the 1962 World Series, but lost in seven.

That 1962 campaign would turn out to be Davenport's one great season. Though he'd play until 1970, the Giant third baseman would never make another All-Star team, never win another Gold Glove, never again hit more than nine home runs in a season, and only once more hit over .252 (the exception was a .275 mark in 1967). Two more things Davenport would never do again: he'd never play in another postseason game—the Giants didn't make it back to the playoffs until 1971, the season after Davenport had retired to manage in the minors—and he'd never again take as many walks as he had during that 1962 season.

Still, Davenport was a San Francisco Giant to the core. He played every one of his 1,501 major league games for the club, managed in their minor league system, and after a short stint as a coach with the Padres, returned to San Francisco to coach for the Giants into the 1980s. In 1985, Davenport was named manager of his long-time team. But with the team's record an abysmal 58–88 in September, and Davenport embroiled in an ongoing feud with Giants star Jeffrey Leonard, the skipper resigned. He would never manage another game in the majors. It's probably a coincidence, but Giants players walked only 488 times in Davenport's single season at the helm, the second-lowest total in the National League.

Two years later, San Francisco would make it back to the postseason—without Davenport.

It is a measure of the lack of fame spawned by Davenport's clutch game-winning walk that a 1982 press release put out by the Giants announcing his return for another season as a coach didn't get the details right. It mentioned in passing that Davenport "drew a bases-loaded walk to *tie* the crucial third game of the 1962 playoffs with Los Angeles." [emphasis added] Davenport's walk actually had produced the *winning* run. Even his own club didn't remember what he'd done for them.

Jim Davenport had just one opportunity for glory. He didn't get the fame, but he got the job done.

THE WOULD-BE SERIES HERO . . .
WHO WOULDN'T EVEN MAKE THE MAJORS

When Yankee shortstop Tony Kubek injured his wrist late in September 1964, Yankee farmhand Chester Trail appeared in an ideal position for fame. The shortstop had been promised a call-up from the minors in the second half of the season anyway. With the starting shortstop out, Trail might have played a significant role during the Yankee pennant drive and the World Series. It didn't happen. The Yankees called up Trail's *contract* after major league rosters expanded, but for some reason they didn't actually call up the player. Trail was a Yankee only on paper. "I never did get an explanation why they did that," said Trail recently. "I always wondered if it had something to do with my being a black shortstop. Only a few years before when I started in the minors I couldn't even eat out with the fellas in some places."

Phil Linz played every inning of all seven Series games at shortstop. He had to. With Trail not on hand, the Yankees didn't have anyone on their bench with significant experience at the position. The Yankees lost to the Cardinals in 1964, and didn't return to the Series until 1976.

Trail was back in the minors the following season. Year after year, he'd make the Yanks spring training roster. Each time he'd be one of the last players cut. In 1967, Trail was sent to the Orioles in a deal for Steve Barber, and again he seemed on the verge of reaching the majors. But just before the final cuts in spring training, Earl Weaver told Trail he'd decided to go with a player who'd played for him in the Orioles system instead. Trail gave up on baseball soon after. He spent a decade in sales for Blue Cross/Blue Shield, and currently is a pastor for two Ohio churches. The man who could have played for the Yankees in the World Series never made it into a single major league game, postseason *or* regular reason, thus denying him even the chance to be known as a former major leaguer.

Buzz Arlett

PART II
WRONG TIME, WRONG PLACE

"Circumstances make a career," wrote Ted Williams in his autobiography, My Turn at Bat. "A man being at the right place at the right time with the right material. Circumstances can make a .400 hitter." Circumstances also can make a 20-game winner or, for that matter, a Hall of Famer. But while circumstances have worked for some players, they've worked against others . . . the home run hitters trapped in times and places more suited to singles . . . the otherwise memorable players stuck on forgettable teams . . . the second men to reach noted milestones. These players' talents and successes suggested they were destined for fame. Circumstances suggested otherwise.

MAJOR STARS OF THE MINOR LEAGUES

4

These days, it's a near certainty that players with major league talent will reach the major leagues. Even ballplayers *without* major league talent have a fighting chance, thanks to teams like the Tampa Bay Devil Rays and 2003 Detroit Tigers. But in the early decades of the 20th century, a number of potential stars spent the bulk of their playing careers in the upper-level minor leagues. Some were viewed as somehow lacking by the majors, despite tremendous minor league success. Others played for minor league teams that simply preferred to keep them. (Minor league clubs have not always been affiliated with major league farm systems.) The Pacific Coast League in particular saw itself as nearly a third major league until the Dodgers and Giants headed west in 1958, and many talented players spent their best years in the PCL.

Stars of the high minors could make decent money by the standards of the time, and some were perfectly happy with their lot. But by playing their best years in the minors they lost their chance at fame. Minor league players, even great ones, are rarely remembered.

GREAT DHS . . . IN AN ERA WHEN THOSE LETTERS MEANT LAWRENCE, NOT BLOMBERG

Arlett, Boone, Jolley, Clabaugh. They were four men, but they have just one story. It's a story that inevitably begins with the words "tremendous hitter," moves on to "stuck in the minors," before wrapping things up with "a wonderful talent who's now forgotten."

What cost these men their chance at major league fame? The explanation is as simple as it is counterintuitive in today's baseball world. They all suffered from the now-obsolete criticism, "good hit, no field." Read a scouting report or article written about any one of them, and after a lengthy discussion of hitting exploits you will inevitably come across the words "but he was no gazelle in the field." (It's always a gazelle, too. No one would expect a puma or a pronghorn antelope to be a serious contender for the Gold Glove, yet the gazelle has somehow acquired legendary status for its defensive prowess.) Buzz Arlett, Ike Boone, Smead Jolley, and Moose Clabaugh were not destined to join the gazelle among baseball's defensive stars. And because of their shortcomings with the glove, these men never got much of chance to become stars with the bat either.

This is, then, the story of four flawed ballplayers. But it's also a story of bad luck. Had just one major league manager decided to live with some bad fielding in exchange for a big bat, any of these men could have been famous. And it's a story of bad timing as well. Since 1973, the American League has offered a refuge for "good hit, no field" players like these. That refuge is known as rule 6.10: the designated hitter. It isn't so far-fetched to wonder how the defensively challenged hitting stars of earlier decades might have fared as designated hitters. Rules similar to the modern DH have been discussed since the 19th century. In the late 1920s, the National League reportedly came close to implementing such a plan—until the American League voted down the proposal.

In the not-too-distant future, Edgar Martinez or another long-time big-name DH might even make the Hall of Fame. And why not? It is the Hall of *Fame,* after all. DHs have that one skill most likely to generate fame in baseball: They can hit.

Buzz Arlett could hit. He hit .341 with 432 homers in the highest levels of minor league baseball between 1918 and 1937. He could pitch, too, winning more than 100 games in his minor league career. Unfortunately, Arlett wasn't much of an outfielder. Just how bad he was defensively is a matter of some debate, but he certainly wasn't good. "He would lose more games with the glove," decided one Cardinals scout, "than he would make up at the bat."

Shaky fielding wasn't the only thing holding Arlett back. The Oakland Oaks, his Pacific Coast League club, reportedly demanded $100,000 for Arlett's contract during his prime. It was a virtually unheard of figure sure to scare off all potential suitors. So Arlett remained in the minors. He remained there after a five-year run in which he hit no less than .344 and no fewer than 25 home runs in any season. He remained there for 13 seasons in all before he got to the bigs.

Finally in 1931, the Philadelphia Phillies convinced Oakland to part with the aging Arlett. At 32, Arlett's best years were already behind him, but at least he'd get a chance to give the baseball world an idea how great he might have been. Arlett posted very respectable numbers that year—a .313 average and 18 homers in 121 games. But injuries slowed him heading down the stretch, and the Phillies dropped Arlett after the season. It would be his only year in the majors.

Arlett was not particularly pleased with his life as a big fish in the small ponds of the minors. He thought—not without some reason—that he deserved to be big leaguer. But when Philadelphia let him go, the other major league clubs weren't interested. With little choice in the matter, Arlett signed with Baltimore of the International League, a top minor league. He hit .339 with 54 home runs in 1932, yet there would be no return trip to the majors. "This time there will be no turning back the hands of the clock," wrote *Baseball Magazine*. "Arlett is too old to try it again."

Arlett moved from Baltimore to Minneapolis, with a brief stop in Birmingham in between. Aside from a four-at-bat stint in Syracuse to end his career in 1937, he hit .313 or better in each of his final 15 professional seasons. Arlett's 432 homers remain the most minor league round-trippers anyone's ever hit on American soil. The former outfielder opened a successful restaurant in Minneapolis after his career, and died in 1964.

Ike Boone's story is much like Arlett's. He was a minor league hitting star whose lack of range in the outfield cost him a shot at major league fame. Boone got a bit more of a chance in the bigs than did Arlett—he played in parts of eight major league seasons with four different teams in the 1920s and early 1930s. Yet for all those seasons, Boone appeared in just 356 big league games. Still, whenever Boone got a shot in the majors, he inevitably hit shots. In his 356 games he hit .321 with

26 homers. In his only two years as a regular, 1924 and 1925 with the Red Sox, Boone hit a combined .333 with 22 homers.

Just how bad was Boone's defense to keep such a potent bat out of the majors? His range was said to be comparable to that of statuary. But based on accounts of the day, he hardly seems to have been the worst outfielder who ever lived. "[Boone was] a fairly sure catcher of a fly [with] a strong throwing arm," wrote *The Brooklyn Eagle* when Boone was cut from the Dodgers in 1933. "Despite lack of speed, it would seem that somewhere there must have been a place in the majors for one of Boone's great hitting ability."

Apparently there wasn't. Boone never made it back to the bigs after leaving Brooklyn. He retired as a professional player in 1936 with 217 minor league homers and an astounding .370 minor league career batting average compiled mainly in the very top levels of minor league ball. His 553 total bases in the Pacific Coast League in 1929 remains the single-season record for all of professional baseball.

Boone's baseball career ended while America was still deep in the Great Depression. He took what work he could find, and eventually became head of plant security for an Alabama foundry. Boone died of a heart attack in 1958 at age 61, shortly after mowing his lawn.

Smead Jolley's offensive statistics are much like those of Arlett and Boone. In the minors Jolley produced a .366 average and 334 home runs. In the majors he hit .305 with 46 homers in just 473 total at-bats with the White Sox and Red Sox in the early 1930s. But Smead Jolley differed from Arlett and Boone in one way: His work in the outfield wasn't just sub-par, it was the stuff of comic legend.

Jolley's pursuit of fly balls was reminiscent, wrote *The Sporting News,* of "a kid chasing soap bubbles." A representative Smead Jolley story holds that the outfielder once let a routine single off the bat of Cleveland's Milt Galatzer bounce through his legs . . . twice—once the conventional way, then again on the rebound off the outfield wall. According to the story, Jolley finally corralled the ball on his third stab, then promptly heaved it over the third baseman's head for his third error on the play as Galatzer came all the way around to score. Some believe this three-error play is apocryphal, or at least exaggerated. If so, that never stopped the good-natured Jolley from telling the story himself.

Jolley's pursuit of airborne baseballs was so poor—yet his potent bat so appealing—that the White Sox even attempted to convert him into a catcher at the age of 30. The experiment lasted a total of five games. Apparently Jolley couldn't catch pitched balls any better than hit ones.

With major league teams unable to find a place to hide Jolley on defense, he and his All-Star-quality bat roamed the minors, playing everywhere from San Francisco to Jersey City. Yet one doesn't get the feeling that Jolley was distraught over his missed shot at fame. When a joke was told about Jolley's defense, Smead would laugh right along with everyone else, then tell one of his own.

Jolley finally retired from baseball in 1941. He and his wife later lived in California, but the Arkansas native apparently still owned some ranch land back in his native state. In the mid-1970s, Jolley recorded one last hit, when oil was discovered beneath that Arkansas property. He died in 1991 at the age of 89.

Moose Clabaugh's eyesight was plenty sharp at the plate, but apparently not up to the job in the field. Throughout his career, Clabaugh blamed his eyes for his poor pursuit of fly balls. Glasses failed to solve the problem. "I'd make easy plays look hard," he'd later admit.

Clabaugh's minor league statistics fit right in with the other players on this list— .339 career average and 346 home runs in 17 minor league seasons. But his taste

OLD OX WAS NO YOUNG BUCK

Like Jolley and company, Ox Eckhardt was a great hitter in the upper levels of the minor leagues. His career minor league average was .367, though he didn't have great power. And like the others, Eckhardt got only a brief trial in the majors—just 52 at-bats. But sub-par glove work wasn't the only thing that denied Eckhardt his shot at fame. His main adversary was age. The University of Texas grad didn't really get going in the minors until he was 26. By the time Eckhardt got his first taste of the majors with the Boston Braves in 1932, he was 30. By that time he'd already played for the New York Giants—the New York *football* Giants. Eckhardt was a highly regarded fullback. Very few players have started so late and still gone on to major league greatness.

Eckhardt returned to Texas after his athletic career and, like any good Texan, became a successful cattle rancher. He died at the age of 49 in 1951.

of the majors was even briefer—just 14 at-bats and one lone hit for the Dodgers at the end of the 1926 season. Those 14 at-bats would be his only chance; Clabaugh never even got an invitation to a major league spring training. "Those were disappointing days," he told the *Arizona Republic* in 1981. "I talked to the major league scouts. They all told me the same thing. They said my fielding was holding me back."

Clabaugh's minor league home-run total would have been even more impressive, except his playing career essentially ended at the age of 35. Clabaugh held out for the entire 1938 season in a contract dispute with Portland of the PCL. When that didn't work, he held out the entire 1939 season as well, joining the Oregon State Police during his extended hiatus. Clabaugh finally returned to baseball in 1940, but retired midseason.

Bad eyes might have cost Clabaugh a shot at stardom, but they didn't stop him from spending the second half of the 1940 season as an umpire, one of the first in pro ball to wear glasses. Clabaugh might have made a career of it, too, but his wife wanted him at home. He took a job as chief of security at Dalles Dam in Oregon. Clabaugh retired to Arizona in 1965, and died there in 1984 at the age of 82.

GREAT EXPECTORATIONS

Perhaps no potentially great pitcher ever had worse timing than Frank Shellenback. Shellenback debuted with the White Sox in 1918 while still a teenager, and spent part of two seasons with the club. But the White Sox were among the best teams in baseball in those pre-Black-Sox-scandal days, and there was little room for a young pitcher still finding his way. Shellenback was back in the minors by the end of the 1919 season.

The return to the minors shouldn't have been a major setback. Shellenback was still quite young, and figured to have a bright big league future ahead of him. But soon something would happen that guaranteed Shellenback would never return to the majors, despite his tremendous minor league success.

In 1920, baseball outlawed the spitter. Frank Shellenback was a spitball specialist. The new rule shouldn't have been a disaster for the young pitcher, since baseball left a loophole: major leaguers who depended on the pitch were allowed to continue throwing it. The trouble was the timing. Shellenback had been farmed out to the minors shortly before the spitball was banned. He was not currently a major leaguer, and therefore was not on the list of players approved to throw wet ones in the majors. Shellenback's big league playing career was over at age 20.

Shellenback *was* allowed to keep throwing the spitter in the minors. He did so for nearly two decades, pitching in the Pacific Coast League until 1938. One year he won 27 games. In two others he won 26. But through it all, Shellenback knew he'd never again pitch in the majors. He retired with a minor league record of 315–192, all of it in the highest reaches of the minors.

In 1939, 20 years after he'd last worn a major league uniform, Shellenback finally made it back to the bigs as pitching coach of the St. Louis Browns. He remained in baseball as a coach and scout into the 1960s. And if one or two of the young pitchers Shellenback coached happened to throw the occasional spitball on the sly, it would be hard to hold it against their coach. The majors owed Shellenback that much. He died in 1969 at the age of 70.

REBIRTH OF THE DROOL

As recently as the 1960s there have been campaigns to re-legalize the spitball. According to *The Sporting News*, both baseball Commissioner Ford Frick and American League President Joe Cronin were in favor of the return of the pitch for the 1962 season. The measure failed to receive sufficient support at the winter meetings.

HECTOR THE KING

Hector Espino is famous. He's just not famous here. Espino hit a record 484 home runs in the Mexican League between 1960 and 1985, a circuit generally considered on par with the top level of American minor league ball. Add Espino's winter league stats, and he hit more home runs in the minors than Hank Aaron did in the majors. Add Espino's .337 career average as well (it would have been higher if he hadn't kept playing into his mid-40s), and you start to get an idea why at least five major league teams tried to sign the first baseman over the years. With one brief exception, they all failed. Espino, a native of Chihuahua, preferred to play in his home country.

Staying home to play ball isn't without precedent. Until fairly recently, all Japanese stars stayed in Japan, either by choice or by contractual obligation. But Japan has a major league of its own. Throughout Espino's career, the Mexican League has been considered a minor league, its top players moving on to the U.S. But not Espino. For a quarter century, Espino was the unquestioned king of the Mexican League, yet all but unknown to Americans—except, of course, to the American scouts and general managers who hoped to sign him.

Espino did play in America once, just 32 games for Cardinal farm club Jacksonville at the end of the 1964 International League season. Espino hit .300 with three home runs in the short trial. Considering he spoke no English, had never before been out of Mexico, and had a wife at home in the middle of a difficult pregnancy, it wasn't a bad first month. The Cardinals were pleased. Espino wasn't.

Some reports have suggested the racism Espino experienced in the American south of the 1960s is what drove the ballplayer away, vowing never to return. Others point to money. Espino was never one to leave pesos on the table, and could earn more as the biggest star in the Mexican League than he could as a young player in pre-free agency America. Or perhaps the problem was homesickness. Whatever the reason, when Espino's suitcases arrived for spring training in 1965, Espino wasn't with them. He'd skipped a connecting flight and headed back to Mexico. The Angels, White Sox, Phillies, and A's all are thought

THE STAR OF THE REDS

In the 1990s, Cuba's Omar Linares often was referred to as the best third baseman in the world. Certainly he was the best third baseman in the third world. While many of Linares' Cuban teammates fled the Communist nation for better baseball opportunities and a better life in the United States, Linares remained behind.

Linares has been with Cuba's national team since he was 17. He's won the Triple Crown in Cuba's Serie Selectiva. His batting average in official international tournaments is over .400. He's reportedly been offered lucrative contracts to play in the U.S. or Japan. But it seems unlikely that Linares, now in his mid-30s, will ever play in the United States. He no doubt will be remembered in Cuba. But for the rest of the baseball world, Omar Linares' story will be a story of what might have been.

to have tried to sign the first baseman in the years that followed. None succeeded.

Perhaps staying in Mexico was the correct decision for Espino. He became a legend in his home country. They even named a stadium after him. But Espino's decision to remain in Mexico cost him any chance he had for fame . . . at least on this side of the border.

THE LAST .400 HITTER

Everything about Artie Wilson suggests he should be remembered. He's the last man to hit over .400 in a top-level professional league. His hitting caused defenses to adopt unique formations. He was a slick-fielding middle infielder . . . even though he was missing half the thumb on his throwing hand, a result of an accident in a pipe factory as a teenager. Yet Wilson is consigned to the small print of baseball history, thanks largely to the leagues in which he played. Despite his considerable talents, Wilson had just 22 at-bats in the majors.

No amount of talent was going to get Wilson to the big leagues early in his career. He started playing professionally in the mid-1940s, an African American in the days before the integration of organized baseball. But young Wilson was a Negro League star. In his five years with the Birmingham Black Barons, the shortstop appeared in four Negro League All-Star games and won two batting titles. Wilson hit .402 in 1948, making him the last man to hit over .400 in either the Negro Leagues or the major leagues.

That .400 average came one year after Jackie Robinson toppled major league baseball's color barrier, so Wilson drew the attention of the major league clubs. But while he drew their attention, he didn't draw all that much of their cash. The Yankees offered Wilson $500 a month to play for their minor league Newark affiliate. Wilson decided it wasn't enough. He'd been making $725 a month with Birmingham in the Negro Leagues. After extensive off-season wrangling (two separate major league clubs believed they had Wilson under contract), the very-much-in-demand infielder landed not in the majors, but in the Pacific Coast League.

In his first year in the extremely competitive PCL, Wilson led the league with a .348 average and 47 stolen bases. The left-handed-hitting

Wilson's opposite-field approach was so pronounced that teams often played their second baseman on the left side of the infield—a sort of reverse Ted Williams shift. "The first baseman was the only player they kept on the right side," Wilson told the *Cleveland Plain Dealer* long after his career. "They would even bring in an outfielder and put him on the left side of the infield."

No defensive alignment seemed able to stop the slap-hitting shortstop from collecting close to 200 singles every year. In early 1951, Wilson got his only taste of the majors, as a 30-year-old rookie with the New York Giants. But Wilson didn't get into many games and by May was back in the minors. It has been suggested that Wilson was farmed out because the Giants wanted to call up Willie Mays and thought five black players was too many. But Wilson has said he asked to be farmed out because he wanted more playing time. The Giants sent him to Minneapolis, but the Oakland Oaks soon brought the shortstop back to the PCL. "He is one of the most popular players in PCL history," said the team's owner. "We need him at the gate."

Wilson hit over .300 in each of the next four PCL seasons before his average began to tail off. He retired in 1957, but after four years out of organized baseball, he returned for one last year in 1962, finishing with a career minor league batting average of .312. Wilson later became a successful car salesman in Portland, Oregon. He always would maintain that he had no regrets about his baseball career. The money was good in the PCL, and he was popular with fans and fellow players. But playing in the minors ensured he wouldn't be remembered.

HAZEWOOD BLOOMS IN MARCH

There's a special corner of baseball fame reserved for rookies who get off to hot starts. Whether it's Bob "Hurricane" Hazle, who hit .403 in 134 at-bats for the 1957 Braves, or Shane Spencer, who hit .373 with ten home runs in 67 at-bats for the 1998 Yankees, such players grab the headlines, at least briefly, as the baseball world debates whether they're truly that talented or merely off to hot starts. The answer almost invariably turns out to be the latter, but nonetheless, these players are rarely forgotten entirely. For the rest of their careers, fans watch the former phenoms closely for any sign they might rediscover their long-departed magic. And their names live on even after they've disappeared from the game, revived for comparison's sake each time another rookie reaches the big leagues on a roll.

The exception to this rule is the uniquely named Drungo LaRue Hazewood. Hazewood, alphabetically Hurricane Hazle's neighbor in baseball history, got off to a Hazle-like start in his 1980 rookie season, hitting .583 right out of the gate. Unfortunately for Hazewood, his hot streak came too soon for fame . . . it was only spring training. The Orioles cut the outfielder before the start of the season, believing he needed more seasoning. "I've never cut a guy hitting that high before," said manager Earl Weaver. "But he was making the rest of us look bad with that average."

No one much remembers spring training stats, so no one much remembers Hazewood's hot start. Spring numbers aren't printed in record books or on the backs of baseball cards. The one-time first-round draft pick did get a cup of coffee with Baltimore that September when rosters were expanded, but he couldn't repeat his spring heroics. Hazewood went hitless in what would be the only five at-bats of his major league career, and struck out four times. It's one of the least-impressive careers in major league history.

FORGOTTEN LEAGUES, FORGOTTEN PLAYERS

5

The American League and the National League weren't the only top-level leagues in the 20th century. Other leagues popped up from time to time, some hoping to gain status as a third major league alongside the AL and NL, others offering refuge for groups not allowed to play in the majors. These alternate top-level leagues have one thing in common: Their players rarely received the fame they were due.

THE NEGRO LEAGUES

Between the 1880s and the 1950s, hundreds of potential stars were denied their fair chance at baseball fame became of the color of their skin. Many of these men did become stars in the Negro Leagues. But with very few exceptions, the greats of the Negro Leagues are not as well known today as they would have been had they played in the majors.

Among those most unfairly forgotten . . .

• Jud Wilson. In the early 1940s, Wilson joined Cool Papa Bell, Josh Gibson, and Buck Leonard as the heart of a Homestead Grays batting order that dominated the Negro Leagues. Today, Bell, Gibson, and Leonard are in the Hall of Fame. Wilson's name is virtually unknown. Yet it was Wilson who Josh Gibson—the man widely regarded as the best hitter in the Negro

Leagues—called the greatest hitter *he* ever saw. And it was Wilson who Satchel Paige—the man widely regarded as the best pitcher in the Negro Leagues—called one of the two best hitters in black baseball.

Statistics weren't kept as religiously in the Negro Leagues as they were in the majors, but based on the box scores that are available, various researchers have placed Wilson's career batting average in the .345 to .389 range. Wilson's record against white teams in exhibition games has been put between .389 and .442.

Wilson was built along the lines of white star Hack Wilson, with a burly upper body that didn't seem quite in proportion to his somewhat stubby legs. Though he stood just 5'8", Jud Wilson was considered one of the toughest players in the game. His plate-crowding hitting style resulted in frequent beanings, yet he rarely left the lineup. When Wilson couldn't field a hot shot cleanly at third base, he'd let the ball bounce off his chest, then recover in time to make the play at first. Stories abound of his fights with opponents, umpires, even teammates who tried a little too hard to wake him up in the morning.

Wilson's playing career ended in 1945, a few years too soon for him to have any chance at the post-integration majors. By the end of his days in the Negro Leagues, Wilson was reportedly suffering epileptic fits and engaging in occasionally unusual behavior. He found work with a Washington, D.C., area road crew for a time after leaving baseball, but the odd behavior apparently continued. Late in life he reportedly was committed to an institution. Wilson died in 1963 at the age of 64.

• Mule Suttles. Josh Gibson would be remembered as the Babe Ruth of black baseball. But before Gibson came along, it was Suttles who owned the title. Suttles, like Ruth, was a big man who swung a big bat. (Figuratively and literally—Wilson's bat was said to weigh in at 50 ounces, which would make it one of the heaviest ever used in a top-level professional league.)

In 22 Negro League seasons, Suttles likely hit somewhere between .329 and .352. His average in exhibition games against white major leaguers is listed at anywhere from .350 to .374. But like Ruth, the muscular, good-natured Suttles was known primarily for his power. In just 87 league games in 1926, Suttles hit 27 homers. For his career he's credited with homering in 6.2 percent of his recorded at-bats. Hank Aaron's major league home run percentage was 6.1 percent. Like Wilson, Suttles was born too soon to make the major leagues. He retired from baseball in 1944 and died of cancer in 1968.

SEPARATE-BUT-EQUAL IMMORTALITY

In 1971, baseball's powers-that-be finally decided to let some former stars of the Negro Leagues take their rightful places in the Hall of Fame . . . sort of. When baseball commissioner Bowie Kuhn announced that Satchel Paige would be immortalized that August, he added that "technically" Paige and any other Negro League stars would not be in the Hall of Fame at all, but in a separate location within Cooperstown's Baseball Hall of Fame and Museum. The rules say you can't be a Hall of Famer unless you've spent at least ten years in the majors, Kuhn explained.

"I'm proud to be in wherever they put me in the Hall of Fame," a magnanimous Paige told reporters. Others were considerably more critical of Kuhn's announcement. Bowing to public pressure, the commissioner and the Hall of Fame reversed their decision that July. Though once denied a chance to be major league ballplayers, the greats of the Negro Leagues would at least have a chance to become full-fledged Hall of Famers.

• Ray Brown. Brown didn't have the flash of Satchel Paige, but the pitcher certainly knew how to win a baseball game. He threw a knuckleball, a curve, a slider, a sinker, and a moving fastball, and reportedly could hit his spots with the best of them. Brown's estimated career winning percentage of .771 is far above that of any 20th century major leaguer with a career of any length. True, Brown did have the advantage of playing the bulk of his career with the talented Homestead Grays. But Brown's stature in his prime was such that when in 1938 the *Pittsburgh Courier* listed five Negro Leaguers sure to star in the majors if given the chance, Brown's name made the list. The other four who made their cut were Paige, Gibson, Buck Leonard, and Cool Papa Bell—all of whom later were inducted into the Hall of Fame.

Brown was still pitching when the integration of the major leagues began—nearly a decade after that *Pittsburgh Courier* article tabbed him as a sure big league star—but by then he was close to 40, too old to get his chance. Brown left the Negro Leagues in 1946 to pitch in Mexico, and in the early 1950s joined Canada's Provincial League. The former pitcher died in Ohio in 1968.

THE FORGOTTEN PENNANT RACE OF THE FORGOTTEN MAJOR LEAGUE
A number of attempts were made in the 20th century to start a third major league to compete with the National and American Leagues. These included the United States League in 1912, which lasted a few days before folding; the Continental League in 1920, which never got off the ground at all; and a second stab at a Continental League in 1960, which didn't fare any better than the first.

The only alternative American major league to survive for any length of time in the 20th century was the Federal League of 1914 and 1915. That 1915 Federal League season produced one of the most exciting pennant races in the history of baseball. But because the Federal League and its teams folded soon after, the pennant race and its hero are hardly remembered, much less celebrated.

With one game left on their schedule, the 1915 Chicago Whales' record stood at 85–66. They were in third place—but with a win they'd claim the Federal League pennant by half a game. The Pittsburgh Rebels, their opponent in that final game, were in first at 86–66, with the St. Louis Terriers in second at 87–67, their season complete. The pivotal final game was actually the second half of a doubleheader. In game one, Chicago had led 4–1 in the 9th, but let Pittsburgh score three that inning to tie, then one more in the 11th to disappoint the capacity Wrigley Field (then known as Weegham Park) crowd. Still, a Chicago win in game two would render the heartbreaking game-one loss moot.

Game two was scoreless into the 6th inning. Pittsburgh's pitcher, the unfortunately named Elmer Knetzer, held Chicago's hitters in check— even though he'd worked the final three innings of game one. Chicago pitcher Bill Bailey matched him goose egg for goose egg. Adding to the drama, any inning could be the game's last. Dusk was approaching, and in those days before stadium lights, dusk meant the end of the day's baseball. "The team that could squeeze over a solitary run," wrote the *Los*

Angeles Times the next day, "would most likely be in possession of the bunting, as the game might be called any minute."

The situation was growing desperate when Chicago outfielder Max Flack stepped to the plate in the bottom of the 6th. With a runner on second, one out, and two strikes against him, Flack hit a line drive that found the gap in right center. The game's first run came around to score. Knetzer seemed to lose his edge after the run crossed the plate, and two more quickly followed. The Rebels didn't score in the top of the 7th, then the game was called for darkness. The Whales took the flag.

"Fortune," wrote the *Los Angeles Times*, "cast Maximillian Flack for the hero role." Flack's double won a pennant-deciding game in his team's last inning of the season. It should have made him famous . . . only it was the last game the Chicago Whales ever played. There would be no life-long Whales fans to retell the story of Flack's key hit. (Of course, it's not as though the Chicago Cubs and Chicago White Sox have had all that many key hits in the years that have followed. Maybe Chicago fans should have gone on rooting for the defunct Whales. At least they wouldn't get their hopes up.) The Whales challenged the American League and National League champs to a three-way round-robin World Series, but were turned down. The other leagues had no desire to further legitimize their upstart Federal League rivals. As it turned out, they needn't have worried. There would be no 1916 Federal League season.

Pittsburgh pitcher Elmer Knetzer hung on for two more years in the majors after the demise of the Federal League, mostly with Cincinnati, without great success. Knetzer continued to pitch in the minors until 1934, his professional baseball career lasting until he was 49. He later worked as a night watchman.

Winning pitcher Bill Bailey had a harder time sticking in the majors after the Federal League disappeared, though he did make brief appearances with Detroit in 1918, then with the Cardinals in 1921 and 1922. He died in 1926 when a blood vessel ruptured in his stomach. Frank Russo, who researches player deaths for his web site, www.thedead ballera.com, reports that there was some speculation at the time that Bailey's hemorrhage might have stemmed from an old baseball injury.

Max Flack landed with the Chicago Cubs after the Federal League folded, and played ten seasons in the National League. He would retire with 200 major league stolen bases and what then was the highest career fielding percentage of any outfielder in history. But Flack would not be remembered for his skill with baserunning or defense. Thanks to the 1918 World Series, he'd be remembered for quite the opposite. In game four of that Series, Flack was picked off base twice in Chicago's 3–2 loss. And if that wasn't enough, the papers also blamed the right-fielder's defense for two of Boston's three runs. He'd played Babe Ruth too shallow, they wrote, opening the door for the Sox slugger's key triple. In game six, Flack dropped George Whiteman's liner, allowing two runs to score. They'd turn out to be the decisive runs of the Series, as the Cubs lost the game 2–1 and the Series 4–2. No Chicago team has won a World Series since.

"Every World Series produces a 'goat,'" wrote *The Sporting News* in 1918, "and Max Flack was it in the one that finished Wednesday." Flack had been the hero of a great pennant race, but he would be remembered instead as the goat of a World Series. He had performed his heroics in the wrong league.

THE DOUG FLUTIE OF BASEBALL

Doug Flutie has had a more-than-respectable career in professional football. He's known as one of the greatest players in the history of the Canadian Football League. He's known as the undersized underdog who proved that quarterbacks don't have to be 6'4" to win. He's known for leading his teams to more than their share of dramatic come-from-behind victories. But none of these things are what makes Doug Flutie a football legend. Flutie is now and forever will be remembered by football fans for a single play that happened before his professional career even began: the shocking, game-ending miracle pass that the then-Boston College star used to beat the University of Miami in a high-scoring game in 1984.

Twelve years later, a second college athlete would deliver another shocking, game-ending play to beat the University of Miami in another high-scoring game. But this athlete wouldn't become famous based on his play. The reason? This time the sport was baseball, and college baseball doesn't make anyone famous.

In the bottom of the 9th inning of the final game of the 1996 College World Series, LSU second baseman Warren Morris came to the plate with two out and one on and his Tigers trailing Miami 8–7. Morris lined a home run just over the right field fence, winning the game 9–8. It was the most dramatic home run in the history of the College World Series. Had it been hit in the major league World Series, it would have been the most dramatic home run of all time. It was, incidentally, Morris' only home run of the season.

Like Flutie before him, Morris was drafted by the pros. Of the two, the pros apparently thought more of Morris—he was selected by the Texas Rangers in the fifth round of baseball's amateur draft six days before his big hit; Flutie hadn't been taken until the 11th round of the NFL draft. In 1998, the Rangers traded their promising minor leaguer to Pittsburgh. There Morris was expected to claim the Pirate second-base job once handled by a man named Bill Mazeroski, who many years before had hit something of a dramatic World Series home run himself. Maz liked what he saw in Morris. "He's going to be around a long time," the hero of 1960 told a sportswriter.

He wasn't. Morris had an excellent rookie year in 1999, hitting .288 with 15 homers and playing solid defense. Then his game fell apart. Morris hit just .259 in 2000, then .204 in limited action in 2001. The Pirates cut Morris in spring 2002. He caught on briefly with Minnesota that year, going zero-for-seven in four major league games. The once-promising second baseman spent 2003 with the Detroit Tigers team that narrowly avoided setting the major league record for losses in a season. Morris' batting average was a credible .272 in 2003, but he hit just six home runs and had an abysmal on-base percentage of .316. Morris will be 30 years old in 2004, and as of this writing, his future in baseball appears very much in doubt.

"Nothing in me is about individual records or things of that nature," Morris told the Associated Press early in his major league career. "I do things quietly." And indeed, Morris soon might drift quietly out of baseball. But this marginal major leaguer might have been famous. College football is nearly as popular as pro football. College basketball is nearly as popular as pro basketball. But not many people care very much about college baseball. If they did, Warren Morris would be a legend.

NO RESPECT FOR THE ELDERLY

Ron Washington did not have a particularly memorable major league career. The utility infielder played parts of ten seasons with five different major league clubs, appearing in as many as 100 games only once. In all, he hit .261 with 20 homers. Tim Ireland's career was even less impressive. Also a utility player, Ireland appeared in just 11 games over two seasons with the Royals. He had exactly one major league hit. Ireland never even hit much in the minors. Yet for one season at the end of Washington's and Ireland's professional careers, it seemed they finally would be stars in—if not the big leagues—at least a league staffed by well-known, big league players.

In 1989, Washington and Ireland joined the Senior League, a brand-new Florida-based circuit featuring players over the age of 35. (Catchers could be as young as 32.) True, starring in the Senior League wasn't quite the same as starring in the majors, but neither was it completely different. The league featured the likes of Ferguson Jenkins, Vida Blue, Rollie Fingers, Bill Lee, Graig Nettles, Cecil Cooper, Mickey Rivers, and Bill Madlock. Washington and Ireland were playing against top talent, if somewhat over-ripe top talent. Yet it was Ireland, a man with one major league hit, who won the league batting title at .374. And it was Washington, a career journeyman, who led the league in RBIs and won the MVP. Old golfers have gained fame on that sport's senior tour. Perhaps Washington and Ireland could gain fame playing senior baseball.

Or perhaps not. Senior baseball didn't catch on as well as senior golf. It didn't even catch on as well as Señor Wences, and that whole talking hand thing got old pretty fast. *USA Today* stopped publishing the Senior League's box scores in the middle of the season, citing lack of interest. The league's average attendance was less than one thousand per game. The Senior League failed to survive its second season. Late bloomers Washington and Ireland had flowered too late in life to be famous. Their Senior League stardom would be all but forgotten.

> **SENIOR MOMENTS**
> World Series near-hero Willie Aikens was second in the Senior League with 12 home runs in 1989, in what would be his swan song in professional baseball. Former Pirate third baseman Jim Morrison finished first with 17. Bob Galasso, a pitcher with a career major league record of 4–8 and a major league ERA of 5.87 posted the second-best ERA in the Senior League that year. Only former 15-year major league pitcher Bill Campbell was better.

IN A LEAGUE OF HER OWN

Jean Faut is arguably the greatest pitcher in the history of women's professional baseball. But since women's baseball never caught on even to the degree that women's basketball or women's soccer has, her achievements didn't earn her lasting fame.

Faut pitched in the All-American Girl's Professional Baseball League during the late 1940s and early 1950s. The league had been around since 1943, and there were other stars before Faut arrived in 1946, but it's a stretch to consider those early stars *baseball* stars. Though the popular 1992 film *A League of Their Own* suggests otherwise, the game played by the AAGPBL then was much closer to softball than baseball. In 1944, the League ball was eleven and a half inches in circumference (the figure for a regulation baseball is a little over nine inches). The League's base paths were only 68 feet long. Pitchers threw underhand from just 40 feet from the plate.

By the time Faut joined the South Bend Blue Sox in 1946, the ball was a bit smaller, the pitching distance and base paths a bit longer, and some sidearm deliveries were allowed. By the end of the 1940s, the league's pitchers threw overhand from 55 feet out and the ball was down to ten inches around. It was baseball, more or less. While some of the league's top pitchers lost their touch after the switch to overhand, Faut became a star. She led the AAGPBL in ERA in 1950, 1952, and 1953. She was named player of the year in 1951 and 1953, finishing second to Betty Foss in a close vote in 1952. There were only two perfect games in league history after the switch to overhand pitching. Faut threw both. Her career record was 140–64, with a league-best 1.23 ERA.

Then she was gone. Faut left the AAGPBL after the 1953 season. She went out in style, throwing a perfect game in her next-to-last appearance

WOMEN PLAYING THE FIELD

Dottie Kamenshak and Doris Sams generally are considered the greatest offensive players in AAGPBL history. Kamenshak, a first baseman (basewoman?) hit .292 and was named to the All-Star team seven times. Sams, an outfielder, hit .290 and made the All-Star team five times.

and retiring as the reigning Player of the Year. Faut didn't want to leave baseball, but her husband, minor league pitcher Karl Winsch, had been named manager of her club, and that apparently caused tension between Faut and some of her teammates. One year later the AAGPBL itself was out of business, and any thoughts of a Faut comeback were gone.

Faut took up bowling after her baseball career and became a charter member of the women's professional bowling tour. She also raised two children, divorced her former manager in 1968, and in 1977 remarried at the age of 52. In doing so, Faut deprived herself of fame in one last way that male athletes never have to consider: she took her husband's name, becoming Jean Eastman. If women's professional baseball occupied an enduring place in American sports, it's likely Jean Faut would be remembered as one of its first great stars. Instead, the only women's baseball players most fans can name are Geena Davis and Madonna.

THE BABE WHO STRUCK OUT THE BABE

When Commissioner Landis ruled in 1931 that women could not play in organized baseball, he denied 17-year-old Jackie Mitchell the chance to earn a living. She had signed to pitch for the minor league Chattanooga Lookouts and already had appeared briefly for the team in an exhibition against the New York Yankees. But did the ruling deny Mitchell fame? A case could be made that it only added to Mitchell's legacy. In her exhibition appearance against New York, Mitchell struck out Babe Ruth and Lou Gehrig. Had Mitchell remained with the Lookouts and later been hit hard by minor leaguers, it only would have spurred the already rampant rumor that Ruth and Gehrig had been convinced to strike out on purpose, as part of a promotional stunt. Instead, baseball fans have been left to wonder just how good Mitchell might have been. Her strikeouts remain part of baseball lore.

With professional baseball no longer an option, Mitchell later settled into a slightly less glamorous job with the Tidy-Didy Diaper Service. She died in 1987 at age 73, always maintaining that her famous strikeouts had been real.

6

STUCK IN THE SHADOWS

On June 21, 1954, Australian runner John Landy ran a mile in less than four minutes, achieving one of the most anticipated accomplishments in all of sport. Landy's feat would have made him a legend . . . but Brit Roger Bannister broke the four-minute barrier 46 days earlier.

There are few better ways to lose fame in the world of sports than to be second-best, second to accomplish a goal, or otherwise overshadowed by another athlete who does whatever it is you do, only to greater acclaim.

THREE MEN, THREE LEGS, ONE MOVIE, NO JUSTICE

Blame it on Hollywood.

In 1949, Tinseltown immortalized former major league pitcher Monty Stratton, who had shot his own leg off while hunting rabbits in 1938 and later tried to return to baseball. Jimmy Stewart played Monty; June Allyson played his wife. *The Stratton Story* won an Oscar for best story that year—but it wasn't even the best real-life story of its kind. Another pitcher, Lou Brissie, had his left leg badly mangled in World War II. And yet another pitcher, Bert Shepard, lost his right leg below the knee during the war. These men had sacrificed their limbs keeping the world safe from Nazis. Stratton lost his keeping the world safe from bunny rabbits. Who's the greater hero? The Brissie and Shepard stories even had better third acts. They each pitched in the majors after their injuries. Monty Stratton never made it back to the bigs. Yet Stratton was the man Hollywood made famous. Brissie and Shepard became, with apologies, footnotes.

True, Lou Brissie didn't lose his leg. But in every other way his story is more compelling than Stratton's. On December 7, 1944, Corporal Brissie led his Army squad out of a creek bed in the Apennine Mountains of northern Italy. They'd advanced only fifty feet when a German shell scored a direct hit. The entire squad was killed—all except Brissie. But shrapnel had lodged in the pitcher's hands, shoulders, legs, and feet. His left leg fared the worst. It was "split open like a ripe watermelon," as Brissie himself would later colorfully put it. Other soldiers and even medics passed him by, assuming the mangled corporal must be dead. Finally, a sergeant noticed that Brissie was breathing.

Army doctors expressed surprise Brissie had made it to the hospital, and even greater surprise when he survived surgery. They held out little hope that they could save his leg. But Brissie begged them not to amputate it. He was a professional ballplayer, he explained, and would be unemployed without it. The doctors saved the leg, but Brissie was a long way from healthy. He became the first wounded soldier in the Mediterranean theater to receive penicillin therapy. He spent two years on crutches and endured 23 operations. Through it all Brissie retained hope. "If God lets me walk again," he wrote to his uncle, "I'll play again."

On the last day of the 1947 season, Brissie kept his word, pitching for the Philadelphia A's in a major league game. The next year Brissie made more than a token appearance. Every step caused him pain, and he was forced to wear a large metal guard under his pants leg when he pitched, yet Brissie went 14–10 in 1948, then 16–11 in 1949. Unfortunately, the A's were a team in decline. They won only 50 games in 1950, and despite posting the best ERA among the team's regular pitchers, Brissie's record fell to 7–19. He was traded to Cleveland the following season and remained in the big leagues through 1953, retiring one year too soon to take part in Cleveland's 1954 pennant-winning campaign. After leaving the majors, Brissie became director of the American Legion Junior Baseball program for a time, then worked for a South Carolina state employee training program. Despite the pain his leg caused him throughout his life, Brissie wasn't one to complain. "I'm here," he told sportscaster Mel Allen. "I'm here. I feel privileged just to have made it."

Bert Shepard's story is just as good as Brissie's. Lieutenant Shepard was scheduled to pitch in the first game of his Army Air Corps baseball team's season on May 21, 1944. His start was slightly delayed: The P-38 pilot was shot down by anti-aircraft fire that morning while flying his 34th mission. He woke up in a German hospital ten days later to find his leg had been amputated below the knee.

Shepard would have been just another casualty of war, except he was one of those never-say-die types who make such great movie characters. A fellow prisoner in his POW camp made him a wooden leg, and soon Shepard was up and walking . . . then jogging . . . then throwing a baseball around. In January 1945, Shepard was sent home in an exchange of prisoners too badly injured to fight. That's when he caught a break: he was one of a small number of former POWs picked by the Under Secretary of War's office to speak to the press about Germany's treatment of prisoners. Asked at the press conference what he planned to do with the rest of his life, Shepard said if he couldn't fly combat, he'd like to play pro baseball.

It was a bold statement. Even with two legs, Shepard hadn't been all that great a pitcher in the minors. But a one-legged war-hero pitcher made for great PR, so the war department convinced the Washington Senators to give him a try. "If I can make the grade, I'm going to visit hospitals during the season and after that I'm going to make a tour of the hospitals," Shepard told the press. "I want all the fellows to get going. If I can make it, then they're going to make it, too."

Shepard did make the Senators, but was little more than a batting practice pitcher for most of the season. For one of the few times in their history, Washington was in a pennant race that year. As far as manager Ossie Bluege was concerned, it was no time to hand the ball to a one-legged rookie. Shepard finally made it into a major league regular-season game on August 4, 1945. He held the Red Sox to one run on three hits in five-and-a-third innings. It was a great debut—and a great finale. Shepard never got into another major league game. The Senators lost the pennant to Detroit by one game.

By 1946, the war was over, and Shepard was sent to the minors. The established major leaguers had returned from military service to reclaim their jobs. Shepard pitched well in the minors—until a follow-up operation on what remained of his leg was botched, leading to two and a half years on crutches and several more surgeries. Shepard tried to return as a player/manager in the low minors when his leg finally allowed—but after the long layoff his arm wasn't the same.

Shepard soon left baseball, and worked at various times as a typewriter salesman, an insurance agent, and a safety engineer. He also was a two-time winner of the National Amputee Golf Championship and has been active in lobbying the medical community on behalf of those who have lost limbs. Since Brissie technically still had his mangled leg and Stratton never made it back to the majors, Bert Shepard remains the only one-legged pitcher in big league history.

In fairness to Monty Stratton, his hunting accident was tragic. Unlike either Shepard or Brissie, Stratton had seemed headed to stardom prior to his injury. He'd posted a 15–5 record for the White Sox in 1937 at age 25, then a 15–9 record in 1938. He lost his leg that November. Stratton tried a comeback in 1946 and managed an 18–8 record in the East Texas League. Unfortunately for Stratton, his leg had been amputated above the knee, putting him at a severe disadvantage even compared to Shepard or Brissie. He would never make it back to the majors. Still, thanks to Jimmy Stewart, he would be remembered.

WRIGHT AND PARTLOW IN ROBINSON'S SHADOW

When Jackie Robinson faced the challenges of his first spring training in the Dodger organization, he didn't face them alone. A pitcher named John Wright shared Robinson's experiences in the less than racially enlightened Florida of 1946. Wright, like Robinson, was an African-American the Dodgers had signed out of the Negro Leagues. Wright, like Robinson, would have to cope with considerable prejudice that spring. Wright, unlike Robinson, did not have a successful career in organized baseball. His role in baseball history is largely forgotten.

Wright's pitching was shaky from the start. The thin right-hander had been able to put his fastball exactly where he wanted it in the Negro Leagues, but he couldn't seem to find the strike zone with the Dodgers that March. In one indicative one-inning spring outing, he walked four and hit a batter. Sent with Robinson to Montreal, the Dodger's top farm club, Wright appeared in only two games, doing poorly in an outing in Syracuse, then rebounding nicely in a relief appearance in Baltimore. Despite the solid game in Baltimore, Montreal manager Clay Hopper decided Wright "wasn't ready." The pitcher didn't appear in another game for Montreal, and in mid-May was sent down to Three Rivers in the Canadian-American League.

Considering Wright's previous success in the Negro Leagues and with the talent-rich Great Lakes Naval Station team during World War II, he should have dominated in the low minors. Instead he continued to struggle. Teammates and sportswriters offered a list of possible explanations for Wright's failures, ranging from his lack of an effective off-speed pitch to the disappointment of his demotion to Three Rivers. Jackie Robinson was quoted as saying Wright simply "couldn't stand the pressure."

When Wright was demoted from Montreal, the Dodgers signed another African-American pitcher, Roy Partlow, to take his place. Partlow was then one of the best left-handed pitchers in the Negro Leagues, not to mention a strong enough hitter to play the outfield when he wasn't on the mound. But Partlow wasn't considered a real prospect. His age was reported as 30, but likely was closer to 36, according to Jules Tygiel, author of *Baseball's Great Experiment*. Like Wright, Partlow initially had some trouble getting his innings in Montreal—the team already was overloaded with pitching. But once he did, he established himself as an effective reliever. Despite this, Partlow, too, soon found himself demoted to Three Rivers.

It's been speculated that Partlow's pitching wasn't the primary reason for his demotion. The Dodgers might have signed Wright and Partlow more to keep Robinson company than for their skills on the field. Partlow had failed in this role, as he and Robinson reportedly were not close. Partlow considered the Canadian-American League below him, and at first balked at reporting to Three Rivers. But when he finally joined the club in mid-July, he put on a show, winning ten of his 11 decisions and hitting over .400. Partlow's presence seemed to rejuvenate the previously mediocre Wright as well. Together they led Three Rivers to the 1946 Canadian-American League title.

Neither man would play in organized baseball again. Wright was released in the off-season and returned to the Negro Leagues, pitching into the early 1950s. He later worked as a driver and janitor for

National Gypsum in New Orleans and died in 1990. The Dodgers invited Partlow to spring training in 1947, but he arrived late, threw poorly, and was released. Partlow, too, returned to the Negro Leagues for a few years, then worked for the American Container Corp. He died in 1987. Wright and Partlow had helped Jackie Robinson integrate organized baseball in 1946, but they were destined to be forgotten.

ELEVEN WEEKS TOO LATE TO BE NEWS

Larry Doby hasn't been forgotten. Baseball fans remember Doby as the first African-American player in the American League. He's even a Hall of Famer. Still, it's hard to look at Doby's baseball career without thinking he doesn't get enough glory for his role in the game's history.

On July 5, 1947, 11 weeks after Jackie Robinson joined the Dodgers, Larry Doby joined the Indians. The pressures on Doby perhaps weren't quite as great as those faced by Robinson—by the time Doby came along, Robinson already had proved that an African-American ballplayer could perform well in white baseball. But like Robinson, Doby was the first black major leaguer to play in many major league stadiums. And like Robinson, he endured injustices and prejudices from fans, opponents, and teammates. "The only difference [between Robinson and I] was that Jackie Robinson got all the publicity," Doby would later say. "You didn't hear much about what I was going through because the media didn't want to repeat the same story."

Fans never did hear too much about Doby during his career—at least not as much as his place in baseball history seemed to dictate. For the better part of a decade, Doby was a steady, dependable presence in the middle of the Cleveland batting order. Steady and dependable has never been a great way to get noticed. His days as a major league player ended in 1959, but by the early 1970s, Doby was back in the big leagues as a coach. In 1975, he again missed a chance to be remembered as a trail-blazer. That year Frank Robinson, not Doby, was named the first African-American manager in major league history.

"Whether I'm the first black manager doesn't matter at all to me," Doby told the *Christian Science Monitor*. "You never hear anybody talk about the first Italian manager or the first Irish manager. I just want an opportunity." In 1978, Doby got his opportunity and became the *second* African-American manager. Not that anyone much remembers. Doby's managerial career lasted just 87 games.

Doby wasn't elected to the Hall of Fame until 1998. One year earlier, major league baseball had celebrated the 50th anniversary of the integration of the major leagues. To mark the event, all major league teams—both National and American League—retired Jackie Robinson's number 42. Though Doby had integrated the AL, his number 14 remains in circulation. Doby doesn't, having died in 2003.

PIPPED BY FATE

Lou Gehrig is one of the greatest hitters in the history of baseball. But had Gehrig not set an unbreakable record of 2,130 consecutive games played (since broken); had he not died tragically of a disease that now bears his name; had he not delivered his famous "luckiest man on the face of the earth" line, he might have gone down in history as little more than Babe Ruth's talented teammate. But if Gehrig spent much of his career in Ruth's shadow, he also was responsible for consigning another player's fine career to the shadows. Because while Wally Pipp is remembered today, he's not remembered for playing baseball. He's remembered, oddly, for *not* playing baseball.

On June 2, 1925, Yankee first baseman Wally Pipp asked out of the lineup, reportedly because of a headache. For the rest of his life, stories of this pain in his head would be a major pain in Pipp's neck.

PINCH HITTING FOR PEE WEE

Though Lou Gehrig's 2,130-consecutive-game playing streak generally is said to have begun the day he replaced Pipp in the lineup, it actually began the day before, when Gehrig pinch hit for Yankee shortstop Pee Wee Wanninger. Remarkably, Everett "Deacon" Scott, the man who'd put together the majors' longest consecutive-games-played streak before Gehrig, had seen his streak broken earlier that same year . . . when he'd been replaced in the Yankee lineup by Wanninger.

Yank rookie Lou Gehrig got the start at first that day—and every other day for the next 14 seasons. (Well, virtually every day. Occasionally Gehrig extended his streak not by starting at first but by playing the outfield, pinch hitting, or even by beginning a game listed in the shortstop's spot in the order.) As Gehrig's streak grew, he became the nation's symbol for a strong work ethic. That left Pipp, the man who asked out of the game that essentially got Gehrig started, as the symbol of slacking off. The single day off came to define Pipp's career. He was no longer a ballplayer. He was a cautionary tale about the dangers of taking time off from work. He was the very image of inadequacy, sitting on the bench while another man did his job. Pipp even became a verb. To this day in baseball, to take another player's job is to "Pipp him." To fall victim to such circumstances is "to get Pipped." It was not the most glamorous way to enter the game's vernacular.

But while the *name* Pipp is remembered, the *player* Pipp is forgotten. The graceful fielder was a key contributor to the original Yankee dynasty, the 1921 through 1923 group that won three straight pennants and the organization's first World Series title. Pipp was the first Yankee to lead the American League in home runs, doing so in both 1916 and 1917. His .329 average led the Yankees in their 1922 pennant-winning season—Ruth hit .315. In both 1922 and 1923, Pipp was second on the Yanks in RBIs behind only Ruth; in both 1921 and 1924, Pipp was third on the club behind Ruth and Bob Meusel.

None of this would be remembered. Wally Pipp is known as the man who cost himself his job by taking a day off. In fact, Pipp's sick day likely did little but set a date on the inevitable. Lou Gehrig was a top prospect. With Pipp off to a slow start in 1925, Gehrig was going to get his shot soon. New York was particularly hot to replace Pipp because the tall, blond first baseman was known for driving hard bargains at contract time. Pipp's sometimes-stormy relationship with Ruth couldn't have helped his situation either—Ruth and Pipp once got in a fistfight on the Yankee bench.

A month after Pipp lost his starting job, Yankee pitcher Charlie Caldwell beaned him in batting practice. Pipp reportedly was near death and spent two months in the hospital with a somewhat more serious headache than the one for which he is remembered. Pipp was sold to the Cincinnati Reds for $7,500 before the 1926 season. There he hit

.291 and helped the Reds stay in the thick of the pennant race. Had Pipp led Cincinnati to victory over his former club, the New York Yankees, in the World Series, it might have changed the way he was remembered by history. But Cincinnati lost the pennant to St. Louis by a narrow two-game margin. The Cardinals, not the Reds, would beat the Yankees in that 1926 Series. It would be Pipp's last, best shot to be remembered for anything other than his day off. In 1927 and 1928, Pipp's Reds fell back to the middle of the pack in the National League, and Pipp's abilities faded as well. He retired at age 35 after the 1928 season.

Unlike many ex-ballplayers, the college-educated Pipp had a successful life after the game. He worked as a writer and in radio and eventually built a solid career as a sales rep in Michigan's growing automotive industry. It was the auto business that brought Pipp to Detroit in early May, 1939, 14 years after he'd so famously lost his starting job. Gehrig was in town as well, to play the Tigers. The two ex-teammates met up at Detroit's Book Cadillac Hotel. There, Pipp would later say, Gehrig told him he didn't feel well and might have to miss a game. Gehrig's 2,130-consecutive-games-played streak ended the next day.

Pipp suffered a fatal heart attack in early 1965 at age 71. His fine career was destined to be overshadowed by a single day off and by the Hall of Famer who took his job.

CALDWELL FINDS HIS GAME

Charlie Caldwell, the man whose errant batting-practice pitch ended Wally Pipp's 1925 season and nearly ended his life, threw only 2⅔ innings in the majors. But he'd make it to the Hall of Fame. The College Football Hall of Fame. Caldwell took over the Williams College team in 1928, then coached at Princeton University for a dozen years after World War II. The Ivy League school put together back-to-back undefeated seasons in 1950 and 1951 under his guidance. Caldwell died of cancer in 1957.

OVERSHADOWED IN LIFE AND DEATH

"Big Ed" Reulbach was a great pitcher with some of the greatest teams in history, the Chicago Cubs of the early 20th century. In the midst of the celebrated 1908 National League pennant race, Reulbach turned in one of the most prolonged shutout stretches any pitcher has ever had, throwing 44 consecutive scoreless innings. Reulbach even threw shutouts in both ends of a doubleheader during that late-season push, a feat no modern pitcher has matched, and in all probability none ever will. Thanks in no small part to Reulbach's efforts, the Cubs won the pennant by a single game. It was the third straight season that Reulbach had ridden his curveball to the best winning percentage in the National League.

Yet Reulbach's success didn't translate into fame. For all his wins, Reulbach labored in the shadows of two even greater pitchers—teammate Mordecai "Three Finger" Brown and "Big Ed" Walsh of the cross-town White Sox. Reulbach's career winning percentage is an impressive .632—but teammate Three Finger Brown's is an even better .648. Reulbach's 2.28 career ERA is eighth best among 20th century pitchers with at least ten years in the majors—but Brown's 2.06 is third best. First on that list is the 1.82 ERA belonging to Big Ed Walsh of the White Sox. Walsh's presence in Chicago ensured that Reulbach wouldn't even be the most famous pitcher in town named Big Ed. Of course, Reulbach owes his high winning percentage in part to the strength of those Cubs teams, and his low ERA has a lot to do with pitching in the deadball era. But plenty of players have become far more famous on the strength of more suspect stats.

Glory and even victory often seemed just inches out of reach for Reulbach in the World Series. In the 1906 Series against the White Sox, Reulbach came within a 7th-inning Jiggs Donahue single of throwing a no-hitter. One-hitters are no path to fame. In the 1907 Series against

DIMAGGIO'S OTHER STREAK

In 1933 Joe DiMaggio hit in 61 consecutive games in the Pacific Coast League, foreshadowing his 56-game streak in the majors in 1941. The PCL hitting streak was ended by pitcher Edward Arthur Walsh, son of Big Ed Walsh, the Hall of Famer. This younger Walsh would spend parts of four seasons in the majors, accumulating an 11–24 record with the White Sox between 1928 and 1932, but die of rheumatic fever in 1937 at age 32.

Detroit, Reulbach was called in to relieve when game one went to extra innings. He threw three shutout innings, but the game was called for darkness still tied after 12. The Cubs had loaded the bases with one out in the 11th, but failed to score. Ties, like one-hitters, are a poor way to be remembered. In game one of the 1908 Series, again against Detroit, Reulbach left with the lead—but the Chicago bullpen gave up the tying run, costing him his win. Though Reulbach had only weeks earlier thrown the century's only doubleheader shutout, he was criticized in the press for his inability to go nine. In the end, Reulbach's career World Series stats would be respectable—2–0, 3.03 ERA—but hardly memorable.

Reulbach's time at the top was brief. By 1913, his arm was sore and his pitching unimpressive. The Cubs traded him to Brooklyn that July and got only mediocre pitcher Eddie Stack and a bit of cash in return. Aside from one successful year in the Federal League, Ed Reulbach's years as a winning major league pitcher were all but over at age 29. Three Finger Brown was elected to the Hall of Fame in 1949, Ed Walsh in 1946. Reulbach never received a single vote.

If any player seemed poised for success after baseball, it was Reulbach. He'd been an engineering student at Notre Dame, pre-med at the University of Vermont, and would later study industrial management at the University of Rochester and law at Columbia. Cub player/manager Frank Chance said Reulbach was a man "full of ideas." Chase recalled that in one close game, Reulbach offered to fill his mouth with soap suds and run onto the field acting crazy so the other team would think he had rabies. The game would be called off, and the Cubs declared winners since they held a slim lead. Reulbach assured Chance he'd checked the rule book, and there was nothing to prevent the maneuver. "And he wasn't kidding, either," noted Chance, who nonetheless declined the pitcher's offer.

Despite his education and creativity, Reulbach was forced to declare bankruptcy after his career. Expenses incurred during his only son's long and eventually fatal illness were at least partly to blame. But the former pitcher rebounded and had an apparently successful career in the construction industry. He also was an active investor in the stock market in the decades following the depression.

Reulbach, 78, died of a heart attack on July 17, 1961. Like his life, the pitcher's death was destined to be overshadowed. Ty Cobb, one of the greatest baseball players in history, had died a few hours before.

FOXX AND RAINES: FAMOUS, BUT SHOULD BE FAMOUSER

Certainly Jimmie Foxx is famous. The man they called The Beast is a Hall of Famer, a Triple Crown winner, and a three-time MVP. But it's worth noting how excruciatingly close Foxx came to becoming one of the most famous players in the history of the game.

In 1932, Foxx nearly set the single-season home run record, perhaps the most celebrated one-year record

> **BREAK UP THE CUBS**
> The famed 1906 Cubs featured not only great pitchers like Brown and Reulbach, but an infield that contained three future Hall of Famers: the famous double-play combination of Joe Tinker, Johnny Evers, and Frank Chance. Chicago won more than 76 percent of their games that year. Asked after his career how any team could win 116 games, Reulbach replied "When I look back, I wonder how we came to lose 36."

in all of American sports. He had 55 homers by the beginning of September, but was slowed in the final month by a sprained wrist. Foxx finished with 58, two short of baseball immortality. A large screen recently added above the right field wall in St. Louis was said to have cost Foxx five homers that year (other sources put this figure as low as three or as high as 12). The screen wasn't there when Ruth hit his 60. Foxx would later claim that rainouts cost him two that year as well.

It wouldn't be the only time Foxx would fall just short of Ruth. In fact, if there hadn't been a Babe Ruth, Foxx might have *become* Babe Ruth. Without Ruth's Herculean home run totals and larger-than-life persona blocking the way, Foxx could have been the fast-living, hard-hitting, home run king of baseball. Not only might Foxx have captured the single-season record, he in all probability would have held the career record if only there had been no Babe. Foxx retired with 534 homers, second only to Ruth's 714. He remained in second till Willie Mays passed him in 1966.

Even allowing for Ruth's existence, Foxx might have had a shot at the career home run record, except The Beast got old fast, reportedly due to his somewhat bestial fondness for drinking and late-night carousing.

Foxx hit just 15 career homers after age 33. Seven more seasons averaging 28 homers a year would have given him the magic 715. That's asking a lot, considering that home run production dropped off league-wide during World War II. But it shouldn't have been impossible for a man who'd averaged more than 40 homers a year through 1940.

Instead, Foxx would retire hidden deep in Ruth's considerable shadow. Despite being one of the greatest hitters of all time, Foxx had to wait till his sixth year of post-retirement eligibility before he earned election to the Hall of Fame. In one of those six years, Foxx received only ten of 161 possible Hall of Fame votes.

Disrespect from the Hall of Fame wasn't the only inequity old age had in store for Foxx. The once-strapping slugger found himself strapped for cash. Foxx hadn't earned as much as other top players during his career, stuck as he was with the penurious Philadelphia A's for his best years. And what Foxx had earned, he'd spent or lost to failed investments. Money and Jimmie Foxx simply had a way of avoiding each other. Sometimes it was bad luck: Foxx bought a Florida golf course in 1941. Later that year the Japanese bombed Pearl Harbor, and Americans suddenly had less free time to hit the links. Other times it was a lack of respect: A restaurant once paid Foxx for the rights to use his name. Soon after the owners of Jimmie Foxx's concluded Foxx's name wasn't a big enough draw and terminated the deal. Another time the Red Sox hired Foxx as minor league hitting coach, only to fire him a season later to cut costs.

Foxx declared bankruptcy in 1961. His only assets, according to the court filing, were his clothes and miscellaneous household items. Foxx then was earning $4,000 a year working for the Bureau of Unemployment Compensation. It was the best income he'd had in years. Sadly, all of Foxx's financial struggles would have been averted had he just stayed in baseball another two seasons, and thus qualified for the pension plan. "I've been on the wrong side of everything," said Foxx in 1960. "I've had nothing but bad luck since I got out of baseball."

By the 1960s, Foxx's health was as poor as his finances. He had high blood pressure and hernias. He suffered a series of heart attacks. He fractured his skull falling down a flight of stairs. Foxx died at the age of 59 in 1967. The Beast choked to death on a piece of meat.

Tim Raines, like Jimmie Foxx, was a great baseball player in the shadow of a slightly greater one. Raines is well known, and probably will make the Hall of Fame. But he's considerably less famous than he might have been if not for the existence of one man: Rickey Henderson.

What Babe Ruth was to power hitting, Henderson was to leadoff hitting. Tim Raines had the misfortune to be almost exactly the same player at almost exactly the same time. Both Raines and Henderson reached the majors in 1979. Both outfielders were still in the game as recently as 2002. (Henderson even managed a few at-bats with the Dodgers in 2003.) Henderson was famous for his ability to reach base, his on-base percentage an impressive .401. But Raines wasn't far behind, at .385. Henderson was famous for his ability to bring power to the leadoff spot. But Raines actually had the higher career slugging percentage, .425 to .419. Henderson was famous for his ability to steal bases—he's the all-time stolen-base champion with 1,406 to Raines' 808. But it was Raines who set the record for highest stolen base success rate, minimum 200 attempts, leading Henderson 84.7 to 80.8 percent.

Raines' best shot at capturing some of the fame later lavished on Henderson came in 1981, when Raines stole 50 bases in his team's first 55 games. If he'd kept up that rate over a full 162 game schedule, he would have had 147 steals, far and away the record. But the 1981 season was shortened by a strike, costing Raines his chance. Henderson stole 130 bases the following year to set the still-standing record.

Raines also played in the wrong place for fame. The first half of his career was spent with the Montreal Expos, off the radar screens of American baseball fans. Raines wanted to leave the Expos as a free agent after the 1986 season. He would have signed with the Dodgers for as little as $1.125 million, a bargain price for a man who'd hit a league-leading .334 that year and stolen 70 bases. But the Dodgers weren't interested, and neither was anyone else. That was the winter baseball's owners covertly agreed not to sign other teams' free agents. This was illegal of course, and the owners later would be found guilty of violating labor agreements. But by that point, Raines was back in Montreal, where he'd remain for another four years.

Tim Raines overcame cocaine addiction early in his career and lupus, a serious disease, late in it. Perhaps he never did overcome Rickey Henderson where fame was concerned, but unlike Foxx, who struggled with alcohol addiction and financial problems, Raines did overcome his personal challenges and build a successful life.

THE GREAT FRITZ OSTERMUELLER

When a highly touted prospect fails to live up to expectations, did that player miss his chance for fame, or did expectations simply outstrip his true ability? If the answer is the former, then the game has an almost unending list of now forgotten potential stars. A 1940 article in *Baseball Weekly* quotes an unidentified veteran umpire about one such player, a 1930s and 1940s pitcher named Fritz Ostermueller. "You fellows don't get the proper slant on him from the press box," said the ump. "When you're right there on the diamond with him you've got to realize that he somehow just misses being one of those pitchers fans'll still be talking about 50 years from now."

"What made [Ostermueller and others] stop short of the pinnacle of success?" asked *Baseball Weekly*. "Is it merely that luck persistently evades them when they seek its finest rewards? Somehow I think that is the answer. Life is so often like that." Ostermueller's career record was 114–115. In the end he didn't just fall short of greatness, he came up one win shy of average.

THE WRONG PLACE FOR FAME, THE RIGHT PLACE FOR WORLD SERIES BONUSES

You can't become famous if you're stuck on the bench. Perhaps no long-time major leaguer ever had less opportunity to show his talents than Yankee catcher Charlie Silvera. From late 1948 through 1956, Silvera's job was to sit in New York's bullpen, warm up the occasional relief pitcher, and watch future Hall of Famer Yogi Berra catch for the Yankees. Silvera's problem wasn't just that he was a backup catcher stuck behind an extremely talented starter. It was that he was a backup catcher stuck behind an extremely *durable*, extremely talented starter. With one exception, 1949, Yogi caught at least 133 of the Yankee's 154 games in each of Silvera's eight full seasons with the club. By the final two years of Silvera's Yankee tenure, 1955 and 1956, his situation was doubly bad: With the emergence of Elston Howard, Silvera was behind two star players on the depth chart. In six of his eight Yankee seasons, Charlie Silvera appeared in 20 or fewer games. He was on the Yankee roster for seven different World Series—yet he appeared in exactly one World Series game.

There's no guarantee that Silvera would have been a star had he played more. Perhaps he was lucky to land with a club where he could warm up pitchers in the bullpen, collect World Series bonuses, and not have his deficiencies exposed. But Silvera's limited playing record hints that he might have had more than a little talent.

Silvera's professional baseball career got off to a slow start thanks to World War II. After just one year in the minors, he spent three years in the Army Air Force. But it was back to baseball in 1946, and Silvera did reasonably well in the minors that year and again in 1947. His work behind the plate was strong, his hitting good enough for a catcher. Silvera got more than 400 at-bats in a season for the first time with Portland in the Pacific Coast League in 1948. Suddenly his bat was as good as his glove, as he hit .301. Silvera got a late-season call-up to the Yanks that year and made the team for good as Berra's backup the following spring. In 1949, Yogi Berra broke his thumb. For six weeks, rookie Charlie Silvera was the starting catcher for the New York Yankees. He hit .315 and caught well. But when Yogi returned, Silvera went back to warming up pitchers in the bullpen.

Silvera had shown that he could step right in and excel when the Yankees needed him, only they'd never need him again. Yogi remained healthy for the next seven seasons; Silvera remained on the sidelines. Yet he always took pride in his six-week stretch as a Yankee starter. "Joe [DiMaggio] and I were the only [Yankees] to hit .300 that year," Silvera recalled in Phil Rizzuto's book *The October Twelve*. "We ended up winning the pennant by one game. I haven't been given much credit for the role I played in 1949. . . . [But] without me I don't know whether the Yankees would have taken that '49 pennant."

In only three other Yankee seasons would Silvera get as many as 50 at-bats. In his more than eight seasons wearing the pinstripes, Silvera accumulated a grand total of just 429 at-bats, fewer than a starter gets in a single season. Despite the infrequent play, he hit .291, an impressive figure for a good defensive catcher. Year in, year out, Silvera quietly did what was asked of him and took glory where he could find it. One season he was named to the All-Star team . . . as batting practice catcher. Some men would have been insulted. Silvera was so pleased he'd get to take part at all that he wrote a thank-you note to AL President Will Harridge. Among his fellow Yankees, Silvera was known more for his wit, smile, pleasant nature, and skill with impersonations than as a ballplayer. The good-natured Silvera certainly never held it against Berra that he hogged all the playing time; the Silvera and Berra families were the closest of friends.

It is a measure of Silvera's lack of fame that his wife Rose struggled to explain to her children what their father did for a living. "She keeps telling them he's a ballplayer," explained a 1956 article. "Comes the question, as soon as the Yankee game is turned on, 'Well, where's daddy?'" Rose knew where he was. "Now and then they switch the camera to the bullpen and I can see Charlie warming up a pitcher," she explained. "I really can't make him out from that distance, but I know it's Charlie."

Silvera claimed to have no regrets about his wasted talents. His World Series bonuses, which totalled nearly $50,000 over the course of his Yankee career, surely softened the blow. "I wouldn't like to be traded," he told a UP reporter in 1956. "I like New York, I like the Yankee organization, and I like the life I'm living."

The Yankees sold Silvera later that year. The timing wasn't great: The catcher had a home under construction in New Jersey. He'd been a Yankee all his life and reportedly was quite shocked he'd have to become a Chicago Cub. "He will be the Cubs' number one catcher," said Yankee manager Casey Stengel after the deal was announced. "It is no secret that he can do a few things catching that have eluded even Berra."

The Cubs gave Silvera a raise and wrote him in as their starter, though scouts and reporters debated all winter whether a 32-year-old man could return to regular play after sitting so long on the bench. Silvera was philosophical about the deal. "I guess I'll have to go back to work," he said.

The 1957 season had barely gotten started when Cubs catcher Charlie Silvera broke his leg, ending his playing career.

In 1958, Silvera became a minor league manager. But unlike Berra, the man Silvera was stuck behind, and Ralph Houk, the man who was stuck behind Silvera in some of those Yankee seasons, Silvera would never get a chance to manage in the majors. He did return to the big leagues as bullpen coach under manager Billy Martin in Minnesota, Detroit, and Texas. Silvera did not, however, join Billy in his many managerial stops with the Yankees. Perhaps he'd seen enough of Yankee Stadium bullpens.

SILVERA'S NORWEGIAN COUNTERPART

Another backup catcher, Arndt Jorgens, had an even longer run with the Yankees and received only slightly more playing time. Like Silvera, Jorgens was stuck behind a future Hall of Famer. Jorgens joined the Yankees in 1929, which also happened to be Bill Dickey's first full season with the club. Jorgens stayed in the majors for 11 years, all of them as Dickey's understudy. Though Dickey didn't play quite as many games each year as Berra later would, Jorgens had more than 100 at-bats in only two seasons and just 738 for his career.

There was, however, one important difference between Silvera and Jorgens: Jorgens' record offers no evidence he could have been a star if given the chance to catch regularly. Despite playing in a hitter's era, Jorgens' career batting average was only .238. It was enough to make him the best ballplayer to hail from Modum, Norway, nothing more.

Like Silvera, Jorgens collected a tidy sum in World Series bonuses during his career. Jorgens was on the roster for five Yankee Series without ever appearing in a single Series game. Apparently that wasn't the only trick Jorgens had for earning money without doing any work. According to sportswriter Dan Daniel, Jorgens also "married into a big chain of grocery stores."

BASEBALL'S INVISIBLE MAN

Great baseball players become famous. Great managers, general managers, and team owners become famous as well. Long-time umpires, coaches, television announcers, even sportswriters can be, if not famous, at least familiar names. But there is at least one type of baseball man for whom fame is all but impossible. Despite the considerable impact they have on the success and failure of their clubs, even baseball's most accomplished scouts tend to remain unknown to all but the players they've discovered—famous only to the men they've helped make famous.

Tony Lucadello was a middle infielder of no great ability in the low minor leagues for two years in the mid-1930s. When his short playing career ended, he took a job with the Fostoria Screw Company. But the tug of the game was too strong, and Lucadello returned to baseball as a scout. Over the decades that followed, he became arguably the most successful finder of baseball talent who ever lived. By the time Lucadello's scouting career ended, he'd discovered and signed at least

50 future major leaguers—two full teams worth of players—quite possibly a record for a regional scout. But as far as fame is concerned, Lucadello might as well have stayed in the screw business.

For 11 years with the Chicago Cubs, then 33 more with the Philadelphia Phillies, Lucadello drove from town to town in the upper Midwest watching baseball games and rating young baseball talent. He signed Hall of Famers Mike Schmidt and Ferguson Jenkins, and was responsible for the Cubs signing of Ernie Banks. He signed All-Stars Toby Harrah, Larry Hisle, Mike Marshall, Alex Johnson, and Grant Jackson. But for all this success, Lucadello, like his fellow scouts, operated in the shadows. Few noted the presence of the small, well-dressed man at high-school ballgames. And if the name Lucadello rings any bells with baseball fans, likely as not it's because of Tony's little brother Johnny Lucadello, who reached the majors for a total of 239 games in the late 1930s and 1940s.

On May 8, 1989, Phillies scout Tony Lucadello drove to an empty high-school baseball field in Fostoria, Ohio. There he put a gun in his mouth and ended his life. None of his friends could offer an explanation. It was a noisy end to a quiet life in baseball.

SCOUTING FOR FAME

Among Tony Lucadello's competition for the title of Greatest Baseball Scout:

• Paul Krichell, New York Yankees. Krichell's signings helped build the Yankee dynasty. His finds included Lou Gehrig, Whitey Ford, Phil Rizzuto, Red Rolfe, Charlie Keller, Mark Koenig, and Tony Lazzeri. After watching Gehrig play a game for Columbia University, Krichell told the Yankees he'd found a new Babe Ruth. The assessment wasn't far off.

• Joe Cambria, Washington Senators. Cambria signed a long list of stars for Washington, a significant achievement considering the Senators never had much money to throw at prospects. Cambria's finds included Early Wynn, Mickey Vernon, Eddie Yost, Camilo Pascual, Pedro Ramos, and Zoilo Versalles. If the stories are to be believed, it was Cambria who rejected a pitching hopeful named Fidel Castro at a tryout.

7

WELCOME TO THE BROWNS. YOUR IDENTITY IS SAFE WITH US.

From the team's arrival in St. Louis in 1902 until its departure for Baltimore in 1953, the St. Louis Browns achieved a depth and consistency of lousiness unrivaled in the history of major league baseball. In 52 years of play, the Browns finished within ten games of the pennant just five times. They went to the World Series exactly once . . . and lost. That lone Series appearance came during World War II, when most of baseball's stars were in the military—in other words, the Browns hadn't played well that year; the rest of the American League simply came down to their level. If not for those four war seasons, the Browns would have finished within ten games of first just three times in roughly half a century of baseball. In 2003, much was made of the poor play of the Detroit Tigers, who finished 47 games behind the division-champ Twins. Four times in their history the Browns finished more than 50 games off the pace. In 1939, they missed the pennant by a mere 64½ games. In their 52 seasons, the Browns finished an *average* of more than 31 games back.

It could have been embarrassing to lose all those ball games, but fortunately for the Browns' players, no one was watching. One year the team drew a *total* of 80,922 paying customers. The Cleveland Indians once crammed more fans into their stadium for a single game.

The Browns always lost, and no one bothered to watch. Being a St. Louis Brown was clearly a poor path to baseball fame. For most of the Browns, of course, fame was hardly an issue. When a team finishes 43–111, its players are lucky to have jobs in the majors. But for those rare Browns with talent, playing for St. Louis meant wasting one's fame on the margins of the major leagues.

THE FIRST SLUGGER AT THIRD

Until fairly recently in baseball history, third base was treated like second or short. Most teams were happy to hand the job to a good glove man, even if he didn't hit all that much. The famed 1927 Yankees were content to start a third baseman, Joe Dugan, who contributed just two home runs and a .269 average, lowest among the team's starters. Even the 1961 Yankees of Maris and Mantle fame got by with third baseman Clete Boyer, who hit just .224 with 11 homers. But by 1961 the expectations for third basemen already were changing. Eddie Mathews had hit 47 homers for Milwaukee in 1953, and by the 1960s, other hot hitters like Ken Boyer and Ron Santo had joined him at the hot corner. Today third basemen are expected to field like infielders and hit like outfielders.

Mathews often is cited as the first third baseman to combine offensive punch and defensive grace. But 15 years before Mathews reached stardom, there was Harlond Clift. In 1937, Clift set a record for third basemen by hitting 29 homers. In 1938, he topped his own record by hitting 34. No third baseman bettered that mark until Eddie Mathews came along in the 1950s. Defensively, Clift set records for assists and double plays at third that weren't matched until Graig Nettles reached his prime in the 1970s.

Throw in Clift's .390 career on-base percentage—he walked more than 100 times in six of his 12 major league seasons—and you can make a case that Clift was the best all-around third baseman of the late 1930s and early 1940s. But since he played for the St. Louis Browns, no one much noticed. In Clift's ten seasons with St. Louis, the team only once finished any higher than sixth in an eight-team league. That one exception was a third-place showing in 1942—but even that year they were 19½ games back of the Yankees. Clift made the American League All-Star team just once and spent that game on the bench.

Harlond Clift didn't spend his *whole* career in St. Louis. Late in the 1943 season a Browns trade finally liberated the 31-year-old from baseball's worst team . . . and sent him to baseball's second-worst team, the Washington Senators. Historically, Washington was nearly as bad as the Browns. In 1944, Clift's first full season as a Senator, Washington was worse than St. Louis. Much worse. Washington finished dead last in the American League that year. Meanwhile, the Browns were winning the only pennant in their history. Against all odds, Clift had escaped the Browns and lost out on a shot for glory in the process.

In 1945, Clift finally got a chance to play for a competitive team, as the Senators finished just a game and a half back of the Tigers. But Clift hit just .211. The third baseman's once impressive skills had deteriorated quickly in Washington, due in no small part to poor health. Clift had been stricken with the mumps in 1943, then hurt his throwing shoulder in a fall from a horse in 1944. He'd retire from the major leagues after the season. He was just 33.

Clift spent the next two years in the low minors as a player/manager with the Yakima Stars of the Class B Western International League. But Clift wasn't well suited to a leadership role. He was a man so taciturn that he'd been in the majors for two full seasons before he'd worked up the nerve to tell anyone his name was "Harlond," not "Harland." Clift switched to coaching and scouting for a time, then left professional baseball in the early 1950s to go home to Yakima, Washington and tend to the family farm. Clift's parents had sold their ranch in Oklahoma to purchase the land in the Pacific Northwest when Harlond was just three. The former ballplayer eventually inherited over 50,000 acres.

He lost it all. By the 1980s, Clift, now in his 70s, was widowed and living alone in a mobile home in Yakima, getting by on his Social Security checks and a small pension. The only cropland he had left was the small garden he meticulously tended next to his mobile home. "Bad management," was how Clift explained the loss of his farm. "I made a lot of mistakes."

Though he'd spent most of his life in Yakima, a UPI sportswriter reported that the ex-ballplayer rarely ventured into town and wasn't even well known locally. Clift had virtually no connection to baseball. "The Browns are gone and the Senators are gone," he noted, "so I have no ballclub anymore."

Clift reportedly broke down and cried when he received an

invitation to an old-timers game at Shea Stadium, so surprised was he to be remembered at all. The once-great third baseman died in 1992 at age 79.

THE 20-WIN SEASON THAT DIDN'T MEAN SQUAT

In 1951, St. Louis Browns hitters finished last in the American League in batting average, on-base percentage, hits, runs scored, walks, strike-outs, and stolen base percentage. Brownie pitchers finished last in earned run average, home runs allowed, walks allowed, hits allowed, opponents' batting average allowed, and opponents' on-base percentage allowed. The Browns defense was last in fielding percentage. The team's bullpen was last in saves. And of course, the club as a whole finished in the American League basement with a record of 52–102, ten games back of the Washington Senators, the next-worst team in the majors, and a scant 46 games behind the league-leading New York Yankees. All in all, a fairly typical year for the Browns.

Wasted in this train wreck of a season was one of the truly heroic single-season performances in major league history. With no defense to assist him, no offense to support him, and no bullpen to provide relief, Browns pitcher Ned Garver won 20 games—38 percent of his team's total. Garver remains the only pitcher since 1900 to win 20 games for a team that lost 100 or more. How little help did Garver have in winning those 20 games? Consider that the best hitter in the Browns' lineup on days Garver pitched was Garver himself. He finished the 1951 season with the highest batting average on the club.

Garver's heroic pitching

MORE WINS FOR LOSERS

There have been other great pitching performances on horrid teams. In 1972, Steve Carlton of the Philadelphia Phillies posted a league-leading 1.97 ERA and won 27 games for a team that all-told won 59 and lost 97. Carlton's 27 were 46 percent of the Phil's wins—the equivalent of a pitcher on that year's league-leading Pirates winning 44 (which would have been a bit rough on the arm). Unlike Garver, Carlton hasn't been forgotten by history. He's widely regarded as one of the great pitchers of modern times, and in 1994 was elected to the Hall of Fame in his first year of eligibility.

earned him a measure of acclaim at the time. It must have been gratifying for Garver when he learned he'd been selected to start the 1951 All-Star game. And surely Garver felt a particular satisfaction the evening that off-season when he received the call congratulating him on winning the American League MVP. That particular satisfaction likely lasted until the following morning, when he received a second call, apologizing for the first one. A final tally of the MVP votes showed he was actually second behind Yankee catcher Yogi Berra. These things happen when you're a St. Louis Brown.

It wasn't Garver's first great season. It was just the first where he'd been so great that even the Browns had little choice but to win his games. The year before, in 1950, the sinker-baller had finished with the second-best ERA in the American League, just behind future Hall of Famer Early Wynn and just ahead of future Hall of Famer Bob Feller. But thanks to the Browns typically abysmal hitting and fielding, Garver's record that year was an undistinguished 13–18. "Even if you're leading in the 8th inning, you still felt something would happen," Garver said in 1990. "[But] I never spent any time worrying about that or dwelling on that or thinking about what would have been."

Garver threw out his back shagging flies in the outfield the following April and was never again quite the same pitcher. Midway through that 1952 season, the Browns traded him to the Tigers. Garver was the closest thing the Browns had to a star, but as Browns team owner Bill Veeck, Jr. reportedly said at the time, the Browns had finished last with him; they couldn't do any worse without him.

The deal should have sprung Garver from the worst team in the American League. Instead, it landed him back in the cellar. His new club, the Tigers, lost 104 games in 1952, and finished behind even the Browns in the standings. Garver was a non-factor. His bad back limited him to one game with Detroit down the stretch that year. The Tigers finished in the bottom half of the standings in each of the next four years as well, as Garver's seasonal won-lost records hovered around the .500 mark. In 1957 Detroit finally returned to the top half of the American League. But it was a year too late for Garver. He'd been dealt to the Kansas City A's the previous December. Garver spent four years in Kansas City, and the team finished in one of the bottom two spots in the

American League each year. Garver was claimed by the Los Angeles Angels in the expansion draft before the 1961 season, but by then the end was near. He made it into only 12 games with the fledgling Angels and showed little of his old form. Garver's major league career was over. The Angels finished eighth that year, keeping Garver's career-long string intact: in 14 years in the majors, he never played for a single competitive team. His lifetime record was a forgettable 129–157. He returned to his hometown of Ney, Ohio and took a job with a local food company.

GARVER'S NEPHEW

Ned Garver's nephew, Bruce Berenyi, got his first extended shot in the majors with the Cincinnati Reds in 1981. The hard-throwing young pitcher did quite well, winning nine of 15 decisions and posting a 3.50 ERA. Cincinnati had the best record in the NL West that year, but true to the Garver family luck, they managed to miss the playoffs. Baseball used a split-season arrangement in 1981 to cope with the players' strike that had interrupted play mid-year. Though the Reds had the best overall record, they didn't have the top record in either the year's first half or its second half.

In 1982, Berenyi continued to look like the pitcher everyone hoped he would become, with a 3.36 ERA and 157 strikeouts. Unfortunately for Berenyi, the Reds collapsed into the basement of the National League that year, losing 101 games. Hurt by his team's anemic .251 batting average, Berenyi's record fell to 9–18. The Reds remained in last in the NL West in 1983, and Berenyi's record remained below .500. But like his Uncle Ned 32 years before, Berenyi was sprung from his non-contending team via a mid-season trade. And where Garver had been sent to the then-toothless Tigers, Berenyi landed with the up-and-coming Mets of the mid-1980s. He responded with a 9–6 record down the stretch for the 1984 Mets. Berenyi was expected to be the Mets' third starter in 1985 behind Dwight Gooden and Ron Darling, and at first it looked like he'd become that and more. But after pitching well in his first two outings that year, Berenyi tore his rotator cuff, ending his season. A 1986 comeback attempt failed. The Mets won the World Series that season, but they did so without Berenyi. His major league career was over.

The Mets reportedly had offered Berenyi a three-year contract before the 1985 season that would have left him comfortable for the rest of his life. But, Garver later told a reporter, Berenyi's agent talked the pitcher out of signing. These things happen when you're related to a St. Louis Brown.

There are, no doubt, some baseball fans who remember Garver's heroic 20-win season. And there probably are others who remember him as the pitcher on the mound for "Grandstand Managers' Day," one of Bill Veeck's stunts meant to boost attendance. But few, if any, remember Garver as a star.

THE BABE'S FORGOTTEN RIVAL

In 1922, Ken Williams became the first player in five years to beat out Babe Ruth for an American League home-run crown. It was the highlight of a seven-season run in which Williams never finished worse than fourth in the home-run race. If not for Ruth and his fellow Yankees, Williams would have won the home-run title in five of those years. Williams also was the first major leaguer to hit 30 homers, steal 30 bases, and hit over .300 in the same year. His career batting average was .319. Yet Williams is far from famous. He never received more than a single vote in any Hall of Fame election.

In part, Williams' lack of fame is a result of his short career. While he appeared in 14 seasons, he was a regular in only nine. Williams spent much of his prime in the Pacific Coast League, after failing to impress the Reds in his first major league trial in 1915 and 1916. Williams was 30 years old by the time his first season as an everyday player in the majors ended, an age by which most hitters start to decline.

Injuries worked against Williams as well. In 1924, a broken ankle limited him to 114 games—yet he still managed to finish fourth in the league in homers. In 1925, Williams was beaned by submarine pitcher Byron Speece. Williams was in the hospital for ten days and ended his season after 102 games—yet finished tied for second in that year's home-run race. Williams wasn't the same hitter after the beaning, hitting just 17 homers in 1926 and another 17 in 1927. He was in his late 30s by then, though, so it's hard to say whether age or injury caused his decline.

Williams' home run total came to only 196 in his abbreviated and oft-interrupted career—not enough to get anyone remembered as a power-hitting great, even if he did once battle the Babe for American League slugger supremacy. It's certainly not enough for a member of the almost-always-irrelevant St. Louis Browns. Only once in Williams' tenure with the team were the Browns competitive. And even that year—the 1922 season in which St. Louis missed the pennant by one game—the only Brown to get much glory was George Sisler, who hit .420. Williams hit .332 and led the league in both home runs and RBIs, but didn't receive a single vote for the MVP award.

Ken Williams was sold to the Red Sox in 1928, but hit just 11 homers in two years with the then-last-place club. It appeared he'd get a shot to play for a contender in 1930, when he signed with the Yankees, but Williams never played for New York. Reportedly, the Yanks just wanted the aging lefty-hitting outfielder as an insurance policy in case their own lefty-hitting outfielder, Babe Ruth, held out for more money. But just as Ruth once had robbed Williams of fame by beating him in home run races, now he robbed him once more, by agreeing to terms with the Yanks. With Ruth in the fold, New York dropped Williams. His major league career over, Williams soon went home to Oregon and opened a pool hall. He died in 1959 at the age of 68.

THE BALLPLAYER FROM NOWHERE

Ed Porray's major league career was not the sort destined to generate much fame. The pitcher went 0–1 in three games for the badly nicknamed Buffalo Buffeds of the short-lived Federal League in 1914, his only major league season. But unlike virtually every other player who's ever made the big leagues, Porray didn't even become locally famous in his native town. He couldn't. The pitcher was born on a ship mid-way across the Atlantic Ocean, and therefore had no native town.

If a letter in the Hall of Fame files in Cooperstown written by Porray's niece is to be believed, then Porray's life was one worth remembering, even if his pitching career leaned strongly toward the forgettable. Porray, his niece wrote, was the son of a Russian baron. The baron had been forced to flee Russia in 1888 because, among other issues, the Czar didn't appreciate his public support of the nation's peasantry. It was during this flight that Ed Porray was born.

After his playing days, the former pitcher wrote and arranged popular songs for Irving Berlin. In 1918, he co-wrote the early jazz hit "Everybody Shimmies Now." Porray himself ceased shimmying in 1954 at age 65, when he died from a fall down a flight of stairs. It was a distinctive end to a distinctive life.

THE BROWNIE WHO JOINED A CONTENDER

Vern Stephens seemed determined to prove it was possible to be a Brown and still be lucky. Through most of his career, Stephens' timing was impeccable. The high-school shortstop signed with the Browns in 1938 because he correctly deduced that the talent-bereft team offered a quicker path to the majors than did the better organizations bidding for his services. When Stephens earned his first starting job with St. Louis in 1942, he was just in time for the greatest run—actually, the only great run—in the club's history. The Browns were competitive for the duration of World War II, even reaching the World Series in 1944. Stephens hit between .289 and .294 for his first four years and averaged 20 home runs a season, tremendous offensive numbers for a shortstop in the 1940s.

Stephens abandoned the Browns in favor of the renegade Mexican League in 1946, when that south-of-the-border circuit briefly lured big leaguers with big bucks. But after a couple games, Stephens returned to St. Louis. "I could see that the [Mexican League] wasn't going to work out financially," Stephens would explain. "After three days I wanted to go home."

Again his timing was perfect. The jump to Mexico prompted the Browns to offer Stephens an attractive contract to return. The jump back to St. Louis prevented Stephens from receiving one of the long suspensions that baseball handed other Mexican League refugees who tried to come back to the bigs after that league failed.

The Browns were back to their usual horrible selves in 1946, finishing in seventh despite Stephens' impressive .307 average. But the shortstop wouldn't have to suffer for long. After the 1947 season, he was traded to the very competitive Boston Red Sox. "Stephens," wrote one publication, "is a fugitive from baseball oblivion."

For four years in Boston, Stephens was one of the best infielders in baseball, posting batting averages often upward of .290 and clubbing close to 30 homers a year. In both 1949 and 1950, Stephens led the American League in RBIs. True, playing for the Red Sox is not a great way to win World Series glory, but Stephens was playing great baseball for a strong team. The former Brownie seemed positioned to become a big name.

Oddly, he didn't. Even during his best days in Boston, Stephens never received the attention given to two apparently lesser shortstops, the Yankee's Phil Rizzuto and the Dodger's Pee Wee Reese. Defense was the typical explanation. But while Stephens wasn't as graceful afield as Rizzuto and Reese, he had a great arm and respectable range.

Soon Stephens' stellar play went from overlooked to just plain over. An old knee injury that had kept him out of the military during World War II now caused him increasing grief. Chronic back problems didn't help either. Stephens was just 30 years old at the end of the 1951 season, his fourth year in Boston. But he never again would produce more than eight home runs in a season, and only once would hit above .262.

After a sub-par 1952 with the Red Sox, Stephens was traded to the White Sox. He played just 44 games with Chicago, then was put on waivers and picked up by the team that had given him his start: the St. Louis Browns. There's no escaping destiny. Stephens experienced a Renaissance of sorts in St. Louis, hitting .321 in his 46 games back with the Browns. His old power was gone, and the trick knee forced a shift to third base, but Vern Stephens was once again the best hitter on a last-place Browns team.

As it turned out, that would be the very last last-place Brownie squad. The club moved to Baltimore in 1954 and became the Orioles. Stephens went with them and spent a little more than a season in Baltimore, then a few final games with the White Sox. Stephens called it quits in 1955. He left the majors at age 35, but his best years were behind him by the time he was 30.

Vern Stephens hit .286 with 247 homers in his career. He'd hit 224 of those home runs by the time he was 31. If he could have managed just 13 a year for six more years he would have had 300, which might even have been enough to earn him a place in the Hall of Fame. Instead, Stephens never received a single Hall of Fame vote, though Rizzuto and Reese have been enshrined. Ten great years might be enough to be remembered as a great player—but not if half of them are with the Browns.

Stephens worked a sales rep for bat maker Hillerich & Bradsby for a time after his playing days, then moved on to sales jobs unrelated to baseball. He reportedly consumed alcohol in unhealthy amounts, and in 1968 died of a heart attack at the age of 48. Until his injuries, he'd been about as lucky in his career as any St. Louis Brown ever had been. It wasn't enough to make him famous.

THE CURSE OF LIVONIA

Playing in the wrong town is one thing. But can *living* in the wrong town cost a player fame? Livonia, Michigan's local paper once ran an article about notable former baseball players who'd called Livonia home. Aside from Tigers players who lived in the Detroit suburb while with the club, the article mentioned the following three men . . .

• Hal Smith. The Pittsburgh catcher and Livonia resident nearly became a legend for his 1960 World Series game-seven home run, until a subsequent Yankee rally made him a footnote. (See page 3) Livonia gave Smith the key to the city and named him an honorary fireman anyway, which isn't quite the same as being famous.

• Eddie Cicotte. Cicotte became *in*famous as one of the Black Sox banned from baseball for throwing the 1919 World Series. If not for the banishment, Cicotte likely would have become famous as one of the top pitchers of his era. He even had a fair shot at a plaque in Cooperstown. Cicotte lived in Livonia while working as head of security for Ford after being forced out of baseball. He also owned a strawberry farm.

• Bernie Carbo. Carbo, a graduate of Livonia's Franklin High School, delivered the key pinch-hit three-run homer that tied up game six of the 1975 World Series for the Red Sox. It was his second big pinch-hit home run of that Series. But Fisk's extra-inning game-winner would be the Sox hit everyone remembered. Carbo nearly hit a key home run early in game seven as well, but his shot hit high on Fenway's Green Monster and stayed in the park for a double. The Red Sox couldn't get Carbo home from second and would go on to lose the game and the Series 4–3.

THE YANKEE WHO SHOULDA BEEN A BROWNIE

It takes bad luck to miss out on fame because you play for a perennial loser like the Browns. But consider how much *worse* your luck must be to play for a perennial winner like the New York Yankees—yet still find yourself stuck on losing teams.

When Mel Stottlemyre was called up to the New York Yankees in August 1964, he was joining a team that had appeared in 14 of the past 17 World Series and won ten of them. He was joining a team that hadn't missed the Series in consecutive years since 1945–1946. He was joining a team that, if not for the war years, might not have gone more than three seasons in a row without winning a World Series since 1919 to 1922. "The secret of success as a pitcher," Hall of Fame hurler Waite Hoyt once noted, "lies in getting a job with the Yankees."

Hoyt would have gotten no argument from Stottlemyre in 1964. The Yankees won the American League pennant by a game over Chicago that year, aided mightily by rookie Stottlemyre's impressive 9–3 record down the stretch. New York leaned heavily on their young sinker-baller again in the World Series. Stottlemyre was pitted against Cardinals great Bob Gibson in games two and five, then once more in game seven on two days' rest. Considering the circumstances, Stottlemyre performed brilliantly. He won the first match-up and got a no-decision in the second as the game went to extra innings tied at two. In game seven, Stottlemyre shut the Cards down through three, but surrendered three runs in the 4th. The runs were earned, though a Phil Linz error didn't help matters. Reliever Al Downing, later to give up Hank Aaron's 715th home run, came in for the Yanks to start the 5th and immediately surrendered a Lou Brock home run, then two more runs besides. The Cardinals were on their way to victory in the 1964 Series. Stottlemyre took the loss.

While this was no doubt very disappointing for young Stottlemyre, the setback must have seemed temporary. He looked like an ace pitcher in the making. He was just 22. He was a New York Yankee.

Stottlemyre did in fact become an ace. And he remained a Yankee for his entire career. But against all odds, this was not enough to make him famous. Stottlemyre had picked the very worst stretch in Yankee history in which to excel. The 1964 World Series would be the last meaningful late-season game in which Stottlemyre would ever throw.

FROM A WASHINGTON TOWN TO A WASHOUT TEAM
Mel Stottlemyre had something in common with Harlond Clift (see page 102) besides playing for the wrong team. Both men resided for most of their lives in the town of Yakima, Washington.

In 1965, Stottlemyre went 20–9. Then he went home. Being a Yankee usually meant playing into October, but in 1965, New York didn't make the World Series. Such things happen on occasion. Even the Yankees can't win the pennant *every* year. But the pennant wasn't the only thing the Yankees missed in 1965—they also missed the .500 mark for the first time since 1925. Mickey Mantle was aging fast, and many of the Yankee's other stars were gone entirely. They'd been replaced by the likes of Hector Lopez and Phil Linz—well, replaced in the sense that those men were now standing in their places on the field. If not for Tommy Tresh's .279 batting average and 26 home runs in 1965, no Yankee regular would have hit more than .261 or as many as 20 home runs.

By 1966, the great New York Yankees stank. New York finished tenth—dead last—in the league that year. Even the St. Louis Browns had never finished *tenth* (if only because there had been just eight teams in the league until the 1960s). Stottlemyre pitched reasonably well, but received little offensive support. His record collapsed to 12–20. That year the Baltimore Orioles—the team that until recently had been known as the St. Louis Browns—swept the Dodgers to win the World Series. Had Stottlemyre been a Brown, he'd have won a championship.

Mel Stottlemyre was among the American League's best pitchers in the late 1960s and early 1970s. He was named to five All-Star teams. His career ERA was below 3.00. He was a three-time 20-game winner, despite the less-than-stellar support from his fellow Yankees. But only once, in 1972, did New York finish any better than 15 games back of the pennant or division title. And even their 6½ game deficit in '72 wasn't as close as it sounds—the Yankees still finished fourth in a six-team division.

The next great Yankee dynasty didn't start to take shape until 1974, Stottlemyre's 11th season with the club. New York finished second that year, just two games behind the Baltimore Orioles. But the 1974 pennant race came a few months too late for Stottlemyre. The Yankee workhorse had torn his rotator cuff early that year and struggled to a 6–7 record. Stottlemyre's season ended in early August. As it turned out, so too did the 33-year-old's major league career. The Yankees released Stottlemyre the following spring. Under the rules of the day, that meant they'd only have to pay him one month's salary.

Six times during Stottlemyre's futile 11-year tenure with the Yankees, the team once known as the St. Louis Browns had won the division or the pennant. Stottlemyre was, then, a contender for the title of the ultimate unlucky player: the Yankee who would have been more famous as a Brown.

A decade and a career change later, Mel Stottlemyre finally got to be a part of a winner. The respected pitching coach was a member of the 1986 Mets team that won the Series. Stottlemyre become pitching coach of the New York Yankees in 1996. This time his timing was better. The Yankees were just beginning their latest dynasty.

LIKE FATHER, LIKE SONS

Two of Mel Stottlemyre's sons, Mel, Jr. and Todd, pitched in the majors, just like their old man. Both suffered torn rotator cuffs, just like their old man.

GOOD HITTERS, BAD STADIUMS

The Houston Astros are not the St. Louis Browns. The Astros have never reached the World Series, but they've been reasonably competitive during their four decades of baseball. Yet for a certain type of ballplayer—the power hitter—there was for years no worse place to play than Houston. The Astros played half their games each year in the Astrodome, a park that had a habit of turning home runs into routine fly outs.

When Jimmy Wynn first reached the major leagues with Houston in 1963, there was no Astrodome. For that matter, there were no Astros. Houston's baseball team had been christened the Colt .45's when added to the National League in 1962. And like every other team in baseball, they played their games outdoors, in Colt Stadium. With its deep fences and steady wind blowing in from right, Colt Stadium wasn't a great home for a slugger like Wynn. (Actually, it wasn't a great home for anyone, except maybe the Cessna-sized Texas mosquitoes that considered it a fine place to take in a ballgame.) But when the Astrodome became the team's home in 1965, life would only get worse for Wynn and his fellow Astro hitters. The dome kept out those huge mosquitoes, but the enclosed park also stopped the big fly. In 1965, the first year of indoor major league baseball, only 57 regular-season home runs were hit in the Astrodome. The first year of the Astrodome also was 23-year old slugger Jimmy Wynn's first full season in the majors. Despite his home-field disadvantage, he managed to hit 22 homers that year and led the team in each of the Triple Crown categories.

Wynn's home run output dipped to 18 in 1966, but only because he missed the final two months of the season after running into an outfield wall. In 1967, Wynn's 37 homers fell just two short of leading the National League. No other Astro had more than ten. Starting that year, Wynn averaged more than 30 homers a season for the next four seasons, all while playing in the worst park for a power hitter in recent major league history. Wynn's battle against the Astrodome was all the more impressive considering he stood just 5'9" and weighed only 165 pounds. He was the ultimate underdog, a short man who hit long balls in baseball's toughest power venue. He should have been a hero. Instead "The Toy Cannon" was criticized for his perceived lack of hustle and his tendency to feud with his managers.

> **THE BIG DEAL**
> Plenty of big-name big leaguers have played in parks not perfectly suited to their talents. A long-standing baseball rumor holds that in 1947, two teams nearly did something about it. The Yankees and Red Sox reportedly considered swapping Joe DiMaggio for Ted Williams. The thinking was that left-handed pull hitter Williams would thrive in Yankee Stadium with its short right field fence, while right-handed hitter DiMaggio would benefit from Fenway's Green Monster, just 315 feet away in left. Obviously, the trade never happened.

"No Astros player has ever had the potential of Jim Wynn or been a bigger disappointment," wrote *Baseball Digest* in June 1972, a common sentiment in baseball at the time. Yet when those words were printed, Wynn had led the Houston Astros in home runs in all but one of the seasons there had been Houston Astros. And while Wynn's batting average was only in the .250 to .280 range most years, few seemed to appreciate the value of Wynn's willingness to work a walk. Wynn walked more than one hundred times in six separate seasons. In 1969, he had more walks than he did hits. Wynn's .269 batting average that year might not have looked like anything special, but his .440 on-base percentage was second in the league, behind only the far-more-heralded Willie McCovey.

Wynn had only two bad seasons in his 11 years with Houston. The first was 1971, when he hit just .203 with seven homers. There were extenuating circumstances, however. Wynn's wife Ruth had stabbed him with a steak knife the previous off-season, one day after the couple's seventh wedding anniversary. (Not to criticize, but stabbing a spouse with a steak knife would have been more appropriate on the 11th, or steel, anniversary. The seventh anniversary gift is supposed to be copper.) Wynn gallantly said he didn't blame his wife. He had, after all, been brandishing a shotgun at the time. "The shotgun was unloaded," said Patrolman J.A. Fortenberry, "but he didn't tell her that, though."

Wynn's second poor year in Houston was 1973, when he managed just 20 homers and a .220 average. That sub-par season got him traded. Leaving the Astrodome should have boosted Wynn's homer totals and been a boon to his fame. Only he was traded to the Dodgers, who played in perhaps the worst hitters' park in the majors outside of Houston. "The Astrodome is one of the toughest home run parks in baseball," said Wynn at the time. "They say the same about Dodger Stadium, but I don't buy it. . . . I expect to hit more than 25 home runs and drive in more than 80 runs."

He was right. Wynn hit 32 out and drove 108 in during the 1974 season, despite a troublesome arm injury. The Dodgers won the pennant, then fell in five to Oakland in the Series. Wynn had surgery on the arm that winter. Perhaps as a result, his batting average dropped to .248 in 1975, his home run total to 18. The Dodgers dealt Wynn to Atlanta after the season. The 34-year-old Wynn finally would get to play in a home park suited to his talents. "It's a hitter's park," said Wynn after the trade. "I think I can do a better job there than I did for the Dodgers last season."

This time Wynn's prediction proved incorrect. He hit just .207 with 17 homers. It went relatively unnoticed that Wynn led the league in walks, quite a feat for a man hitting so poorly. After the 1976 season, Wynn was sold to the Yankees. Yankee Stadium was yet another poor place for a right-handed power-hitter to play, and Wynn lasted only 30 games in New York. A final 36 games with Milwaukee later that season closed out his career.

Wynn's lifetime stats aren't all that impressive at first glance—a .250 career batting average and 291 home runs. But that .250 batting average doesn't take into account his 1,224 career walks, and his 291 home runs don't take into account his difficult home parks. Wynn never received even a single vote in a Hall of Fame election. It didn't have to be that way. Wynn originally was in the farm system of the Cincinnati Reds. Had he remained in the Cincinnati chain, he would have started his career in Crosley Field, one of the best hitters parks in the National League.

One season after Jimmy Wynn left Houston, Jose Cruz arrived. Cruz had begun his major league career in St. Louis in 1970. And while he was acknowledged to be the best of the three Cruz brothers to appear in the St. Louis outfield in late 1973, the Cardinals gave him credit for little else. Cruz was relegated to a platoon or pinch-hitting role. After the 1974 season, St. Louis sold the outfielder to the Astros for the bargain price of $20,000. It was the best and worst thing that could have happened to him. Already 28, Cruz finally got his chance to play everyday— but he'd play half those days in the Astrodome. It wasn't the most auspicious venue for a man who liked to swing for the fences.

In his first year in Houston, it looked like the difficult conditions would be too much for Cruz. He hit just .257 with nine home runs in 1975. But everything changed before the 1976 season when new Astros coach Deacon Jones asked Cruz "Do you want to hit 10 or 20 homers and bat .260, or be a consistent .300 hitter?"

With Jones' help, former pull-hitter Cruz started hitting to all fields. The former slugger even chopped down on pitches and legged out Astro-turf hits. At 29, an age when hitters' skills typically begin to slip, Cruz's batting average topped .300 for the first time. From 1976 through 1985, Cruz was the consistent .300 hitter Jones had told him he could be. His numbers would have looked even better if he'd played in a different park. In 1984, Cruz hit .343 with 12 home runs on the road. The Astrodome held him to .277 with no home runs. Cruz hit 165 home runs during his career. Only 59 of them were in his home parks.

Thanks perhaps to the Astrodome's inhibiting effect on his power numbers, Cruz was never even close to famous. He was never an MVP, except in the Puerto Rican winter league. He never won a Gold Glove, despite raves about his play in left field. He appeared in the All-Star Game just once, that at age 37. "It's just too bad the players don't vote for the All-Star team," Mets pitcher Ed Lynch told *USA Today* in 1985. "He'd be on there every year."

DEACON'S BAD WING

Deacon Jones, the coach who helped Jose Cruz become a top hitter, once seemed destined for greatness himself. Jones hit .409 for Dubuque of the Midwest League to lead all of professional baseball in 1956. He also led all Midwest League second basemen in fielding average and narrowly missed the Triple Crown that year, finishing first in RBIs, but second in home runs. Then Jones was drafted into the military and missed the next two seasons. When he returned in 1959, he badly injured his shoulder in a head-first slide. The shoulder would never recover. Jones still could hit—he won the winter league Triple Crown one year, batting .420—but the once-reliable second baseman couldn't throw the ball.

Jones became a defensive liability even at his new position, first base. One year with Indianapolis, Jones' team lost a game when a runner rounded third and scored on a routine play at first, knowing Jones couldn't get the ball home. The next day Indianapolis Manager Rollie Hemsley tried to teach Jones to throw left-handed. The result: two sore arms. With the DH rule still a decade away, Jones' bad shoulder kept him from finding a place in the majors. He had a grand total of only 49 big league at-bats in the majors spread over three seasons in the 1960s.

The intelligent, college-educated Jones could have given up and made a decent living outside of baseball. But he loved the game too much to leave it, and he later became a respected hitting coach, radio commentator, and one of the first African-American managers in the minor leagues. Though Jones had lost a potentially great career to injury, he was not the sort to complain. Not usually, anyway. There was the one time he voiced some concerns about a minor league assignment. "They told me I'm being sent to Lynchburg," the African-American Jones said to White Sox coach Tony Cuccinello. "I just don't like the sound of that name."

Instead, Cruz frequently was confused with Julio Cruz, a career .237-hitting infielder with the Mariners and White Sox. Throughout his 13 seasons in Houston, articles about Cruz inevitably sported headlines like "Jose Cruz: Astros' Invisible Superstar," "Astros equipped with secret weapon," or "He's been doomed by the Dome, or he'd be on everybody's best list."

At the age of 40, Cruz left Houston, the years having finally caught up with him. His average had tumbled from .300 in 1985 to .278 in 1986, then .241 in 1987. Cruz signed a non-guaranteed free agent contract with the New York Yankees for the 1988 season. For a left-handed hitter with good power, there are few better parks than Yankee Stadium. And certainly there are few better cities for fame than New York. The Yanks expected the aging Cruz to provide nothing more than a bat off the bench, if he could make the team at all. Instead he was the hottest Yankee hitter in spring training, and quickly was written into the team's plans as DH against right-handed pitching. But Cruz stopped hitting when the team went north. He was released in July after just 80 at-bats, his average a forgettable .200. It was, incidentally, the failure of Cruz in the left-handed power-hitting DH role that led the Yankees to swap young Jay Buhner for an aging Ken Phelps that July. That deal is widely considered one of the worst Yankee trades in history.

In 1994, Cruz received a grand total of two votes in the Hall of Fame election (342 were needed for election that year). Wes Westrum once got two votes. Morrie Martin once got two votes. Jose Cruz deserved better. Instead, his name was removed from future ballots due to lack of support.

In 1991, three years after Jose Cruz left Houston, Jeff Bagwell arrived. Like Wynn and Cruz before him, Bagwell was a power hitter. Like Wynn, he'd started his career in the farm system of a team that played in one of the best hitters parks in baseball—in Bagwell's case, Boston's Fenway Park. But Bagwell had some distinct advantages over the doomed domed Astros sluggers of the past. He played in a hitter's era, and he played a decent portion of his career in a hitter's park. The Astros moved to a new home, the homer-friendly Enron Field (now Minute Maid Park) in 2000, making Bagwell one of the few people this side of Enron CEO Jeff Skilling to profit from the failed energy conglomerate. With 419 home runs and a .300 average through the end of the 2003 season, it seems likely that Bagwell will find his way to the Hall of Fame.

ANOTHER OVERLOOKED ASTRO

Jeff Bagwell's long-time Astros teammate Craig Biggio has been called one of the overlooked greats of modern baseball. But then Biggio's greatness was overshadowed even on his *college* team. As a senior at Seton Hall in 1987, Biggio hit .407 with 14 home runs . . . yet was overshadowed by teammates Mo Vaughn, who hit .429 with 28 homers that year, and Marteese Robinson, who stole 58 bases and led all of Division I with a .529 batting average. Vaughn would go on to have six great seasons in the majors before his career was derailed by injury. Robinson never advanced beyond the minors, left baseball to enter law enforcement, then returned to the game as a scout. Biggio keeps rolling quietly along, reaching base and playing whatever position the Astros ask of him.

8

ASSORTED EXAMPLES OF BAD BASEBALL TIMING

itting is timing," said Hall of Fame pitcher Warren Spahn. "Pitching is upsetting timing." Fame, too, is timing. And there are plenty of ways in which the timing required for baseball fame can be upset. The game's history is full of men who seemingly did everything required for fame, but did so too soon or too late to be remembered.

GRAYS BEFORE BLACK SOX

Shoeless Joe Jackson, Ed Cicotte, and their fellow Black Sox earned lasting baseball infamy as the men who accepted bribes from gamblers to throw the 1919 World Series. But they weren't the first ballplayers to throw key games. In 1877, four members of the Louisville Grays threw the National League pennant. (or at least threw games during the pennant race). The main reason "The crime of '77" and the players responsible aren't infamous today is that it was superseded by 1919's scandal.

In August of 1877, the Louisville Grays led heading the pennant race into their final road swing through the East in the National League's second year. Yet when the season ended, Louisville was seven games behind Harry Wright's Boston club. It looked suspicious to just about everyone, and rumors of intentional dumping were widespread. An investigation turned up damning telegrams, and the players confessed. The culprits were Jim Devlin, a pitcher who had been second in the league in wins and winning percentage that year and third in ERA; outfielder George Hall, who'd led the Grays with a .323 batting average; starting shortstop Bill Craver; and a marginal player named Al Nichols. All four were permanently banned from professional baseball. The scandal was the final nail in the coffin of the Louisville Grays franchise, which was dropped from the National League after the season.

For Devlin and Hall, the scandal was the end of what might have been great major league careers. Devlin, only 28 when he was banned, had recently developed a "down shoot" pitch that had turned him into one of the league's most effective pitchers. His 2.05 career ERA (1.89, according to some sources) is fifth best all-time among pitchers with at least one thousand innings pitched and one hundred decisions. Hall, also 28, had hit a combined .345 in his two National League seasons and won the home run crown in 1876.

There were other baseball scandals before this, and there would be others in the decades that followed. But as recently as 1918, *The Sporting News* wrote that "the 'crime of '77' easily takes precedence over all other baseball scandals." One year after *The Sporting News* printed those words, the White Sox threw the 1919 World Series, and the events of 1877 became yesterday's news. The names Devlin, Hall, Craver, and Nichols have been replaced in the minds of baseball fans with those of Jackson, Cicotte, Gandil, Weaver, and company.

The players involved in the 1877 Louisville scandal made numerous appeals for reinstatement in the years after their expulsion. Devlin was particularly persistent, reportedly once visiting the office of National League president William Hulbert dressed in rags, insisting the banishment had led his family to ruin. A *Chicago Tribune* article dismissed Devlin's claims of poverty as an attempt to gain Hulbert's sympathy, but *The Sporting News* wasn't so sure. "Everything about the man's appearance betokened weariness and woe," wrote a *Sporting News* reporter who claimed to have witnessed Devlin's supplication. "His face was a picture of abject misery."

Whatever Devlin's circumstances, all appeals for forgiveness were unsuccessful. Little is known of the remaining years of Al Nichols and George Hall, though Hall is thought to have died in Ridgewood, New York in 1923. Devlin died of consumption in 1883, roughly 34 years old. He continued to ask the National League for forgiveness until the end. Craver died of heart disease at age 57 in 1901.

Devlin and Craver found work in the same profession following their forced retirements from baseball. The perpetrators of the so-called "crime of '77" became policemen.

TOO SOON THE REBEL

Curt Flood had a fine career by any standard. He played 15 seasons in the big leagues, hit .293, and won two World Series (though Flood's defensive misplay hurt his team's chances of winning a third). But Flood instead is remembered first and foremost for the role he played in the birth of free agency, one of the most dramatic changes in major league baseball of the past 50 years. In 1970, Flood sued the major leagues in an effort to strike down the reserve clause that bound players to their teams in perpetuity. Two years later, the U.S. Supreme Court ruled against Flood. But today Flood's failed case is remembered as an important skirmish in the larger legal war for freedom that the players soon won.

Two decades before Curt Flood, another man challenged baseball's reserve clause. That man, George Toolson, wasn't a star like Flood. He wasn't even a major leaguer. And he didn't have a powerful players' union on his side. George Toolson was a minor league pitcher of only modest abilities who found himself stuck in the farm system of the New York Yankees. When the Yankees tried to demote Toolson within their system in 1950, the pitcher refused and brought suit against the Yankees on antitrust grounds. In 1953, the Supreme Court ruled against Toolson by a 7–2 margin—just as they later ruled against Flood—claiming in their wisdom that baseball was not commerce. The suit ended Toolson's professional baseball career. He had rebelled against the system 20 years before the courts and his fellow ballplayers were ready to join him in the fight.

Curt Flood, the man who would become famous for unsuccessfully standing up to baseball, was felled by cancer at age 59, gone before his time. George Toolson, the man who *wouldn't* become famous for unsuccessfully standing up to baseball, was stricken with cancer at the age of 60. Surgeons removed one of Toolson's kidneys in 1982, and the ex-minor league pitcher's health improved. But the cancer returned in

TOOLSON'S NEPHEW

Considering the unpleasant end to George Toolson's pitching career, it would have been understandable if he'd become bitter and stopped following pro baseball. But in the late 1970s and early 1980s, Toolson found himself rooting for the Blue Jays. He was more or less obliged to—his nephew was a struggling infielder with the club. But perhaps deep down Toolson was just as happy when the young man gave up on baseball and moved on to a different line of work. It turned out for the best anyway. The struggling infielder, Danny Ainge, found more success in his new field, basketball, than he had in baseball.

After his NBA playing career, Ainge—the nephew of a man who once battled against professional sports' powers-that-be—became one of the powers-that-be himself, as Executive Director of Basketball Operations for the Boston Celtics.

1987, and Toolson passed away at the age of 65.

George Toolson might not have been a great pitcher, but as the Orange County Register noted with his Supreme Court case in mind, he was just "one victory from becoming a household name."

A BAD TIME TO BE IN A BAD SPOT

The first act of Benny Kauff's drama is pure triumph. The second act is pure tragedy. His reversal of fortune was, as much as anything, a result of bad timing.

Kauff was born into an Ohio coal-mining community in 1890. At age 11, he began the life that seemed all but certain to be his destiny: He went down into the mines. All the men in Kauff's family were coal miners, and his friends were coal miners, too. For eight years, Kauff spent 12 hours a day in the mines. By late in his teenage years, he was earning around ten cents an hour.

According to Kauff, he was nearly killed by falling rock on two separate occasions.

Sundays were Kauff's refuge. On Sundays, and on the occasional Saturday afternoon, Kauff could go outside when the sun was still in the sky. To Kauff, sunshine meant baseball. The game was his passion, and by the time Kauff neared age 20, it also was the only hope he had of escaping the mines. In 1910, he begged a local low-level minor league club for a tryout. They must have been hard up for players, Kauff would later theorize, because they agreed to take him.

Only two years later Kauff was playing for the New York Yankees (at that point still better known as the Highlanders). Kauff hit well, but New York sent him back to the minors after a brief trial. According to reports, the optimistic young Kauff had an unfortunate habit of continuing to try for additional bases until he was thrown out.

The birth of the Federal League in 1914 offered Kauff his escape from the minors, and he took full advantage. Kauff hit .370 in the new major league in 1914, then .342 in 1915. He also stole 130 bases during those two years. The combination of batting skill and speed earned Kauff the title "The Ty Cobb of the Federal League." But that moniker wouldn't have much meaning after 1915. The Federal League folded.

Kauff landed with the New York Giants in the National League. He hit just .264 in 1916, but his .308 average in 1917 seemed to suggest Kauff was more than just a Federal League phenom. His two home runs in game four of that year's World Series helped the Giants even the Series at two, though they'd eventually lose to the White Sox in six. In the first half of 1918, Kauff compiled an average of .315, but he spent the remainder of the season in the military fighting the final months of World War I.

The war ended later that year, and Benny Kauff's storybook life appeared ready to resume. He had left the dark and dirt and poverty of the coal mines behind him and never looked back. Kauff was known throughout baseball for his seemingly insatiable appetite for loud, expensive clothes, diamond jewelry, and cash. Always cash. Big rolls of cash. Kauff sometimes carried thousands of dollars in his pockets, a huge amount of money in the 1910s. It was quite a change for someone who less than a decade before had toiled in the mines for a little over a dollar a day. Kauff talked big and lived fast. He was said to have wrapped more than one expensive car around a tree. His fellow ballplayers expressed admiration for Kauff's ability to chew tobacco, smoke cigars, and drink beer *at the same time.*

Then things went wrong for Kauff. It was 1919. He'd had a sub-par season, and in December came the incident that would change his life. Charges later filed against Kauff alleged that on the night of December 8, 1919, he and two accomplices stole a Cadillac belonging to a James E. Brennan of New York. The car was allegedly repainted and sold for $1,800, the money split three ways.

An indictment was handed down in early 1920. Kauff maintained his innocence, but his play suffered, and the former star found himself back in the minor leagues part-way through the year. New York's justice system moved slowly, and when spring training began in 1921, Kauff's case still hadn't come to trial. The delay proved disastrous for the outfielder.

In 1920, the news had broken that the 1919 World Series had been fixed. Major league baseball installed the capricious, dictatorial Judge Kenesaw Mountain Landis as commissioner to deal with the problem. Landis' mandate was to clean up the game's image, and an outfielder under indictment for auto theft wasn't exactly the image he had in mind. Though Kauff hadn't been convicted of anything—his case was still pending—Landis summoned the outfielder north from spring training in 1921 and suspended him from baseball.

Kauff's auto theft trial finally got underway later that year. It turned out the state's case against the ballplayer was not very strong. The main evidence against him was the testimony of his alleged accomplices, James Shields and James Whalen, both former employees of an auto accessory business Kauff had owned on the side. Their testimony was countered by Kauff's evidence that he had purchased the vehicle in good faith before reselling it. Further, Kauff's wife testified that she had been eating dinner with her husband on the night the prosecution witnesses claimed the loot was divided. Also appearing in Kauff's defense were Giant manager John McGraw and teammate George Burns. Both noted that Kauff had served honorably in the war, and that he had a history of honesty—once offered a bribe to throw a ballgame, he'd turned it down and reported the incident to Christy Matheson. The jury took less than an hour to render their verdict: not guilty.

The whole episode might have been a hiccup in a fine baseball career. Instead it was the end. Despite the acquittal, Commissioner Landis refused to lift Kauff's suspension. Landis, never the fairest of arbiters, reportedly decided that Kauff looked guilty to him, whatever the jury had ruled. (Others have speculated that Landis' harsh treatment of Kauff might have been in part a punishment for the ballplayer's habit of contract jumping during the Federal League era.)

In 1922, Kauff sued both Landis and the National Exhibition Company, the owners of the Giants, for reinstatement into baseball. The judge hearing the case agreed that "an apparent injustice" had been done to Kauff, but ruled that he had no power to lift the suspension.

Kauff was in large part a victim of bad timing. His legal problems had played out in 1920 and 1921. With baseball desperate to clean up its image in the wake of the Black Sox scandal, it was the very worst moment in baseball history to have ethical issues hanging over one's head. Kauff was out of the game forever. When his career ended, he had a .311 lifetime average. He was just 30 years old.

In 1931, a reporter met Kauff in New York. Like so many in those depression years, the formerly flush Kauff was looking for work. "I could play ball again," he said. "But they won't let me. I'm only 42 years old . . . .But I know I never will, not as long as Landis is on the job. One jam— and I was through for life. But it's too late to holler 'foul' now.

" I never did anything wrong in baseball, although they tried to get me to. They tried to bribe me in Chicago and I went right to Matty who was my roommate and told him about it. Never mind who tried to bribe me; I'm no squealer."

As the years passed, Kauff's career largely slipped from memory. Five full seasons and three partial seasons in the majors isn't enough for lasting fame, even for a flashy one-time New York star. According to his obituary in *The Columbus Citizen*, Kauff later spent more than two decades as a scout—but this fact is unconfirmed by other sources, and

THE BRAVE LAWYER

Kauff's attorney in his 1921 trial was a New York lawyer named Emil Fuchs. As it happened, Fuchs had more of a future in baseball than did his client. For much of the 1920s and into the 1930s, Fuchs served as head of the group that owned the Boston Braves. In 1929, the German-born Fuchs even named himself manager, though he reportedly left most of the decision-making to coach Johnny Evers. The Braves finished last that year, at 56–98. No other owner would manage his own team until Ted Turner gave it a try for one game, also with the Braves, in 1977. Turner did no better, ending his managerial career at 0–1.

likely would not have been permitted for a player who'd been expelled from baseball. It's more certain that he worked for some years as a salesman with a company that makes dusting cloths. Kauff had risen from rags to riches in his life, but he ended up selling rags. He died of a cerebral hemorrhage in 1961.

THE BRIEF AND VARIED GREATNESS OF GUY HECKER

Many of the great players and great performances of the 19th century are all but ignored today. When people refer to the record for wins in a season, they inevitably mean Jack Chesbro's 41 in 1904, not Charley Radbourn's 60 in 1884. When they refer to the most stolen bases in a season, they mean Rickey Henderson's 130 in 1982, not Hugh Nicol's 138 in 1887. If the subject is strikeouts, they're after Nolan Ryan's 383 in 1973, not Matt Kilroy's 513 in 1886.

Segregating old numbers from new isn't without some justification. The game was very different in its infancy. When Old Hoss Radbourn won 60 in 1884, he had the distinct advantage of starting 75 times. When Nicol stole those 138 bases in 1887, he was given credit for steals when he went from first to third on singles. But paying heed to the differences in the game is little excuse for ignoring the stars of the 19th century entirely.

Among the most interesting of the forgotten is pitcher Guy Hecker, who once did just about everything you can do in baseball and did it well. But he quickly faded from the sport, and today is hardly remembered at all. Hecker joined Louisville of the then major league American Association in 1882 as a 26-year old rookie first baseman/pitcher. Two years later, Hecker led the league with 52 wins and a 1.80 ERA. Only two pitchers in history have won more than Hecker's 52 games in a season, and both of them did so for dominant pennant-winning teams. Hecker had no such elite talent around him. Remove his 52–20 record, and Louisville was well below .500. Unfortunately for noted ladies' man "Blond Guy" Hecker, those 52 wins came at a price. He threw 671 innings, the third most any pitcher ever has thrown in a major league season.

Louisville asked Hecker to carry the club again in 1885. He threw 480 innings, fifth most in the league, and won 30 games. Hecker's 2.18 ERA was second in the American Association, and his 385 strikeouts were tops. But all the innings caught up with Hecker, and he developed a sore arm.

**ONCE THE GREATEST EVER, NOW JUST
ANOTHER PLAQUE ON THE WALL**

Buck Ewing *is* in the Hall of Fame, so it isn't fair to say he's forgotten. But it is worth noting how far his star has fallen since his own times. When Ewing died in 1906, *Sporting Life* referred to him as "the only absolutely perfect ball player" and "the greatest ballplayer that ever wore a spiked shoe." He was "perfect in all departments and had not a weakness." The *Cincinnati Enquirer* called Ewing "The Greatest of Them All" and said he was "pretty generally acknowledged to be the greatest all-around ballplayer that the world has ever seen." That's pretty heady stuff, considering Ewing hit a good-but-not-great .303 (or .307, depending on who you ask) with 71 home runs in his 18 years in the majors.

"Fifty years from now," Brooks Robinson once said, "I'll just be three inches of type in a record book." Whatever Ewing did to earn the praise lavished on him in his day, it obviously isn't fully conveyed in his three inches. With all those who saw him play long since deceased, the greatness of Buck Ewing has been lost forever.

By 1886, Hecker's pitching career was clearly on the decline. His once-devastating sinking fastball had deserted him, leaving Hecker to hang on as a junk-ball specialist. His strikeouts decreased, and his walks more than doubled, but Hecker's 2.87 ERA still was good for sixth in the league. He was, however, no longer the star pitcher of his team. Louisville concluded Hecker's days as an ace were behind him and signed Toad Ramsey to pick up the slack.

So Hecker found a completely different way to be the best in the league. With his pitching arm hurting, he became a star hitter. Hecker hit .341 in 1886 to lead the American Association. He remains the only player in baseball history to capture season titles for both wins and batting average. But Hecker received no glory for his feat. Due to a miscalculation in the tabulation of that year's batting averages, New York first baseman Dave Orr was credited with a league-leading average of .346. The mistake wasn't noticed for more than 70 years. Hecker did receive some mild acclaim that year for becoming the first pitcher to hit three home runs in a single contest, and he remains to this day the only man to score seven runs in a major league game. But that wasn't enough to make him famous.

Hecker's pitching career took another blow in 1887, when the pitcher's box was shrunk in size. (In those days, pitchers didn't deliver the ball by pushing off a pitching rubber on top of a mound. They were allowed to throw from anywhere in a marked-out "pitcher's box"— hence the expression "knocked out of the box" for pitchers who are hit hard.) Hecker had always been one to take full advantage of the pitcher's box, running forward on his delivery; the smaller box cramped his style. Hecker's record was a good-but-not-spectacular 18–12 that year, his ERA up to 4.16. It would be his last winning record. Hecker hit .319 in 1887, but he never again hit above .300 for a season. He was released in mid-1889. The ever-versatile Hecker served as an umpire in the league for the remainder of the year. Louisville fell to 27–111 that season, dead last in the American Association.

In 1890, Hecker became pitcher/first baseman/manager for Pittsburgh of the National League. He had a tough year in all three roles. Hecker's batting average was just .226, his ERA a hefty 5.11. Meanwhile his team was one of the worst in history, most of its best players having jumped to Pittsburgh's entry in the new Players' League. Hecker's club finished the season at 23–113, effectively ending his major league managerial career. *Sporting Life* would note that between Louisville in 1889 and Pittsburgh in 1890, "Hecker enjoys the distinction of having figured in more defeats in two years than any other player on record. . . . Sir Guy ought to be a right jolly loser by this time."

It was a dramatic turn for a man who had been the toast of Louisville a few years before. "Babies and cigars were named after him," wrote the *Louisville Courier-Journal*. "Nothing that he could wish for wasn't somehow forthcoming. The king has fallen. None now are so poor as to do him reverence."

Hecker managed and played some first base for a few years in the minors, then returned home to Oil City, Pennsylvania to enter the oil business, which must have seemed like the thing to do thereabouts. In 1926, he moved to Wooster, Ohio where he worked for Ohio Fuel Gas Co. Five years later, a serious car accident left Hecker's former pitching arm crippled. He lived another seven years, but never fully regained his health. Hecker died at age 82, never knowing he'd won a batting title.

Guy Hecker had been, if only briefly, arguably the best in his league as both a pitcher and a hitter. Babe Ruth might be the only other man in the game's history who could make such a claim. The rare combination of talents should have made Hecker famous. But he came along too soon and was gone not long after.

THE DEADBALL SLUGGERS

In 1918, 98 total home runs were hit in American League games. No one player had more than 11. In 1920, 370 home runs were hit league-wide. Babe Ruth alone hit 54. The new lively baseball was flying out of parks, and the sluggers who played in the "deadball era" prior to 1920 were destined to be forgotten. Who's going to be impressed by 11 homers when the record is 54—or for that matter, 61 or 73? But just as we can't blame Roger Clemens for never winning 41 games in a season like Jack Chesbro, neither can we blame the deadball sluggers for never hitting 54. They simply played at the wrong time to accumulate such gaudy stats. Two deadball sluggers who deserve to be remembered . . .

• Buck Freeman. When Freeman hit 25 home runs in 1899, he got screwed. Twice.

First, by all rights Freeman's 25 should have captured the single-season home run record with room to spare. But because of an oddly shaped field 15 years before, the record actually stood at 27. In 1884, the National League Chicago White Stockings played in a park that featured the closest outfield fence in history—just 180 feet down the line in left, 196 to right. That year four Chicago players became the *only* four major leaguers prior to Freeman to hit more than 20 home runs in a season. One of them, Ned Williamson, hit 27. Had Freeman's 25 homers counted as the record, it would have stood until Ruth hit his 29 two full decades later.

Second, Freeman hit his 25 in 1899, one year too soon to claim the so-called "modern" record. Though there was no significant change in the way the game was played between 1899 and 1900, many record books split baseball history into pre-1900 and 1900 onward. Freeman missed by one year falling on the correct side of this line for lasting recognition.

Freeman would never again approach 25 homers, though he

did lead the American League with 13 in 1903. His career total was 82 in eight full seasons and part of three others. That's more impressive than it sounds, considering how tough home runs were to hit in those days. After his playing career ended, Freeman did some managing and umpiring in the minors, scouted for seven years, then ran a pool hall in his hometown of Wilkes-Barre, Pennsylvania. He reportedly lived quietly, though like most people he did enjoy a good cockfight. Freeman wasn't a man to spend his time recounting his glory days. "The fans don't give a whoop about what went on 25 or 35 years ago," he told an interviewer in the late 1940s. "They live in the present and all this guff about the game being better in the old days does not interest them. Besides, it's a pretty good game as it stands and probably a trifle more interesting . . . than it was in my day."

Freeman died in 1949 at age 77 after a short illness. "Freeman was the greatest home run hitter of all time," said Ira Thomas, a catcher whose career in the American League began just as Freeman's was ending, and ended just as Babe Ruth's was beginning. "Freeman hit a ball that was hard to make go far. . . . 'Bucky' Freeman did the world's best job when he [hit 25 homers in a season], and he has never been equaled."

• Gavvy Cravath. Between 1913 and 1919, Cravath led the National League in home runs six times. Had he managed one more homer in 1916, he would have won or shared the home run crown seven years running. His 24 homers in 1915 was the 20th century record until Ruth hit 29 in 1919. Cravath, known as "Cactus" for his sometimes-prickly personality, did have an advantage over other deadball sluggers in assembling these stats—he played in Philadelphia's Baker Bowl, the greatest home run-hitter's park of its day. Of Cravath's 119 career homers, 93 were hit at home. But Cravath also had a substantial disadvantage—he didn't really get his start in the majors until he was 31. Cravath had failed in three previous major league trials, but his 29 home runs and .363 average with minor league Minneapolis in 1911 earned him one last try. The Phillies bought his rights for $9,000, and this time Cravath stuck in the bigs. But thanks to his age, he had just seven and a half seasons as a star. His playing days ended just as home-run hitting started to come into style. The 39-year-old Cravath had 45 at-bats in 1920. It was the first season of the new livelier ball; it was the last season of his major league career. Cravath spent a couple years managing in the minors, then moved back to California. After a few years selling real estate, he became a justice of the peace in Laguna, California. Cravath died in 1953 at the age of 82.

Though his home run records don't look like much today, Cravath was the godfather of the modern power hitter, at least in terms of philosophy. "I am a slugger or nothing," he said in 1914. "There is no advice that I can give in batting except to hammer the ball."

Somewhere, Dave Kingman just said "Amen."

9

TRAILBLAZING
FORGOTTEN
TRAILS

Jackie Robinson wasn't the only minority major leaguer to topple an ethnic barrier. He's simply the man who toppled the most entrenched, most iniquitous, and longest-lasting of the barriers. Before Robinson other men overcame other prejudices, great and small, to make it to the major leagues. Most have been forgotten.

SOCK'S SHORT RUN

Lou Sockalexis, a Penobscot Indian, became the first racial minority major league baseball star when he reached the majors with a splash in 1897, precisely 50 years before Jackie Robinson. Sockalexis was a hugely talented five-tool player, long before anyone even knew what a "five-tool player" was. (It's someone who can run, field, throw, hit, and hit for power.) A once-popular series of children's books seems to have been based on his life. A major league team is, in a round-about way, likely named after Sockalexis. Any one of these facts should have been sufficient to make Lou Sockalexis famous. But fame proved fleeting.

There had been other minorities in the majors before Sockalexis. African-American brothers Fleet and Welday Walker played with Toledo of the American Association in 1884. And some believe that Jim Toy, an American Association player in 1887 and 1890, was part Sioux. But it's far from certain that Toy was Native American, and at any rate, none of these men were stars. Sockalexis unquestionably was a star. He made headlines, for his play and for his race. That "Sock" was soon forgotten owes to the small number of years he spent in the majors, the large number of years that have passed since his career ended—and the fact that his presence in the game failed to open the door for a large number of great Native-American players the way Jackie Robinson's later would for African-American players.

Baseball was easy for Lou Sockalexis. Life was not. Sockalexis starred for college teams at Holy Cross

JUST WALK IT OFF

In the 1960s, Baseball Hall of Fame historian Lee Allen reported that a man named James Madison Toy, not Lou Sockalexis, deserved to be known as the first Native American major leaguer. Apparently a relative of Toy had written Allen claiming that the long-since-departed ballplayer was part Sioux. Debate about Toy's ethnicity continues. What is known is that whatever his race, Toy had one of the most unpleasant departures from the majors in history. He was catching for Brooklyn in 1890 when a low pitch took an odd hop off home plate and struck him in the groin. The protective cup was not then in use. The injury ended Toy's career, and reportedly caused him pain for the remaining 29 years of his life.

and Notre Dame, then was an instant sensation in the majors. In 1897, his first season in the bigs, Sockalexis hit .338, stole 16 bases, and fell just one short of leading Cleveland in homers despite playing in only 66 games. His throwing arm and foot speed were considered among the best in the league. When New York newspapers reported that Amos Rusie planned to strike out the phenom, Sockalexis responded by homering off the future Hall of Famer in their first meeting.

Yet Sockalexis would appear in only eight games after July 3 that year, and in only 28 games after his rookie season. The trouble was alcohol. Drinking and carousing had gotten Sockalexis kicked out of Notre Dame, now late nights and alcohol cost him his major league career as well. Cleveland finally gave up on Sockalexis in 1899, and he disappeared from the majors forever.

Sockalexis' story wasn't forgotten outright. Bert Standish's once popular Frank Merriwell children's books appear to have been based

THE OTHER SOCK

Lou Sockalexis' cousin Andrew Sockalexis also was an athlete of some note. This younger Sockalexis narrowly missed winning the Boston Marathon in 1912, finishing second. He also narrowly missed medaling in the 1912 Olympic marathon, finishing fourth. He later would lament that he might have won the gold, if not for the tactical mistake of starting his finishing kick too late. Andrew Sockalexis' luck wasn't any better away from sports. He contracted tuberculosis and died at age 27.

loosely on Sockalexis. And baseball luminaries who'd seen Sockalexis play continued to extol his talents for the rest of their lives. Hall of Famer Hughie Jennings said Sockalexis "should have been the greatest player of all time." Ed Barrow, the man who built the great Yankee teams of the 1920s and 1930s—teams that included Babe Ruth—called Sockalexis "the greatest outfielder in history."

The very name of the Cleveland Indians likely derives from Sockalexis' career. When Sockalexis had his brief moment in the sun, the Cleveland club frequently was called the Indians by the press, thanks, of course, to his presence. (Team nicknames were less formal in the 19th century than they are today. Clubs were known by whatever names sportswriters called them in print.) When the American League Cleveland team needed a new nickname years later, Indians was chosen in part because the name had been used by a Cleveland ball club in the past. Of course this doesn't mean that the Cleveland Indians are so named to honor Sockalexis' memory, something the Cleveland Indians organization once claimed.

After leaving the majors for good in 1899, Sockalexis spent a few years drifting around the minor leagues, then landed back in his home state of Maine as a logger and occasional umpire in local leagues. He remained a sports fan and was said to be a voracious reader of *The Sporting News*. On Christmas eve, 1913, Sockalexis was found dead at the age of 42, an apparent victim of chronic alcoholism. Legend has it that newspaper clippings recounting his days as a star were found in his pocket.

ABBATICCHIO TOPPLES A FORGOTTEN ETHNIC BARRIER

Lou Sockalexis wasn't the only man scaling baseball's ethnic walls in

POWERS DOWN

Mike "Doc" Powers was Lou Sockalexis' closest friend in baseball. The two were teammates at both Holy Cross and Notre Dame, and they played together on semi-pro teams before reaching the majors. Unlike Sockalexis, Powers was no star. He spent the bulk of his professional career as a weak-hitting backup catcher for the Philadelphia A's. Still, it's a bit surprising that he isn't better remembered for the way his career ended in 1909.

During the first game ever played in Philadelphia's Shibe Park, the first modern concrete and steel stadium, Powers began to experience pain in his midsection, perhaps brought on by a dive for a foul ball. Though he initially diagnosed his own injury as a pulled muscle—Powers wasn't just nicknamed "Doc," he actually had a medical degree—it turned out to be a serious intestinal problem. Gangrene developed, and two weeks and several surgeries later, Powers was dead. If Powers' injuries were in fact the result of his dive for a foul ball as some have claimed, then Powers should stand alongside the much-better-remembered Ray Chapman as a major leaguer killed as a result of on-field play.

1897. That same year, an infielder named Ed Abbaticchio debuted with Philadelphia. Abbaticchio was considered the first major leaguer of Italian origin. That might not sound like a big deal these days, but in 1897 it was a significant ethnic breakthrough. Most ballplayers in the 1890s were of German or Irish extraction, and prejudice against Italians was considerable. "What is baseball coming to?" asked an article in the *New York Clipper.* "For nearly half a century things ran smoothly enough until they began to rope in a few ringers, such as Abbaticchio, Sockalexis [and other ethnic minorities]."

Abbaticchio did have one advantage over other trail-blazing ethnic minority ballplayers: He didn't have to battle so hard to prove he was the social equal of his teammates—mainly because it was common knowledge that he was their social *better,* at least where economic status was concerned. Unlike virtually all of his fellow players, Abbaticchio came from a wealthy family. As one sportswriter put it, he "plays the game merely because he loves it."

Abbaticchio apparently didn't love it with all his heart. He skipped the 1906 season to run an upscale Pittsburgh hotel. The rumor at the time was that Abbaticchio's father did not approve of his son's career in baseball and gave him the hotel on the condition he renounce the sport. If so, dad got a bum deal. In 1907, Ed returned to the field—once he determined that his status as a ballplayer wouldn't affect his hotel's license to sell beer.

At first glance, Abbaticchio's baseball career wasn't all that memorable. He hit just .254 in nine seasons. But it's possible that with Pittsburgh in 1908, Abbaticchio hit what *should* have been one of the most fame-generating regular-season home runs in baseball history, only to have it unfairly taken away. According to numerous reports, Abbaticchio hit an apparent grand slam into the left-field stands in a crucial late-season game between Pittsburgh and Chicago during the famously tight 1908 pennant race. The hit should have won the game for his Pirates . . . except the umpire ruled it foul. After a long argument, Abbaticchio returned to the plate and again hit a long drive to left, but this one wasn't long enough, and the Cubs won the game. When the season ended, Pittsburgh had lost the pennant by that one game. According to the story, a woman sued Abbaticchio for damages after the season, claiming she'd been struck and injured by his nearly famous grand slam foul. When her ticket was put into evidence, it showed she'd been seated in fair territory.

It's a great story, but baseball researchers have cast serious doubt on whether it's a true story. Abbaticchio's "apparent grand slam" actually might have been an apparent ground-rule double into the overflow crowd standing behind a rope in the outfield. The hit, while potentially important to the Pirates, would not have been an automatic game winner, and thus would not have brought Abbaticchio instant fame. As for the court case, no record of it ever has been found.

Abbaticchio's most lasting impact on the world of sports might not have been on the baseball diamond at all. He played fullback on the 1895 Latrobe, Pennsylvania squad that's generally considered the first pro football team, earning up to $50 a game. Abbaticchio also handled the punting duties for Latrobe, and is credited by some with being the first to learn how to put a spiral on a punt, adding to its distance. Unfortunately for Abbaticchio's legacy, 19th-century professional football players are even less likely to be remembered than are early-20th-century major league baseball players.

For all his brushes with sports fame, Abbaticchio's name would be remembered only by the patrons of the Abbaticchio Hotel he ran after his playing days ended. He died in 1957 at the age of 79.

BILL ZUBER'S "FRIVOLOUS" CAREER

American League pitcher Bill Zuber has received surprisingly little lasting fame for being baseball's first Amish player. That's just as well, since Zuber wasn't really Amish at all, though he often was labeled as such during his career. Zuber was in fact a member of the Amana Church Society, a lesser-known and somewhat Amish-like religious sect that lived a largely pastoral existence, spoke German, handled work communally, and looked askance at dancing, cars, ostentation, and, yes, games like baseball. "Baseball was frowned upon by the elders as a frivolous sport," explained Zuber's son years later.

Zuber played anyway, and eventually was discovered by famed scout Cy Slapnicka. According to the legend, Slapnicka arrived at the Amana compound in Iowa during the 1930 onion harvest. Since Zuber didn't have a baseball, he showed off his arm by throwing an onion.

Zuber was never a top pitcher, but his conscientious-objector status made him a useful member of the Yankees staff during World War II. When an arm injury ended his career in 1947, Zuber returned to the Amana community, by then no longer communal, and opened a restaurant called Bill Zuber's Dugout. Zuber died of a hemorrhage in 1982 at age 69. His lifetime record was just 43–42, not particularly noteworthy. But considering his unique background and the obstacles Zuber had to overcome to become a professional athlete at all, his career seems worth remembering.

Charlie Hollocher

PART III
INJURIES, ILLNESSES, AND OTHER INTERRUPTIONS

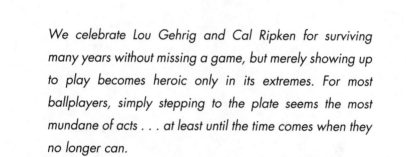

We celebrate Lou Gehrig and Cal Ripken for surviving many years without missing a game, but merely showing up to play becomes heroic only in its extremes. For most ballplayers, simply stepping to the plate seems the most mundane of acts . . . at least until the time comes when they no longer can.

Though often overlooked, the ability to stay on the field is an attribute crucial to the pursuit of baseball fame. It is impossible to deliver a key hit while on the disabled list . . . or win a World Series after being drafted into a war . . . or throw a perfect game if you've been thrown out of the game. As the lottery people are so fond of pointing out, you have to be in it to win it.

10

INJURY

Bad timing, bad bounces, and bad teams have denied many ballplayers their chance at fame over the years. But nothing has broken more hearts than broken bones, torn tendons, and the ever-popular frayed rotator cuff. A serious injury can keep a baseball player off the field or curtail his abilities while on it. Neither alternative is conducive to fame. As Cleveland Indians owner Bill Veeck noted, "Suffering is overrated."

It would be foolish to try to recount the stories of all of the players whose careers have been derailed by injury. Their stories are too many, and too similar besides. This chapter will offer only a cross section of potentially great careers cut down, a mere melange of misery. Just one representative sore-armed pitcher story will be included; no one wants to read two dozen tales of woe all turning on the words "then he blew out his arm."

Many of the injuries described in this chapter were incurred by players who simply seem to have been in the wrong place at the wrong time with the wrong protective equipment. "He said it was broken in two places," said former pitcher Steve Stone after one of pitcher Jose Rijo's trips to the disabled list. "I, of course, told him to stay out of those places."

ONE REPRESENTATIVE SORE-ARMED PITCHER STORY

Karl Spooner had only two games in the majors to show his talents. He showed plenty. The Brooklyn Dodger prospect made his first start on September 22, 1954, against the soon-to-be World Champion New York Giants. Matched up with Johnny Antonelli, that season's NL leader in winning percentage and ERA, Spooner threw a 3–0 shutout, allowing just three hits, all singles, and striking out 15. His second start came against the Pittsburgh Pirates four days later, in the Dodgers' final game of the season. This time Spooner shut out Pittsburgh 1–0 on four hits, striking out 12.

The Dodgers finished second in 1954, five games back of the Giants. With the 23-year-old Spooner now on board, many thought Brooklyn had an excellent chance to win the pennant in '55. The six-foot-tall star-in-the-making had a blazing fastball, a great curve, and a left arm that any pitcher in the country would have given his right arm for. "Ask anyone who saw him," said former teammate Don Zimmer decades later. "They will tell you he would have been another Koufax."

In a way, he *was* another Koufax. Spooner, like Koufax, injured his valuable left arm and was forced from baseball far too soon. Only for Spooner, far too soon came even sooner.

It was just a spring training game, a chance for players on the Dodgers and White Sox to work off any unnecessary pounds they might have acquired over the winter. Nothing depended on the result. They kept score only out of habit. Johnny Podres was scheduled to work the first three innings for the Dodgers that March afternoon in 1955, Karl Spooner the next three. Only Podres got shelled by Chicago, so Dodgers manager Walter Alston decided to call in Spooner an inning earlier than planned.

The young pitcher hadn't expected to work in the third, so he hadn't been warming up. Spooner threw some hurried pitches in the bullpen, then a few more on the mound—no more than 15 altogether, he would later estimate—before the umpire signaled for the Chicago batter to step in. Spooner could have told Alston he wasn't ready. He could have taken it easy on his first few pitches in the game—it didn't matter if he gave up a few runs in an exhibition game. But Spooner was young and wanted to impress, so he did what he'd always done, the only thing he knew how to do. He gave it all he had.

By the time Spooner left the park that evening, his shoulder was throbbing. He tried to convince himself it was normal spring stiffness, but of course it wasn't. The shoulder would never recover. Spooner tried to pitch through the pain in 1955, and managed an 8–6 record with a 3.65 ERA. It was impressive under the circumstances, but a far cry from the pitcher he had until so recently been. Spooner hadn't led Brooklyn to the '55 pennant, but the Dodgers won it anyway. They even won the World Series. Spooner got into two Series games, but his 0–1 record and 13.50 ERA said volumes about the health of his arm.

Spooner faded back to the minor leagues after the 1955 season. By 1957 he was desperate enough to have shoulder surgery—a risky move in those relative dark ages of sports medicine. Nothing helped. Spooner officially gave up on his baseball career in 1959 at the age of 26. "I had a wife and . . . kids," he explained in the 1970s. "[I] had to put food on the table."

Karl Spooner's story is not his alone. The greatest risk of injury in baseball always has fallen on the shoulders (and elbows) of pitchers. Each decade it seems there's a young Mark Fidrych or Joe Wood who blows away the league for a season or two, then blows out his arm and makes a slow, painful exit from the game, his formidable talents suggested but barely revealed. The headline of a 1956 *Sport* magazine article put it best: "A pitcher's arm has got to go." But the fact that a sore-armed pitcher's tale is trite makes it no less tragic.

After baseball, Spooner found work as a floor refinisher, a bartender, and in fruit packing. "I wasn't trained to do anything but pitch," he said in 1981. "I certainly didn't have any skills. I remember shoveling s––– just to make ends meet. I was always in debt."

Eventually he settled into a position as packing-house manager for the Hatfield Citrus Corporation. The company was located in Vero Beach, Florida. Vero Beach also is the spring training home of the Dodgers. Every March the team came to town, and Spooner was reminded once again of what might have been. "I've tried to forget the misery . . . to go on with life," Spooner said in the early 1980s. "But let's be honest. After pitching didn't work out, I was heartbroken."

In 1970, Spooner admitted to a sportswriter that he was "very envious of all these five-figure guys in baseball." In 1981 he'd tell another writer that "my biggest frustration nowadays is reading the sports pages and seeing these six-figure contracts some guys get." In 1984, Karl Spooner died of cancer at the age of 52. If there was any consolation in premature death, it's that it spared him from witnessing the era of seven-figure contracts.

ONE REPRESENTATIVE SORE-ARMED PITCHER SIDEBAR

In 1911, rookies Vean Gregg and Grover Cleveland Alexander both reached the major leagues. By the end of the 1913 season, they were considered virtual equals. Gregg was 63–33 with a 2.23 ERA in his first three seasons, Alexander, 69–38 with a 2.71 ERA. (Alexander's ERA was inflated a bit by his hitter-friendly home park.) Gregg got off to a hot start in 1914 as well, but the Cleveland pitcher hurt his arm and was largely ineffective thereafter. He barely hung onto big league jobs with the Red Sox in 1915 and 1916 and with the Philadelphia A's in 1918 before sliding back to the minors.

Gregg continued to pitch in the minors off and on into his 40s, whenever his arm felt up to it. Most years he didn't have much success, but in 1924 he threw well enough in the PCL to earn a return trip to the majors. The 40-year old did reasonably well in 26 appearances for the Washington Senators in 1925, but it would be his swan song in the big leagues. Gregg's major league record came to just 92–63. Alexander's added up to a slightly more impressive 373–208.

Alexander was elected to the Hall of Fame in 1938. Gregg returned to his farm in western Canada after his career and was forgotten. He died in 1964.

RIGGS KNOWS SHOULDER INJURIES

Before there was Bo Jackson, there was Riggs Stephenson. Stephenson, like Jackson, was an Alabama-born star running back who also could play a bit of baseball. And Stephenson, like Jackson, saw a football injury wreck his promising baseball career.

Stephenson played 14 seasons in the majors and hit well in the first 13 of them, so his career wasn't precisely injury-shortened. It might more accurately be referred to as injury-marred. Stephenson badly damaged his right shoulder playing fullback for the University of Alabama football team before he reached the major leagues. Even with the injury, he could hit as well as anyone, though not for much power. It was Stephenson's defense that suffered: His throwing arm was robbed of all its strength. Once a fine infielder, Stephenson now was a defensive liability anywhere on the field. A man without a regular position, he collected as many as 400 at-bats in only four of his 14 seasons.

Stephenson reached the majors with Cleveland right off the Alabama campus in 1921. During the next five years, his batting average was an impressive .337—yet he played in an average of just 66 big league games per season. In 1924, Stephenson hit .371 in 240 at-bats—yet the next year he found himself in the minors. As far as Cleveland was concerned, Stephenson's bat didn't make up for his injury-related deficiencies as an infielder.

Not until 1926 did the Cubs acquire Stephenson from Cleveland, stick him in left field, and accept the fact baserunners would take occasional liberties with his arm. Stephenson rewarded Chicago with annual batting averages between .319 and .367 for the next eight years. Though an ankle injury cost him half of 1931, Stephenson was essentially a regular in Chicago through 1932. When he left the majors in 1934 he had a .336 career batting average.

Had Riggs Stephenson been an everyday middle infielder throughout his 14-year career, his .336 batting average likely would have put him in the Hall of Fame. But Stephenson was neither an everyday player nor a middle infielder. His injury had turned him into a weak-armed outfielder who played in approximately 60 percent of his clubs' games during those 14 seasons. In 1960, 26 years after his playing days ended, Stephenson received four of the 202 votes needed for election to the Hall of Fame. It was the closest he'd ever get.

The gentlemanly Stephenson played and managed a few years in the minors, then returned to his hometown of Akron, Alabama, where he ran a sawmill and owned a lumberyard. He died in 1985 at the age of 87.

TWO PITCHES, TWO CAREERS

On August 18, 1967, 22-year-old Boston slugger Tony Conigliaro was struck just below the left eye on a pitch thrown by Jack Hamilton of the California Angels. Before that pitch, the handsome, popular

Conigliaro had been one of the most promising young players in baseball. Despite time in the military and a string of injuries, the outfielder had reached one hundred homers at a younger age than anyone who'd come before. His teammates were certain he was headed for 500 homers and the Hall of Fame. After that pitch, Conigliaro was out of baseball until 1969, and would never again see properly out of the damaged left eye.

Conigliaro somehow managed two more solid seasons after the beaning, even as his vision grew steadily worse. In 1971 he was traded to the Angels—ironically, the team whose pitcher had ruined his career in the first place. But Conigliaro was hitting just a shade over .200 with little power by midseason. On July 11, he announced his retirement. He was just 26. A comeback attempt with the Red Sox in 1975 failed.

Conigliaro remained in baseball as a broadcaster, and in 1982 auditioned for a spot in the Red Sox television booth. Considering his popularity in New England, he seemed a good bet to land the job. But on his way to the airport after the audition, the 37-year-old Conigliaro suffered a massive heart attack. The broadcasting job was no longer an issue. Instead, Conigliaro would require 24-hour nursing care for the rest of his life. He died of kidney failure in 1990 at 45.

On April 8, 1984, 25-year-old Astro shortstop Dickie Thon was hit just above the left eye on a pitch thrown by Mike Torrez of the New York Mets. Before that pitch, Thon was a top defensive shortstop who the year before had hit .286 with 20 home runs. Houston's general manager called him a future Hall of Famer. *The Sporting News* named him their NL All-Star shortstop. After that pitch, Thon would miss more than a season and never again see properly out of the eye. "I was young and stubborn and crowding the plate," Thon said later. "I was giving the pitcher no respect."

Thon returned in 1985, but played sparingly and hit poorly for the next three years. The vision in his left eye was blurry and his depth perception gone. Thon was out of baseball entirely for much of the 1987 season. But with rest, he found his sight began to improve. In 1988, Thon returned and hit a respectable .264 as a platoon player with the Padres. The next year he was an everyday player with the Phillies. Thon started slowly that year, but hit upwards of .310 in the second half to finish at .271 with 15 homers. Encouraged by Thon's performance down the stretch in 1989, Philadelphia signed the shortstop to a million-dollar contract. He was just in his early 30s; there was still time to salvage something of his lost talent. But the second half of 1989 proved the exception, and Thon's hitting went back into decline in 1990. He retired in 1993 not a Hall of Famer, but a journeyman infielder with a .264 career average.

Two pitches had altered the course of two potentially great careers. But was it just bad luck that put Conigliaro and Thon in the paths of these beanballs? For what it's worth, the famous beaning wasn't Conigliaro's first major injury, nor would it be his last. A noted plate-crowder, he had bones broken by pitched balls at least five times in his baseball life—and not always by flamethrowers trying to crowd him inside. Conigliaro once had his shoulder broken by a batting practice pitcher. On another occasion his wrist was broken on a pitch thrown by his uncle during the off season. Perhaps Conigliaro lacked the ability to get out of the way. If so, his story was destined to end poorly from the start. Had it not been that pitch from Jack Hamilton, it likely would have been another pitch, another pitcher.

Unlike Conigliaro, Thon did not have a long history of injuries to suggest that his career was destined for an unhappy end. Thon merely had been looking for an outside pitch when he got an inside one. Then again maybe there was something in his genes. Dickie's younger brother Frankie once was a baseball prospect himself. Some said he was even more talented than Dickie—at least until an ill-fated American Legion game in Puerto Rico. Frankie, an infielder like his brother, was standing at second base between innings when the catcher threw the final warm-up pitch his way. It's something catchers always do to keep their arms loose and send a warning to any potential bases-stealers who might be watching. Even a young infielder like Frankie Thon would have handled such throws hundreds of times. Only this time Thon wasn't watching. The throw struck him just below the left eye. Three operations failed to correct Frankie's blurry vision. The San Francisco Giants signed him anyway, but he wasn't the same player. Frankie Thon's career had turned on a single throw, just like that of his older brother.

LOSING SCORE

In 1955, Indians rookie Herb Score went 16–10 with a 2.85 ERA, led the American League with 245 strikeouts, was named to the All-Star team, and won the Rookie of the Year Award. The next year Score was even better, posting a 20–9 record and 2.53 ERA. Again he made the All-Star team and led the league in strikeouts. On May 7, 1957, in the fifth start of Score's third season, a hard come-backer off the bat of Yankee infielder Gil McDougald hit the 23-year old pitcher in the eye. He spent the following week in a darkened hospital room and missed the rest of the season.

The personable, dedicated Score returned to the mound in 1958, but the remaining five years of his career produced just a 17–26 record. Score, like Conigliaro, stayed in baseball as a broadcaster after his pitching days ended.

As with Conigliaro and Thon, Score's career seemed to turn on one tragic play. Only Score claims his eye injury wasn't the issue. According to the pitcher, he was as good as ever in the spring of 1958, but injured his arm early in the 1958 season. Score, it seems, was just one of many young, hard-throwing pitchers to have his arm give out.

JOE HAUSER'S BAD BREAK

A broken kneecap turned Joe Hauser from a star on the rise to a star of the minor leagues. Unfortunately for Hauser, "star of the minor leagues" is more-or-less the same as not a star at all.

In 1922, 23-year-old rookie Joe Hauser hit .323 as the starting first baseman for the Philadelphia A's. His average declined a bit in 1923 and 1924, but his power improved. By 1924, Hauser's 27 home runs were second only to Babe Ruth in the American League. Hauser appeared on his way to becoming one of the best hitters in baseball—until an exhibition game on April 17, 1925. It was a simple infield grounder, and Hauser trotted to cover first. There was nothing special about the play; Hauser did not recall tripping or twisting oddly or stepping in a hole. Yet his left kneecap fractured, for reasons known only to the kneecap. The first baseman toppled to the ground and soon toppled right out of the majors.

The bone was rebuilt, but such surgical procedures were far from perfect in the 1920s, and the leg would never fully recover. Hauser didn't return until 1926, and when he did, he hit just .192 with eight homers. Sent to the minors in 1927, Hauser showed he still could swing the bat, hitting .353 with 20 homers. In 1928 it was back to the majors, and the season started reasonably well for him. But soon his knee started acting up, and the gimpy first baseman lost playing time to rising star Jimmie Foxx. Hauser ended the year at .260 with 16 homers in just 300 at-bats. Sold to Cleveland for the waiver price in 1929, Hauser got into just 37 games and once more disappeared from the big leagues.

Hauser clearly was too good for the minors. For four consecutive years, he led an upper-level minor league in homers. With Baltimore of the International League in 1930, he set a new record for all of organized baseball with 63 homers. With Minneapolis of the American Association in 1933, he bettered his own mark by hitting 69. Yet the majors weren't interested in the now-34-year-old slugger. "He hasn't said so publicly," wrote the Associated Press that October, "but Joe Hauser probably is wondering just what a fellow has to do in the big minors to get a tumble from the major leagues."

The trouble of course was the knee and other assorted leg injuries Hauser had sustained over the years. "I had those broken legs," Hauser explained in the 1990s. "They were scared to take me."

Hauser had one more great minor league year, hitting .348 with 33 homers in 1934. But by 1937, the 38-year-old had departed the upper reaches of the minors, spending the next six seasons as first baseman/manager of Sheboygan in the Wisconsin State League. Hauser retired as a player in 1942 with 399 minor league home runs and a .299 batting average. By all accounts, the affable Hauser was not one to agonize about what might have been. Instead he managed in the low minors and cheerfully ran the Joe Hauser Sport Shop in Sheboygan with his brother-in-law for more than 40 years—Joe Hauser is world famous, in Sheboygan. In 1967, he was elected to the Hall of Fame. The Wisconsin Hall of Fame. Hauser died in 1997 at age 98.

WALLY BERGER'S SEVEN YEARS OF WASTED HEROICS

Wally Berger's career was played out in two acts. In act one, Berger was a great player—but was stuck on an uncompetetive team and in a stadium ill suited to his talents. In act two, Berger finally got a chance to play for solid teams—but was too injured to be a star.

Between 1930 and 1936, Berger's first seven years in the majors, he hit .305 and six times finished in the top three in the National League home-run race. Berger's 38 home runs in 1930 stood as the rookie record until Mark McGwire clubbed 49 in 1987. Berger did these things despite playing his home games in the majors' toughest park for a power hitter and despite weak-hitting teammates who never gave him any protection in the batting order. In three of his seasons, not one of his teammates hit more than five home runs. Berger also did these things without anyone much noticing. His team, the Boston Braves, was never in contention.

The most dramatic moment in his time in Boston came in 1933, when Berger pinch-hit a game-winning 9th-inning homer on the final day of the season despite a high fever. It would be one of the great hits in baseball history, except for one thing: It was virtually irrelevant. With the win the Braves clinched *fourth* place in the National League. Getting the big hit that secures fourth isn't exactly the sort of thing that gets one remembered—except perhaps by one's teammates. The Braves pocketed $400 apiece in playoff money for finishing fourth, which might explain why they carried Berger off the field on their shoulders. (No doubt while chanting, "We're number four," and holding four fingers aloft.)

The Braves would finish no higher than fourth during Berger's tenure. Many years they'd fare much worse. The Braves were an appalling 38–115 in 1935. Berger won the National League home run crown that year, but of course most of his homers came in a losing cause.

Berger's career might have been played under conditions far more conducive to fame. In the late 1920s, his contract was controlled by the Chicago Cubs. Chicago was extremely competitive in the 1930s, reaching the World Series three times. They also played in Wrigley Field, one of the best home run parks in the majors. But the Cubs outfield then featured Kiki Cuyler, Hack Wilson, and Riggs Stephenson. In 1929, each had hit .345 or better, with over one hundred RBIs and double-digit homers. There wasn't any room for a rookie centerfielder, however talented. The Braves outbid a number of other interested clubs for Berger's services.

If that was all there was to Wally Berger's story, he would have been little different from the top players of the St. Louis Browns: great, but forgotten. Only the greatest tragedy of Berger's career isn't that his first seven seasons are ignored, it's that they were the only healthy seasons he got. In 1936, the slugger suffered a shoulder injury that held his batting average to a career-worst .288, his home run total to 25, Berger's lowest total since 1932. He was just 30 years old, but the injury spelled the end of his days as an elite player.

The following June, Berger was traded to the Giants. It was his first chance to play for a top-quality club, but Berger was no longer a top-quality player. Used mainly against left-handed pitching, he posted respectable numbers, hitting .291 with 12 homers in his 199 at-bats with New York. The Giants won the pennant, but were steam-rolled by the Yankees in the 1937 Series. Berger had just three World Series at-bats. He made three outs.

Berger was traded to the Cincinnati Reds during the 1938 season. He responded by hitting .307, though the formerly formidable slugger managed just 16 home runs. By 1939, his average was down to .258, his home runs down to 14. The Reds reached the Series that year, but Berger went an embarrassing 0–15 as the Reds were swept by the Yanks. Berger was cut after just two at-bats in early 1940. That October the Reds won the Series without him. Berger signed briefly with the Phillies, but was released after just 41 at-bats.

The faded star returned to the minors briefly, then joined the Navy in 1942. After World War II, Berger did some scouting and managed in the minors. In the 1950s, he took a job with defense company Northrop, where he stayed until retirement. Once among the greatest power hitters in baseball, Wally Berger now was responsible for keeping track of the tools used by aviation mechanics in training.

Berger never received more than two votes in any Hall of Fame election. In 1968, he was invited back to Boston to be honored at an annual sportswriter's dinner. For most great players, such events are commonplace. For Berger it was a rare moment of recognition. "I couldn't believe it," he said of the dinner. "I thought everybody forgot me."

WALLY B. AND TONY C.

Wally Berger remained a base-ball fan in retirement. In 1967, the former Boston power-hitting phenom followed another Boston power-hitting phenom with great interest. The player's name was Tony Conigliaro. "Tony's a right-handed batter like myself, you know," Berger told the *Boston Record American*. "I love his aggressive style at the bat. He hangs right in there."

"Berger had a more personal reason for liking Conigliaro," the paper noted. "Looking at Tony he undoubtedly was looking at himself when he was hitting those tape-measure jobs into the railroad tracks beyond Braves Field. Berger stands about 6'2" and a half, about the same as Tony, and weighs 242. But in his heyday, he went 195, same as Tony."

The 1967 season provided one additional parallel between Berger and Conigliaro. On August 18, Conigliaro suffered an injury that derailed his prom-ising career.

THE FALL OF THE GREAT ALEXANDERS

Dale "Moose" Alexander was not a well-rounded player—all he could do was hit. But Alexander could do that like few others. In 1928, he won the International League Triple Crown, punching his ticket for the majors. The rookie first baseman hit .343 with the Tigers in 1929, and was fifth in the American League in homers. His average was in the mid-.320s in each of the next two years. Even in the hitter-friendly 1930s, it was an extremely impressive start for a young player.

Early in the 1932 season, Detroit sent Alexander to the Red Sox in a deal for outfielder Earl Webb. Alexander's .367 batting average that year led the American League, but the batting champi-onship led to grief, not glory. Many fans felt his 392 at-bats that season shouldn't have been enough to qualify for the title. He'd have even fewer at-bats the following year. On May 30, 1933, Alexander wrenched his knee running the bases in the first game of a double-header—you don't earn the nickname Moose by running gracefully. It was a minor injury, but it would have major consequences.

In the clubhouse between games the Red Sox trainer hooked Alexander up to a diathermy machine, a device that uses small electrical impulses to stimulate tissue healing. At the time diathermy was a relatively new procedure. Obviously it was new to the Sox trainer—he let the machine run so long that Alexander received third-degree burns on his leg. Gangrene later set in, and there was talk of amputation. Doctors saved the leg, but they couldn't save Alexander's career. The Red Sox unceremoniously dumped their hobbled first baseman later that season, apparently without suffering much guilt over the fact that it was their trainer who had hobbled him in the first place. Alexander never returned to the majors. "I couldn't run and I couldn't field," Alexander would later say. "When I got hurt, that was the end."

Alexander continued in the minors, first as a player, then as a manager. Later he became a scout. The .331 career hitter also owned a tobacco farm in his home state of Tennessee, and once lost a close election for the position of county sheriff. He died in 1979 at age 75. His major league career had lasted just 662 games.

Hugh Alexander, no relation, had a major league career that made Dale Alexander's 662 games look like an eternity. Hugh reached the major leagues for a cup of coffee late in 1937, four years after Dale had been burned to a crisp and sent on his way. Like Dale, Hugh appeared on his way to stardom. In two seasons in the minors, Hugh had hit over .340 twice with close to 30 homers each year. He got 11 at-bats in that late-season call-up with Cleveland, managing one hit, a single. He was just 20 years old. The one hit should have become one of many.

Alexander took a job working in the oil fields of Oklahoma during the off-season. On an oil rig in Seminole, Oklahoma that December he got his left sleeve caught between two of the mechanism's large gears. His hand was crushed before he could pull the sleeve free. Alexander drove himself 14 miles to the nearest country doctor for treatment. The physician gave him two gulps of whiskey for anesthetic and lopped off the mangled hand. Alexander's playing days were over.

The following season Cleveland gave the 20-year old Alexander a scouting job. It was an act of sympathy on the Indians' part—they certainly didn't expect someone barely out of his teens to be a success as a talent evaluator. But Cleveland figured the scouting gig would buy Alexander some time to decide what to do with the rest of his life. As it turned out, they'd answered the question for him. The first player the young scout signed was future All-Star Allie Reynolds. The second was future All-Star Dale Mitchell. Alexander spent more than 60 years in scouting with a number of teams, signing the likes of Steve Garvey, Bill Russell, Davey Lopes, and Don Sutton. He did, however, turn down Mickey Mantle without ever watching him play. Alexander had been told the boy had bad knees. He wasn't interested in players with disabilities.

An oil rig cost Hugh Alexander his shot at baseball fame, but it didn't stop him from having a successful life. Alexander was reportedly content as a scout, though the travel it required contributed to his string of failed marriages. Still, Alexander wouldn't have been human if he didn't wonder about what might have been. "Driving down the highway, I might reminisce to myself," he allowed a few years before his death in 2000. "But I'm not going to be sad about it. I said [when the accident happened] 'I'm not going to let this kill me.'"

GOOD BATS, BAD KNEES

Johnny Hodapp made it to the major leagues as a 19-year-old infielder with Cleveland in August 1925. Unfortunately, his early start in the bigs didn't guarantee him a long career. Just three games into the 1926 season, Hodapp badly injured his knee and was out for the rest of the year. He was back in time to play 79 games the following season, hitting .304. Hodapp was hitting .323 late in the 1928 season when he again injured his knee, tearing ligaments and missing the rest of the year. In spring training in 1929, Hodapp re-tore the same ligaments, though he returned to hit .327 in 90 games. Hodapp had been in the majors five years. The score thus far was knee injuries, three, healthy seasons as an everyday player, zero.

Hodapp finally played a full season in 1930. He hit .354, a gaudy figure for a middle infielder, even considering the inflated batting averages of the era. It would be his only healthy year. Yet another knee injury in 1931 marked the beginning of the end of Hodapp's career. He got into just 75 games in 1932, and though he bounced back to hit .312 in 115 games for Boston in 1933, both his range at second base and his batting average declined badly down the stretch. He was a 28-year-old middle infielder with a .311 career batting average, but his baseball life was over. Hodapp returned home to Cincinnati and spent the next four decades working with his brothers in the family's funeral home business. He died in 1980, and no doubt got a great deal on a coffin.

Four decades later, another bad knee felled another great player. Minnesota outfielder Tony Oliva was in the top three in the American League batting race in seven of his first eight years in the bigs. He made the All-Star team every year. He won a Gold Glove. He averaged more than 20 home runs a season. He became the only man in history to win batting titles in his first two seasons. For eight years Oliva was, without question, one of the top players in baseball.

Oliva appeared on his way to the best season of his career in 1971, his eighth full year in the majors. He was hitting .375 as the season neared the All-Star break, far and away the best in the league. But in the 9th inning of a June 29th game against Oakland, Oliva tore cartilage in his right knee diving for a ball hit by Joe Rudi. Minnesota won the game, but essentially lost their star. Oliva played through the pain in 1971, but his average dropped precipitously, ending the year at .337. That was still good enough to lead the American League, but only because Oliva had been so far out ahead of everyone else through June. Knee surgery limited Oliva to just ten games in 1972. It would be only the first of seven operations on the knee over the years ahead. Oliva played four more seasons, but the man who had been one of the greatest offensive talents in baseball would never again hit .300 or play in an All-Star game.

In one way, Oliva was fortunate. The American League instituted the DH in 1973, without which the gimpy former star might have disappeared from the majors entirely. Instead he was able to limp along as best he could, getting by but not getting much glory. Oliva retired after the 1976 season at age 35. By the end he was reduced to serving as Minnesota's first-base coach and occasional pinch hitter, a bulky brace always on his knee. "Watching his career curtailed due to that knee is the saddest experience I've had as Minnesota's manager," said Gene Mauch.

As the years passed, Oliva, now a coach, became increasingly frustrated that the Hall of Fame never called. "I see the list of others who get more votes and I can't believe it," he told the *New York Daily News* in 1987. "Sometimes I want to kill people."

Oliva's seven and a half great years apparently weren't enough for Hall of Fame voters, as he never came particularly close to being elected.

Perhaps if Oliva had played in more of a hitter's era his stats would have been more impressive to future Hall of Fame voters. Perhaps if he'd played his career in New York instead of Minnesota he'd be better remembered. Or perhaps Oliva wasn't meant to be famous. How else can you explain a top player whose name wasn't well known even in his prime—his *real* name, that is. The ballplayer known as Tony Oliva was really Pedro Oliva. Pedro borrowed his brother's passport to help him reach the U.S., and has been known by the wrong name ever since. Oliva's career might be overlooked because of injury, but knee or no, his name was never destined to be known.

A SORE-LEGGED PITCHER STORY

It's hardly a surprise when a pitcher's arm goes bad. But his leg? On May 28, 1983, Kansas City's 32-year-old three-time 20-game winner Dennis Leonard collapsed to the ground after delivering a 1–0 pitch to famously durable Oriole shortstop Cal Ripken, Jr. Writhing in pain, Leonard first thought he'd been hit by a line drive—except he distinctly remembered hearing the umpire yell, "strike."

It turned out he had ruptured his left patellar tendon, sending his kneecap flying out of place. Leonard's leg was repaired, but the rebuilt tendon deteriorated. Doctors tried again using tendons from corpses, but Leonard had no more luck with them than did their original owners: An infection developed. The former star didn't start another game until four knee operations and nearly three full years had passed. "People think I've disappeared," Leonard said in 1985, "that I'm out of the game."

His talented right arm remained on the shelf all those years while the Royals waited for his left leg—not even his push-off leg—to heal. In the first start of his comeback, April 12, 1986, Leonard threw a three-hit shutout to win 1–0. But Leonard's record in 1986 was just 8–13, with a 4.44 ERA, and he retired that winter.

THE ULTIMATE INJURED STAR STORY

Other great players got carried off the field on teammates' shoulders. Pete Reiser got carried off on stretchers. His career history reads like the casualty report from a small war. He dislocated a shoulder. He broke a collarbone. He broke both ankles, tore knee cartilage, and ripped any number of muscles. He fractured his skull on multiple occasions. He was knocked unconscious in collisions with outfield walls five times. Eleven times he was carried from the field on a stretcher. Reiser generally is credited with being the inspiration for padded outfield walls and warning tracks.

Reiser raised injury to the level of art, and in doing so acquired a sort of fame. But even those who do remember Reiser's career remember it the way people remember a car crash. They remember it for being the waste of a perfectly good car. Reiser's career was the waste of a perfectly good ballplayer. And whether one's referring to Pete Reiser or an auto accident, there's only one positive that ever can be found: At least no one was killed. This nearly wasn't so. After colliding with an outfield wall in 1947, Reiser was administered last rites in the clubhouse.

Before Pete Reiser became known for hitting walls, he was known, briefly, for hitting baseballs. In Reiser's first full season, 1941, the 22-year-old center fielder led the league in batting average, slugging percentage, doubles, triples, and runs scored. He also led the Dodgers to their first World Series in more than two decades. Yet there already were signs of the troubles ahead. In April he strained a muscle swinging too hard. Later that month, he spent a night in the hospital after a beaning. In May he needed stitches after running into an outfield wall. He returned to the hospital for another night that August after a second beaning. Pete Reiser checked into the hospital the way most of us check into the Holiday Inn.

In 1942, Reiser's hitting was even better, his survival instinct even worse. In early July, Reiser ran headlong into the concrete centerfield wall in St. Louis. He wound up in the hospital. Reiser's average, over .380 at the time of the injury, fell to .310 at year's end. Any other man would have been on the disabled list. "An umpire once asked him if he felt all right," wrote Jim Murray of the *Los Angeles Times* about that 1942 season. "Pete answered 'Well, if that pitcher's got five eyes I'm all right. Otherwise I'd have to say I'm having dizzy spells.'"

Reiser spent the next three years in the Army. All things considered, a World War probably was the safest place for him. Reiser did suffer a separated shoulder during the war, but he got it playing in a service ball game. As long as Pistol Pete was kept around bullets and not baseballs, he'd come through okay.

He hit just .277 when he returned from the war in 1946. But while Reiser's hitting suffered, his ability to suffer was doing just fine. At various times that year Reiser dislocated a shoulder, broke bones, tore muscles, and knocked himself unconscious. Somehow he found time to lead the league with 34 stolen bases.

In 1947, Reiser suffered the worst of his outfield wall collisions, fracturing his skull and dislocating both shoulders. He spent ten days in a coma, and was famously given last rites. "I never was the same ballplayer after that," Reiser later admitted to *The Sporting News*. He did, however, come back in time to play in the World Series that year . . . where he broke his ankle.

Reiser was asked to address the student body at the Missouri School for the Blind that winter. It was the fifth time he'd spoken at the school. "Look, I don't mind coming here," Reiser would later say he asked the school's director, "but why do you keep asking me?" "Our children here always have problems with walls and they hear you have the same problem," the director reportedly replied. "They figure you're one of them."

Reiser spent five more seasons in the majors, but he would never again play in more than 84 games, hit above .271, or remain with the same club for more than two seasons in a row. His career officially ended at age 33, but it had been all but over since he was 28. Between injury and war, Reiser had played just four seasons of at least one hundred games. His career average was .295, but it could have been much more. "He could have been," said Dodger manager Leo Durocher, "one of the all-time greats."

Considering how many of Reiser's injuries involved testing the solidity of concrete outfield walls, it's tempting to wonder if his career might have been longer had he not been shifted out of the infield after his rookie year. But such speculation is pointless. Pete Reiser would have run into outfield walls even if he had been playing third base; it just would have taken him a little longer to get there. It was the nature of the man. "No, I don't have any regrets," Reiser said after his career, "not about one damned thing."

Reiser remained in baseball as a coach and scout into the 1970s. On May 6, 1973, 53-year-old Chicago Cubs coach Pete Reiser was knocked unconscious when he was hit or kicked in the neck during a bench-clearing brawl against the Giants. He was carried off the field on a stretcher and spent the night in a San Francisco hospital. The old boy hadn't lost his touch. Reiser died in 1981 at age 62. "Pete may have been born the best baseball player that ever lived," wrote Red Smith of *The New York Times*, "but there never was a park big enough to contain his efforts."

11

ILLNESS

Star athletes are young, strong, and, by all appearances, the healthiest of us all. Perhaps that's why it's so discomforting to hear that a ballplayer has been laid low by a serious medical problem beyond the torn tendons and such that are an athlete's lot in life. If it could happen to them, it could happen to anyone.

HOLLOCHER'S UNCERTAIN CONDITION

There seems little question that Charlie Hollocher would have been a star if not for his health problems. The question is whether those health problems were in his stomach or in his head.

In 1918, 21-year-old rookie shortstop Hollocher led the Chicago Cubs to the World Series. He was graceful in the field and potent at the plate, his .316 average good for fourth in the National League batting race. "It looks as though the National League has discovered the player who will be the successor of Honus Wagner as the league's leading star," wrote *The Sporting News* that October. "For a time it seemed as though Rogers Hornsby of the Cardinals would win the honor, but of the two, Hollocher seems destined for the greater career."

Even after the season, things went Hollocher's way. Drafted into World War I that September, Hollocher and the rest of that month's inductees were told not to report—an influenza epidemic made the crowded Army training camps too dangerous. Hollocher finally was ordered to appear on November 11. He arrived to find that the Armistice had been signed that very day, ending the war. "Seems harder to break into the Army than into the big league," quipped the shortstop.

Hollocher's batting average dipped to .270 in 1919, but he was back well over .300 in 1920 when the troubles began. The young Cub had a history of believing himself ill, but in 1920 his health concerns blossomed into continual complaints of serious stomach pains. The Cubs sent him for tests, but doctors and X-rays found nothing wrong. Hollocher played in only 80 games that year, hitting .319. He played more regularly in the two years that followed, hitting .289 in 1921 and .340 in 1922. Yet Hollocher never considered himself healthy.

The situation finally came to a head shortly before the 1923 season. The Cubs were at their spring training camp on California's Catalina Island when Hollocher decided he could no longer carry on and returned home to St. Louis. He later said his private doctor told him that playing baseball that year could ruin his health for good. The Cubs doctors continued to insist there was nothing wrong with the shortstop, aside from his state of mind. *Baseball Magazine* later lent support to the state-of-mind theory, reporting that an unnamed Cub teammate once saw Hollocher cough a few times and become convinced he had consumption.

Cub manager Bill Killefer talked Hollocher into returning, promising he could skip games when he didn't feel up to playing. But Hollocher deserted the team in August, leaving a note for Killefer. "Tried to see you at the clubhouse this afternoon but guess I missed you," he wrote. "Feeling pretty rotten so made up my mind to go home and take a rest and forget about baseball for the rest of the year. No hard feelings, just don't feel like playing anymore. Good luck." The shortstop didn't return that season. He'd played just 66 games in 1923, but his .342 batting average offered no hint of ill health.

Hollocher returned once more in 1924, but again decided to go home midseason. Though he hinted at comebacks from time to time in the years that followed, Hollocher never played again. His career was over at age 28.

There was some speculation that Hollocher's health wasn't the real reason for his hesitation to play. Some said it was because he didn't get along with teammates, others said that he'd invested his money wisely and no longer needed his baseball income. Hollocher denied such claims. "I miss baseball," he said in 1933. "All of [the speculation about not wanting to play] is the bunk. If I had my health I would be playing baseball even if I had a million dollars. I love the game."

Hollocher spent one season, 1931, scouting for the Cubs. Otherwise he and his wife lived on their farm in Des Peres, Missouri, 16 miles outside St. Louis. But while Hollocher lived on a farm, he wasn't a farmer. He claimed his bad stomach still forced him to avoid strenuous exercise like farm work—though Hollocher was known to be an avid golfer. The one time Hollocher had tried to farm, he'd discovered that being a good fielder doesn't necessarily translate to skill in tending to fields. His carrot crop had been a disaster. He returned to the work force in the late '30s, opening a tavern in St. Louis County. The tavern didn't last long, however. Hollocher became an investigator for the county and was employed as a watchman for a drive-in theater. Hollocher's wife divorced him in 1939. It wasn't a particularly glamorous life for the man once expected to replace Honus Wagner.

In August 1940, Hollocher pulled his car into a stranger's driveway. In the car with him was a shotgun he'd recently purchased. He got out, pointed the shotgun at his throat, and ended his life. He was 44. Hollocher had complained recently that he was once again suffering severe stomach pain. "Hollocher wins the nomination as the forgotten man of baseball," wrote *The Sporting News* some years prior to his death. "Never, probably, did another recognized star drop out of the public eye more completely."

MIND GAMES

Jim Eisenreich's rise to the majors had been swift. Selected by the Twins in the 16th round of the 1980 amateur draft, the Minnesota native was playing center field for his hometown team after just a season and a half in the minors. The 23-year-old rookie hit .302 in 99 at-bats that year. "A natural ballplayer like this might come along only once in a lifetime," said Twins owner Calvin Griffith.

Eisenreich would have had more than those 99 at-bats, had he not

ANOTHER GUT FEELING

Charlie Hollocher wasn't the only top player whose career was ended by stomach distress. Cleveland's Elmer Flick was one of the best hitters in baseball between 1898, his rookie year, and 1907. Seven times in those ten seasons Flick finished in the top ten in his league in batting and slugging percentage, eight times in on-base percentage, and six times in stolen bases. Following the 1907 season, Detroit offered Ty Cobb for Flick even up. Cleveland turned the deal down.

The following Spring, Flick complained of indigestion at the team's New Orleans training camp. The condition turned serious, and Flick lost 30 of his 170 pounds. The 32-year-old would get into just nine games that year, and hit .229. Never before in his career had Flick hit less than .296 in a season or appeared in fewer than 121 games. Never again would he hit above .265 or play in more than 66 games. His major league career ended in 1910. "My last three years . . . were awful," Flick would later say. "I had a nervous stomach that I never did get over. I shouldn't have played at all."

After a few failed comeback attempts in the minors, Flick made his living in real estate and building. He also owned and drove harness horses. Flick's abortive career might have been forgotten like Hollocher's, except Flick managed ten years as a top hitter before his stomach problems forced him from the game. In 1963—more than half a century after he last played—that proved enough to land Flick a place in Cooperstown. "Mr. Rickey told me I had been put in the Hall of Fame," said the 87-year-old Flick, "and I thought he was kidding."

Flick died in 1971, two days short of his 95th birthday.

suffered from a neurological disorder known as Tourette's syndrome. The disorder made him twitch and hyperventilate, particularly under the stress of the major leagues. Mean-spirited chants of "Shake! Shake! Shake!" from fans in Boston made Eisenreich hyperventilate so severely that he was forced to rush off the field. In 1983, Eisenreich went home after just two games. "It's too hard to play," he said. "It isn't any fun."

The potential big league star spent that summer playing for an amateur team. In 1984, the Twins called in a hypnotist, hoping to cure Eisenreich of what the team called his "nervous problem." It didn't help. Medications that reduced the twitching also slowed Eisenreich's reflexes, making it impossible for him to play. After just 12 games that year, Eisenreich announced his retirement. He was 25 and had a grand total of 138 major league at-bats.

For nearly three years, the only baseball Eisenreich played was at an amateur level. But during those years he discovered that smaller doses of the medications that he'd been prescribed could control his condition without making him feel listless. In late 1986, Eisenreich decided to stage a comeback. "If there's a hint of any trouble again, I'll just quit," he said. "That's all there is to it."

The Twins weren't interested in their aging former prospect, so for the price of $1, the Kansas City Royals claimed his contract. Eisenreich was sent to Memphis of the Southern League. There he hit .382 and came within four doubles of setting a new league record for two-baggers . . . even though he was with Memphis for only 70 games. "He just made a mockery out of the league," said his Memphis manager.

Kansas City called Eisenreich up to the majors late that season and again for part of 1988. He finally reached the big leagues to stay in 1989 and that season hit .293 and was voted Kansas City's Player of the Year. Most hitters reach their peak around age 28. Eisenreich was 30 years old and just starting out—yet he'd hit over .300 in five of the next seven seasons. In 1996, at the age of 37, Eisenreich hit .361 in 338 at-bats for the Phillies. Time finally caught up with him in 1998, when the 39-year old hit just .215.

Eisenreich was denied the first half of his playing career. But he preferred not to speculate about what might have been. "I don't look in the past," he said after the 1989 season. "Whatever happened long ago is history. It'll never come back—at least I hope it doesn't."

THE ASTRO WHO FELL TO EARTH

J.R. Richard should have been one of the most famous pitchers of modern times. He was a frightening figure staring down at National League hitters, his 6'8" frame looking all the larger atop the pitching mound. He threw a fastball that topped a hundred and a slider in the mid-90s. He won between 18 and 20 games a year from 1976 through 1979. In 1978, he became the first National League right-hander in the 20th century to strike out more than 300 in a season. In 1979, he did it again, and led the league in ERA besides. Richard was Randy Johnson in his prime, only right-handed and not so ugly.

Unfortunately, 1980 wasn't a great year for Texans named J.R. The fictional J.R. Ewing took a bullet that March, and the real-life J.R. Richard took a blow of his own four months later. The season had started quite well. Richard's record was 10–4 by July, his ERA 1.90. His Astros looked like they had a shot at the postseason. Richard often had complained that he would be famous if only he played in New York. Playing in the World Series might have boosted his public profile without a change of address.

There was just one dark cloud: Richard had been complaining of a dead arm since mid-July, and even missed a start. But team doctors assured the Astros nothing was wrong. Though Richard always had been a workhorse in the past, he now was accused of malingering.

He wasn't.

During a light workout on July 30, 1980, Richard collapsed to the Astrodome turf. His dead arm had been caused by a blood clot. Left untreated by the Astros doctors, the clot had reached Richards brain, causing a massive stroke. The 30-year-old survived, but the left side of his body was paralyzed. Physical therapy helped him regain some use of those muscles, but it wasn't enough to regain his pitching career, and a 1981 comeback attempt ended in failure. J.R. Richard would never throw another regular-season pitch in the major leagues.

The Astros made the playoffs in 1980 despite the loss of their ace, but they fell short of the World Series. Just short. Houston lost by a single run in the deciding game of the National League Championship Series. Had Richard been available to the Astros, he very well might have made the difference. Instead, close to a quarter century later, Houston continues to wait for its first trip to the Series.

Baseball wasn't all that J.R. Richard lost in the 1980s. An oil scam was said to have cost him $300,000 of his baseball savings. An ex-wife reportedly fared even better than the con men, pocketing $669,000 in a divorce settlement. By the 1990s, Richard was homeless and living under a bridge in Houston. Fortunately, the ex-pitcher rebuilt his life, his situation improving considerably when he became eligible for his major league pension at age 45.

Had J.R. Richard continued to pitch until age 37 or 38, he likely would have had a shot at the Hall of Fame. The Astros in all probability

ORR'S STROKE

Dave Orr was one of baseball's heaviest hitters in the 1880s. In each of his seven full seasons he finished in the top five in his league in batting. Four times he was in the top five in RBIs, three times in homers. But Orr was a heavy hitter in another way as well: though he stood just 5'11", he weighed between 250 to 265 pounds, and it wasn't all muscle. Orr lacked self discipline in his physical conditioning and in most other phases of his life besides. In 1888, he was stripped of the Brooklyn captaincy when it was discovered he'd skipped a game claiming to be ill, then spent the day enjoying himself at Coney Island. On another occasion, he was accused of assaulting a law clerk who tried to serve him divorce papers.

Orr had his best season in 1890. His .371 average with Brooklyn in the Players' League was a close second in the batting race. He also finished second in the league in RBIs, despite missing time with two broken ribs. Shortly after the end of the regular season, Brooklyn was playing an exhibition game in Renova, Pennsylvania when Orr collapsed. The 31-year-old had suffered a stroke. Some in the baseball world believed his excessive weight was to blame. Whatever the cause, the left side of Orr's body was paralyzed and his baseball career was over. His .342 batting average today ranks him among the top ten hitters of all time . . . though with just 791 games played and 3,289 at-bats, he often isn't included on all-time leader lists. Big Dave Orr has been largely forgotten.

Orr worked at Ebbets Field in various capacities after his stroke, including a stint as press box attendant for the Federal League Brooklyn Tip-Tops in 1914. He died of heart disease in June, 1915.

would have reached at least one World Series, perhaps more. Instead, the best that can be said for Richard's major league experience is that he survived it.

12

DEATH

When a talented young ballplayer dies, his tragedy extends far beyond the field. But from a baseball standpoint, death is like any other career-ending injury, only with less talk of a comeback.

Deaths of major league prospects fortunately are rare. But every now and then an apparent star in the making is called to meet his maker.

FERGUSON'S FATAL FEVER

In the 1880s, Charlie Ferguson was one of the greatest all-around players in the game.

- As a pitcher, he had a record of 99–64 despite playing for a mediocre team, with an ERA estimated to be around 2.67. "It was generally conceded," maintained Frank Hough of the *Philadelphia Inquirer* in 1908, "that [Old Hoss Radbourne] could do nothing with a ball that Fergy could not duplicate." Radbourn was the greatest pitcher of his day and a future Hall of Famer.

- As a hitter, Ferguson had the best batting average on the Philadelphia club in two of his four years with the team.

- As a baserunner, Ferguson won an 1887 running contest against Tommy Poorman, an outfielder considered among the fastest men in the league.
- As a fielder, Ferguson reportedly could play any position with skill.

Ferguson was, at least according to the *Inquirer*'s Hough in 1908, "the one man who stood out clean cut and away above all the players of his time or of the present as a player without weakness."

Shortly before the start of the 1888 season, the 24-year-old college-educated Ferguson contracted typhoid fever and was consigned to a sickbed in the home of Philadelphia team captain Arthur Irwin. Local newspapers reported regularly on Ferguson's progress. In mid-April the star rallied, and his doctors proclaimed him to be on the road to recovery. But the unseasonably hot weather of April 29 proved too much for the weakened man. "He cannot live," Ferguson's doctor told the three teammates keeping vigil that evening. "He is in a state of collapse."

Ferguson died at 10:30 that night. He left a widow, but no children, his only daughter having died in 1887. Philadelphia had closed to within three and a half games of the National League pennant in 1887, Ferguson's final year with the club. They wouldn't come within seven games of the pennant again until 1915.

TERRIBLE TIMES FOR TWO TERRIERS

Freshman Tommy Gastall seemed to have Boston University's starting quarterback job locked up in 1951—until Harry Agganis returned from the Marines to resume his collegiate career. Agganis wasn't just the greatest athlete in Boston University history. More than a few sports fans considered him the greatest athlete the state of Massachusetts had ever produced. Agganis' athletic talents were such that the Marines hadn't drafted him to fight in the Korean War—they just wanted him to lead their football team at Camp Lejeune. When Agganis' military stint ended, would-be quarterback Gastall shifted over to end.

In 1953, the Cleveland Browns made Agganis their first-round pick. Red Grange called him the best college player he'd seen that year. Yet Harry Agganis would never play in the NFL. "I've already proven myself in football," Agganis explained, and signed a $35,000 bonus contract to join the Boston Red Sox. New England's greatest sports hero would stay home and play baseball.

With Agganis playing baseball, Tommy Gastall finally became BU's everyday starting quarterback in his senior year, and led The Terriers to a 7–2 record. Like Agganis, Gastall was considered an NFL prospect and was drafted by the Lions. But like Agganis, he chose baseball instead, signing a $40,000 bonus contract with the Baltimore Orioles—$5,000 more than Agganis had received.

Meanwhile, Agganis was making good on his athletic potential.

IRWIN'S END

Canadian-born Arthur Irwin, the man at whose home Charlie Ferguson spent his final days, played in the majors for 13 years, managed for eight, and remained in the game as an executive through the first two decades of the 20th century. The one-time shortstop is credited with developing perhaps the first infielder's glove.

In July 1921, more than 30 years after Ferguson's death, Irwin disappeared from a steamship heading from New York to Boston. He is presumed to have committed suicide. Some sources suggest Irwin took his own life because of failing health, but there also were reports that problems created by an extended extramarital affair might have played a role. His body was never found.

After just one year in the minors, "The Golden Greek" landed in Boston. He hit just .251 with 11 homers in 1954, then got off to a tremendous start in his second season. Through 25 games, Agganis was hitting .313 batting cleanup behind Ted Williams. The *Boston Globe* reported that Agganis was "regarded by many as the next Lou Gehrig." No one was very worried when health problems including pneumonia, chest pains, and a high temperature forced Agganis from the Boston lineup—he was a great athlete in the prime of life. What could hurt him? By mid-June, Agganis' malady landed him on the disabled list. It was considered a minor setback.

Agganis was still on the DL on June 21, 1955, when Gastall made his major league debut for the Orioles. A new rule required that bonus babies like Gastall remain in the majors for their first two professional seasons. The rule was an attempt by baseball to control the proliferation of big bonus contracts offered to prospects, but for young players like Gastall it meant two years sitting on the bench when he should have been improving in the minors. The Orioles used the young catcher sparingly. He got just 27 at-bats in 1955.

While Gastall was sitting, Agganis was suffering, his seemingly minor health problems having grown more serious. Agganis had developed phlebitis in his leg, an inflammation of a vein. The usual treatment would have included an operation. But Agganis declined, concerned what a leg operation might do to his athletic career. Instead his leg was packed in ice. Agganis' doctor told the press the treatment seemed to be working. The ballplayer was said to be in good spirits. On June 27, Agganis died suddenly, the victim of a massive blood clot.

The name Harry Agganis still is known, particularly in New England. He's remembered for his unfulfilled potential. He's remembered as the man who showed a generation of young baseball fans that death could come to anyone, even one as strong and healthy as The Golden Greek. He's *not* remembered as a major league star. Agganis played just 157 games in the big leagues.

Tommy Gastall's career is even less well-remembered. The Orioles expected Gastall to develop into a great catcher, but Baltimore already had two fine catchers in Gus Triandos and Hal Smith. Gastall would have to wait his turn. As the 1956 season neared its end, he had just 83 career at-bats.

The Orioles had a rare off day on their schedule on September 20, and Gastall intended to make the most of it. After a morning workout, he told teammates he was heading to the airport to go up in the small plane he'd purchased two months before with some of his bonus money.

"Don't go up in that thing," cautioned Orioles shortstop Willie Miranda. But Gastall was bored with his life sitting on the bench, and wasn't about to give up his exciting new hobby. Besides, Gastall had to log more flight time or he wouldn't be allowed to fly his plane back home to Massachusetts after the season ended in a couple of weeks.

Gastall took off from Harbor Field southeast of Baltimore at 3:50. At 6:21, the control tower received the call "75 Hotel, I'm going into the water." Five days later, Gastall's body was found floating off Riviera Beach in Chesapeake Bay. It was identified by the catcher's Boston University class ring. Gastall left a widow and 15-month-old son.

There's no guarantee that Tommy Gastall would have become a famous baseball player. Highly touted bonus babies had flopped before, and Gastall had done little in his 83 major league at-bats to suggest greatness. But like Harry Agganis before him, he wouldn't even get a chance to try.

TONY BOECKEL'S DECADE OF BASEBALL

On February 15, 1924, Boston Braves third baseman Norman Doxie "Tony" Boeckel and New York Yankees outfielder Bob Meusel were passengers in a car driven by "theatrical man" Bob Albright. According to reports, a large truck swerved into the side of Albright's car, sending them careening into the path of an on-coming vehicle. Albright's car flipped over. Albright escaped with minor cuts, and Meusel was virtually unhurt. But Boeckel was pinned beneath the car. His pelvis was fractured and his bladder punctured. He died the next day.

Boeckel was 30 when he died. His career batting average was a respectable but unspectacular .282, his defense at third wasn't great, and he played on a second-division team. It would be easy to dismiss him as a man not destined for fame even before the accident. But the rapid end to Boeckel's playing days was only half his story. His late start was the other half. According to Paul H. Shannon of the *Boston Post,*

Boeckel had "never had a baseball in his hands until he was fully 19 years of age."

Apparently in 1912, the 19-year-old Boeckel was working as a clerk for a Los Angeles oil company. The company had its own semi-pro team, and Boeckel was persuaded to take part in a practice. To everyone's surprise, "the stocky little German showed amazing proficiency." When one of the team's players was injured, Boeckel was added to the squad. By the end of that season—reportedly his first year playing baseball anywhere—Boeckel had signed a pro contract. Five years later, in 1917, the 24-year old was in the majors . . . then he was right back out of baseball a year later, spending 1918 with the Navy during World War I. Finally in 1919, the 26-year-old Boeckel got to start his major league career in earnest. He hit a roundly mediocre .250. But his average improved in his second year, and between 1921 and 1923, the final season of his life, his overall average was just north of .300.

Most hitters decline after age 30, but as someone still learning the game, perhaps Boeckel would have been the exception. At the very least, one wonders what Boeckel's career might have looked like if his time in baseball had started sooner and ended later. Instead, the glimpse the baseball world got of Norman Doxie Boeckel has long since been forgotten.

BOSTOCK'S SHOT

In 1976, 25-year-old Minnesota Twin outfielder Lyman Bostock hit .323, good for fourth in the American League. In 1977, he hit .336, second in the league. That winter, Bostock signed one of the richest free-agent contracts to that point in the sport's history, a five-year deal with the Angels worth between $2 million and $3 million. (Bostock's father, former Negro League All-Star Lyman Bostock, Sr., had never made more than $5,000 in a season.)

Lyman, Jr. wasn't the typical spoiled rich star. When the pressure of the big contract led to a slow start with the Angels in 1978, Bostock tried to give his April paycheck back to the club, feeling he hadn't earned it. Angel owner Gene Autry refused to take the money, so Bostock gave it to charity instead. Bostock soon turned his season around, and by late September, his average was in the mid-.290s—it was well over .300 since the end of April. Sparked by his hot bat, the Angels—fifth in a

HIS ONLY ERROR WAS PILOT ERROR

Ken Hubbs set a record with 78 consecutive errorless games at second base on his way to winning both the Gold Glove and National League Rookie of the Year in 1962. The Chicago Cub hit .260 that year, and though his batting average fell to .235 in his second season, he still was just 21 years old and had an excellent chance to develop into an excellent player.

That chance died with Hubbs on February 13, 1964, when he crashed his Cessna into a Utah lake. Investigators concluded that Hubbs had lost his bearings in a snowstorm. He'd earned his pilot's license only two weeks before.

Hubbs' father later would lament the string of circumstances that had led up to his son's death. Hubbs normally played basketball on Wednesdays, but on this particular Wednesday for some reason no game had been scheduled. Hubbs and friend Denny Doyle (not Denny Doyle the ballplayer) had planned just a one-day excursion, but had been talked into staying overnight. The weather would have been clear if they'd followed the original schedule. Doyle's sister heard her brother was in town the following morning and rushed to the airport to visit, only to find he'd just taken off. The airport manager reportedly said he was too busy to radio Hubbs and tell him to come back. The sequence of circumstances proved fatal, as Hubbs and Doyle flew into the teeth of a snowstorm.

The remains of Hubbs' plane were found on February 15, 1964, 40 years to the day after another National League infielder, Tony Boeckel, had his fatal vehicular accident.

seven-team division the year before—had climbed to second. Five back with eight to play, they even had an outside chance to catch the Royals for the division title.

On September 23, the Angels trailed the White Sox 5–4 in the 9th inning in Chicago. Bostock, already 2-for-3 with a walk, came to the plate with two on and two out. He grounded back to the mound and the Angels came up one run short. After the game, Bostock decided to visit relatives in nearby Gary, Indiana. At 10:40 that night, Bostock, his uncle Thomas Turner, and Turner's goddaughters, sisters Barbara Smith and Joan Hawkins, were in Turner's car heading to a late dinner. Smith and Bostock were in the backseat. Apparently unbeknownst to Bostock, Smith had told her husband only hours before that she intended to file for divorce. Also apparently unknown to Bostock, Leonard Smith, the

Lyman Bostock's untimely passing led the Associated Press to note that the Angels franchise had been "stalked by tragedy from the beginning." Angels pitcher Dick Wantz died of a cerebral hemorrhage in 1965, just a month after his debut in the majors. Another pitcher, one-time AL saves leader Minnie Rojas, was paralyzed in a car crash in 1970. Angel shortstop Chico Ruiz died in a car accident in 1972. Highly regarded pitching prospect Bruce Heinbechner died in another car accident during spring training in 1973. He'd been considered a sure bet to make the Angels that year. Shortstop Mike Miley, the team's first-round pick in 1974 and perhaps the best prospect in their system at the time, died in a car crash in 1977.

husband, was trailing close behind them with a loaded shotgun. Smith pulled his vehicle alongside Turner's and fired a shotgun into the back seat. His wife, reportedly the intended target, received pellet wounds to her face. Bostock took the brunt of the shot in his left temple. He died in the hospital at 1:30 the following morning. Bostock's career and life were over at 27. His batting average was .311 in four big league seasons. "It's very shocking," said teammate Don Baylor. "Here one day and gone tomorrow."

Leonard Smith, the man who had killed the star ballplayer, was found not guilty by reason of insanity. He was released from Logansport State Hospital in June, 1980, less than two years after Bostock's death.

AN OUTFIELDER TRIES TO END HIS OWN CAREER

Johnny Mostil's career didn't end with his death—but it wasn't for a lack of trying. Mostil had gotten something of a late start on his major league career. He didn't get a real shot in the bigs until 1921, when the Chicago White Sox found themselves in desperate need of players to replace those banned from baseball in the wake of the Black Sox scandal. Mostil, a 25-year-old rookie center fielder in '21, stepped right in to hit .290 or better in each of his first six full seasons, though without much power. He also was regarded as perhaps the best defensive outfielder in the American League. According to one story, Mostil once caught a foul ball in an exhibition game in Nashville—even though he'd been playing *center* field.

In 1926, Mostil had the best offensive season of his career, hitting .328 and leading the league in stolen bases for the second straight year. Thanks in part to his efforts, the White Sox finished within ten games of the pennant for the first time since eight of their players were banned following the 1920 season. The 1927 campaign seemed to hold considerable promise for the Sox and their 30-year-old outfielder.

Mostil reported to White Sox training camp in Shreveport, Louisiana on March 7, but rain precluded the first day of practice. Teammates who saw Mostil that day would say he appeared to be in good spirits. Yet late that afternoon Mostil was discovered unconscious on the floor of his hotel bathroom, bleeding profusely from numerous self-inflicted cuts to his throat and body.

Friends at first wondered if his actions might have been precipitated by a recent medical check up—but aside from bad teeth and high blood pressure, Mostil's health was fine. The suicide attempt officially was chalked up to a temporary bout with depression—though a persistent rumor holds that Mostil's teammate Red Faber had discovered his wife was having an affair with the outfielder, and confronted him that afternoon.

Doctors initially feared for Mostil's life, but the outfielder pulled through. He spent much of the season recuperating in Wisconsin, rejoining the Sox in August, to "generous applause" from Chicago fans. Mostil got into 13 games late that year, hitting just .125. Chicago slid to 70–83, 40 games back of the Yankees in the American League.

Mostil played a full season in 1928, but hit only .270. His average was .229 in 1929 when an ankle injury ended his major league career for good. Mostil's career batting average before the

THE TIME OF LIFE IS SHORT
Another promising 1920s outfielder, Austin McHenry, hit .350 for the Cardinals in 1921, second in the National League behind Rogers Hornsby. The next year the 26-year-old was hitting .303 when he took ill. Later diagnosed with a brain tumor, McHenry died that November leaving a wife and two children. His career average was a good-but-not-spectacular .302. It would have been more impressive, but the first two of his three full seasons were played in the deadball era when league batting averages were in the .250s.

suicide attempt was .307. His batting average after that day in March was .264. (Incidentally, Red Faber went just 4–7 with a career-worst 4.55 ERA in 1927. His record had been 15–9 with a 3.56 the year before. Perhaps there *was* something on his mind that season.)

Mostil remained in the White Sox organization as a scout and minor league manager until the late 1960s, when arthritis and a circulatory problem finally forced him to retire. He died in a Chicago nursing home in December, 1970.

13

CASUALTIES OF WAR

F or the past half century, baseball fans have debated how many games Bob Feller might have won had he not spent nearly four years of his prime serving in World War II, and how many home runs Ted Williams might have hit had he not spent close to five years serving in World War II and Korea. But Feller and Williams are famous despite the years they sacrificed to military service. Other ballplayers lost their shot at fame to war. A few even lost their lives.

WAR DRAWS ACES FROM CARD DECK
The Cardinals' farm system was loaded with young pitching talent in the early 1940s. Future major league arms in the St. Louis chain included Harry Brecheen, Preacher Roe, Al Brazle, George Munger, and Murry Dickson. But in the eyes of many, the team's top pitching prospects were Johnny Beazley and, most promising of all, Johnny Grodzicki. In 1941, Beazley went 16–12 with a 3.61 ERA for New Orleans in the Southern Association. Grodzicki went 19–5 with a 2.58 ERA for Columbus, leading the American Association in both winning percentage and ERA. "Grodzicki was a legend," said fellow Cards prospect Joe Garagiola years later.

Both pitchers were given cups of coffee with St. Louis in 1941. Beazley won his only game, throwing nine innings and surrendering just one run. Grodzicki pitched a total of 13⅓ innings, giving up two runs on six hits and earning a 2–1 record. Both pitchers were considered likely to make the Cards in 1942. Grodzicki was considered a potential star.

Johnny Grodzicki had a first-rate fastball and a changeup that was every bit as effective. But what the Cardinals organization liked best about the pitcher was his attitude. Grodzicki never shied away from throwing at a batter. And if that didn't work, he never shied away from throwing at him again. He'd had a tough childhood and didn't expect anyone to hand him anything. He was ready to fight for every win.

Johnny Beazley was more taciturn than Grodzicki, but no less tough. He'd once competed in Golden Gloves tournaments and had his sights set on a boxing career. Only the pleas of his widowed mother pulled him away from the ring. Mrs. Beazley already had lost one son to a high school football accident. She didn't want to lose another to boxing. Baseball was safer, so Johnny agreed to switch his focus to the diamond.

By the time the 1942 season neared, the more promising of the Cards' two young Johnnys was in military training, not spring training. Grodzicki had been drafted into the Army as a paratrooper. Beazley, however, made the Card rotation that year. Though considered the lesser of the two prospects, the rookie went 21–6 with a 2.13 ERA and followed that up by beating the Yankees twice in the Cardinals' five-game World Series victory. After the final game, Babe Ruth burst into the Cardinal locker room bellowing, "Where's that guy that whooped my Yankees?" The Babe shook Beazley's hand. Johnny Beazley was a star on the rise. But by November he, too, was in the Army.

"I'll never go back to pitching," Beazley was quoted as saying after one week in the Army Air Corps. "Baseball is a thing of the past for me. I'm going to make a career out of the army." It was just talk; good press for the sake of good war morale. But any way you slice it, it can't be good luck for a ballplayer heading off to war to say he's done with baseball.

Beazley's stellar 1942 season had given him some advantages in the war. Now a well-known name, his role would be to pitch exhibition baseball games for the sake of military morale. It should have been a safe job. Beazley should have come out of the war unscathed and returned to his career. Instead he developed a sore arm. According to later reports, Beazley was ordered by a superior officer to pitch in an exhibition game though he hadn't had a chance to warm up properly. His arm would never recover.

John Grodzicki had nowhere near as cushy a military life as Beazley. He'd been called into the war a year sooner, before he'd had a chance to establish himself in the big leagues. Without the preferential treatment accorded many big-name sports stars, Grodzicki was assigned to the Army's 17th Airborne Division. Grodzicki's unit parachuted into Germany in March, 1945, to assist in the final push for Berlin.

On March 30, five weeks before the end of the war in Europe and two weeks before the start of the baseball season back home, Grodzicki and three fellow soldiers were hit by a German shell. It ripped a large chunk out of Grodzicki's upper right leg, tearing away nerves and muscles. He was lucky. His companions had been killed. Months of therapy in an English hospital followed, but Grodzicki still had no strength in the leg. Walking was difficult; pitching seemed out of the question. Grodzicki was a right-handed pitcher. With no strength in his right leg, he couldn't push off the rubber to get velocity on the ball.

The sore-armed Beazley tried to continue pitching after the war, but his fastball never returned. He won seven games in 1946 for the Cards, then two more in 1947 for the Braves. Four more games spread over 1948 and 1949 concluded his major league career. Beazley went on to a successful career as owner of a Nashville beer distributorship. He died of cancer in 1990 at age 71.

Grodzicki was invited to spring training with the Cards in 1946, but could make the club only as a batting practice pitcher, his bulky leg brace visible through his uniform. He did find his way onto the roster and into a few games that year, then 16 more in 1947, but was never effective.

Grodzicki remained in baseball, drifting around the minors until 1953, pitching with no great success. He had more luck as a scout and then as a long-time minor league pitching coach in the Detroit Tiger system. In 1979, Grodzicki made it back to the majors as a coach under new Detroit manager Les Moss. Unfortunately for Grodzicki, Moss was replaced by Sparky Anderson two months into the season. By 1980, Grodzicki was back in the minors, his final stay in the majors almost as brief as his first. He died in 1998.

MORE CARDS PITCHERS LOST TO WAR

Cardinal pitcher Howie Krist wasn't quite as highly regarded as Johnny Grodzicki and Johnny Beazley, nor quite as young, but Krist did have a phenomenal 37–9 major league record before heading off to war in 1944. Krist was badly wounded in the leg during fighting near Nancy, France in 1944. His post-war major league career would amount to less than 19 innings. (Even before the war, Krist had been no stranger to injury. He'd already lost time in his professional career to appendicitis, a sore arm, a broken ankle, and bone chips in his elbow.)

Yet another highly regarded Cardinal pitching prospect, Hank Nowak, was killed in action in Belgium. He'd won 13 games for Houston in the Texas League in the last season of his life. Nowak very well might have been the top prospect to die in the war. Another contender for that title is Gene Stack, a pitcher who was about to be called up to the White Sox when he instead was called into service. Stack, however, died of a heart attack unrelated to combat. His weak heart might have finished him even without the war.

FIRST IN WAR

Perhaps the most enduring joke about the perennial also-ran Washington Senators held that Washington was first in war, first in peace, but last in the American League. That joke can't be very funny to Cecil Travis. War and last-place finishes conspired to cost the Senator infielder his shot at fame.

From 1934, Travis' first full season in the majors, to 1941, his last season before leaving for World War II, he hit between .317 and .359 in seven of eight seasons and played respectable defense at shortstop and third. They were great numbers for an infielder, yet humble Georgia farm boy Cecil Travis wasn't regarded as a big star. The reason: he played his whole career for the Senators. The team never finished higher than fourth during Travis' seasons as a regular with the club.

Travis' timing was off in another way as well. In 1941, his smooth left-handed swing produced a .359 batting average. It was easily the best season of his career—but that same year Ted Williams hit .406 and Joe DiMaggio hit in 56 straight. No one much noticed Travis' efforts . . . even though he, not DiMaggio, finished second in the batting race behind Williams. Travis was a distant sixth in the 1941 MVP vote.

By January 7, 1942, Travis was in the Army. War was nothing new for his family. Travis' grandfather had given his life for the Confederacy during the Civil War, taking a bullet on Kennesaw Mountain, the Georgia geographical feature that gave baseball's first commissioner his name. Two generations later, Cecil Travis and the rest of the 76th infantry found themselves in Belgium in the winter of 1945, shortly after the Battle of the Bulge. The German Army was in retreat, and Travis and company took up the pursuit, right behind the front line troops. "It was the cold that got us," he'd later say. "Why, we just shivered all night long. I'll never forget that cold as long as I live."

Sargent Travis' feet were badly frostbitten, and he spent three weeks in the hospital recuperating. Yet when the war ended late in 1945 season, Travis called Senators owner Clark Griffith to tell him he was in playing shape despite the frozen feet and his three-and-a-half-year absence from the game. Perhaps Travis was anxious to get into a pennant race. Washington and Detroit were neck-in-neck heading down the stretch. The infielder's initial swings in practice that September were encouraging. "Timing?" wrote *The Washington Evening Star*. "It took Travis only one minute to acquire it."

The optimism proved unfounded. Travis hit just .241 in 15 games for the Senators late that year, and Washington lost the pennant by a game and a half. Travis' rusty performance was disappointing, but hardly shocking. Most fans assumed Travis would return to form in 1946. He was just 32 years old and figured to have had some good years left. Instead, Travis hit a weak .252. Most put the blame on the shortstop's frozen feet, but Travis himself denied they were the problem. "I just lost my timing is all," he'd explain.

When Travis' average slid to .216 in 1947, he announced his retirement. "I could keep playing a couple of more years, and I could keep on drawing top salaries," Travis said. "But somehow I just couldn't stand to go out there and stumble around."

Travis was offered a job managing in the minors, but instead returned to his small farm 15 miles southeast of Atlanta. He was just a simple Georgia country boy at heart, and it was time to head home. Travis was only 27 years old in his final season before the war. His career batting average was .326. He'd already accumulated 1,370 hits. Whether by freezing his feet or fouling his timing, the war in all likelihood had cost Travis a place in the Hall of Fame.

THE FALLEN STAR OF THE RISING SUN

In 1934, a team made up of some of the greatest American ballplayers in history barnstormed across Japan. Babe Ruth, Lou Gehrig, Jimmie Foxx, and Lefty Gomez all were there, and the Japanese all-stars they faced were out of their league—all except a teenage pitcher named Eiji Sawamura. Sawamura struck out Charlie Gehringer, Babe Ruth, Lou Gehrig, and Jimmie Foxx in his start and held the Americans scoreless most of the way. He lost the game 1–0 on a Gehrig home run, but still won acclaim in Japan and respect from the American team. "The Japanese can field [and] run the bases," American manager Connie Mack later wrote, "but they can't hit and have only one real pitcher." He was referring, of course, to Sawamura.

Sawamura continued to excel in the newly formed Japanese professional league. Between 1936 and 1943, Sawamura went 63–22 with a 1.74 ERA. He threw three no-hitters—no pitcher in Japanese history has thrown more. The Pittsburgh Pirates tried to lure the Japanese star to America, only to discover that Sawamura was caught up in the rabid anti-Americanism sweeping Japan in the 1930s. "My problem is I hate America and I cannot make myself like Americans," Sawamura explained, refusing Pittsburgh's offer.

Apparently the American Navy didn't think much of Sawamura either. The pitcher was killed in the Battle of Ryukus in 1945, shortly before the end of World War II. He was just 26. Since 1947, the Eiji Sawamura Award has served as Japan's answer to America's Cy Young. The war hadn't cost him fame in his home country—he remains well-known in Japan despite his early death. But the political

> ### TATUM'S TWELVE AT-BATS
> Dodger outfield prospect Tommy Tatum hit .347 in the Southern Association in 1941, earning him a promotion to the majors that August. The blazing-fast outfielder got just 12 major league at-bats that year. He was drafted into the military before the 1942 season. By the time Tatum returned from the war, he'd missed more than three seasons of baseball and had injured his arm. He would get just 182 more at-bats in the majors. He tried managing in the minors for a while, then left the game to become an insurance broker. Tatum died of lung cancer in 1989.

tensions preceding the war had caused Sawamura to decline offers to pitch in America, and thus cost him his chance to be famous in the U.S.

GOING OUT IN STYLE. ALMOST.

World War II didn't prevent Larry French from becoming famous. But the war did set the stage for French's near miss with fame.

Larry French was a dependable workhorse lefty in the 1930s and early 1940s. He made the All-Star team in 1940, but that was the exception. The typical Larry French season featured perhaps 15 wins, an ERA in the mid-threes, and 250 innings pitched. He'd appeared in three World Series, but had been on the wrong side in each. After 13 seasons in the league, French's record was 182–167. It was the sort of career that earns a pitcher respect, but not fame.

By 1942, French was 34, an age when the end of an athletic career is considerably nearer than its beginning. The end must have seemed particularly near for French when his 14th season in the majors began. His record had been just 5–14 with the Cubs the year before, his stock falling so low that the Brooklyn Dodgers had been able to claim him off waivers late in 1941. And the shaky season wasn't even the greatest threat to French's pitching career. The U.S. had become embroiled in World War II, and French, like all American men, knew there was a chance he'd soon be drafted. For a player of French's age, any prolonged stint in the military likely meant the end of his days in baseball. But if 1942 was to be French's farewell performance, he seemed determined to make it a great one. As the season headed into its final week, his record was 14–4, his ERA below 2.00. Never before in his career had French ended a season as many as ten games over .500, never had he ended a season with an ERA below 2.70. Larry French was having a career year in what well could be his final year.

Brooklyn battled St. Louis for the pennant all season, but by late September the Dodgers trailed in the standings and were running out of time. On September 23, Larry French took the mound against the Phils for what he knew might be the last start of his career. He came up just inches short of history. In the second inning, Phils first baseman Nick Etten hit a hump-back liner just out of the reach of Pee Wee Reese at short. Etten was erased moments later on a double play. When the game ended, that scratch single was the only thing standing between Larry French and the major league's first perfect game since 1922.

Brooklyn lost the pennant by two games that season, and French entered the Navy shortly after. Had he thrown a perfect game in his last start before leaving for war, it surely would have made him a legend. Instead French had to settle for leading the National League in winning percentage. His final record that year was 15–4, his ERA 1.83.

Lt. French began his Naval career working in the Ordinance Department at the Brooklyn Navy Yard. Since he was still in Brooklyn, French petitioned the Navy to let him throw for the Dodgers in his off-duty hours. He wanted the three last wins he needed to push his career total to an even 200. French even offered to donate his baseball salary to the war effort. The Navy turned him down. Still, French wasn't complaining. While the war took many American men away from their families, it gave him more time with his. "For the first time in years I've had some home life in the summer," he noted. "My wife loves it."

He wouldn't find the whole war so cushy. As a landing craft material officer, French reached the French coast on D-Day plus 2. "This beach was plenty hot," he wrote to Dodger outfielder Augie Galan soon after. "88 mm fire, mines everywhere you stepped, and the darndest fireworks each night you can imagine . . . I had a darned good friend blown up yesterday by a mine not 50 feet from me. . . . It really gives one plenty to think of."

French still harbored dreams of returning for those three wins after the war and was added to the Dodgers roster in the spring of 1946. But after giving it some thought, French decided that working all the way back into playing shape just to get three wins was frivolous at his age. He officially retired from baseball and for the rest of the 1940s made his living working for an auto dealership and an insurance agency.

In 1951, French was recalled to active duty by the Navy for the Korean War. The war soon ended, but this time French didn't return to civilian life. He remained in the Navy until 1969, retiring as a highly decorated Captain and veteran of two wars. French died in 1987. He had come up inches short of fame one day in 1942, but he was every bit a hero.

In 1918, Ralph Worrell was 25–10 with a 2.25 ERA for Baltimore in the International League. Those 25 wins were tops in the league, and Worrell was expected to pitch in the majors in 1919. But World War I was raging, so Worrell joined the Army at the end of the 1918 season. The Army sent him to the automobile truck training school they'd established on the campus of the University of Virginia.

Worrell was still in the United States, but that didn't mean he was safe. The greatest killer of World War I was disease, and by late 1918, an influenza epidemic had reached the United States. Military training camps were particularly hard hit, and Worrell soon took ill. A short item appeared in *The Sporting News* in mid-November, one of many of its kind during that year. "Ralph Worrell, who as a left-handed pitcher with Baltimore in the International League last year, made a wonderful record—one that promised for him the brightest career in baseball—died on November 6."

The war ended on November 11.

DANGER ON THE HOMEFRONT

World War II didn't rob Frank "Creepy" Crespi of anything as grandiose as the Hall of Fame. His career never appeared destined for such heights. But Crespi had seemed poised to become one of baseball's top defensive second basemen before the war. Marty Marion called his Cardinal double-play partner "by far the best second baseman I ever teamed up with."

Defensive brilliance coupled with Crespi's memorable nickname "Creepy" might have been enough for the second baseman to carve out a niche for himself in baseball history. (Some attribute the nickname to the fact that Crespi looked like a film noir gangster, others to his low-to-the-ground fielding style. The ballplayer himself evaded questions about his moniker's meaning.)

In early 1943, Crespi was drafted into the war. He was his mother's sole supporter and probably could have gotten a deferment, but Crespi refused to file an appeal. "I don't think I'm too good to fight for the things I've always enjoyed," he said.

Crespi never made it overseas, but even in the U.S. he found military life full of danger. First Crespi suffered a compound fracture of his left leg while turning a double play in an Army baseball game in Kansas. The leg healed, but Crespi broke it again when his tank overturned in training. Recuperating in the hospital, the leg broke a third time when orderlies staged an impromptu wheelchair race featuring Crespi and another injured soldier. Finally an Army nurse misread her instructions and applied 100 times the proper amount of boric acid to his bandages, badly burning the leg. The series of mishaps took a once fleet middle infielder and left him with a limp for life. His playing days were over.

Crespi tried to return to the majors as a coach after the war so he could qualify for the pension plan—even a brief coaching stint in the big leagues could have been worth a tidy sum to Crespi in retirement. But no major league team offered him a coaching job. Instead, Crespi settled into a 20-year career as a budget analyst at aerospace firm McDonnell-Douglas. Just as he was retiring from this second career, a fortuitous fact was uncovered about his first: technically, he'd been on the disabled list, not retired, when the major league pension plan began back in the late 1940s. Though he hadn't played baseball in 30 years, Crespi suddenly qualified for his major league pension. An unusual and unnecessary series of wartime accidents had cost the man known as Creepy any chance at baseball fame, but at least he had a comfortable retirement. Crespi died of a heart attack in 1990 at age 72.

Did World War II cost Dick Wakefield his fame, or did the much-hyped prospect simply not pan out? The Detroit Tigers signed the 6'4" University of Michigan outfielder to a then-hefty $51,000 bonus contract in 1941. In 1943 and 1944, it appeared their money had been well spent. Wakefield hit .316 and led the league in doubles in 1943, then .355 with 12 homers and 53 RBIs in the first 78 games of 1944. Had he kept that pace for the rest of the year, Wakefield had a shot at the Triple Crown. Instead, he spent the second half of the 1944 season in the Navy air cadet program.

Wakefield's numbers weren't anywhere near as good upon his return to baseball in 1946. He played regularly in just three more seasons, hitting between .268 and .283 with only glimmers of his former home run power. By the 1950s, Wakefield was a faded phenom. He had two at-bats with the Yanks in 1950 and two more with the Giants in 1952. But by age 31 he was finished in the majors. By the middle of the 1950s, Wakefield, now in his mid-30s, was paying his own way down to Florida in the spring in the hopes of landing with a team. He'd lost most of his bonus money to bad investments and fancy living.

When he finally realized his baseball career was over, Wakefield tried selling insurance. Later he worked for the state of Michigan. He even ran for U.S Congress, but lost. Twice. Wakefield died of heart disease in 1985.

Everyone had an explanation for Wakefield's post-war baseball failure. Some sportswriters felt he didn't care enough about the game. Others argued that that his stellar 1943–1944 stats were the product of weak wartime pitching and he'd never really been all that good in the first place. But there is at least a chance that Wakefield really was every bit the player he seemed to be before the war, but couldn't regain his timing after missing a season and a half in the military. That certainly isn't how history remembers him. When Dick Wakefield's name comes up at all, the subject is either wasted potential or young players who weren't worth the money they were paid.

14

JUST WALK AWAY

Plenty of players have missed out on potential fame. Only a few have done so of their own volition. Potential lost by choice is still potential lost, and it's hard not to wonder what might have been.

A STAR WHEN HE WISHED TO BE

There was never any question that "Turkey" Mike Donlin *could* play baseball with the best of them. The only question was whether he *would* play baseball at all. Though his major league career began in 1899 and didn't end until 1914, Donlin had just five seasons of more than 300 at-bats. By and large it wasn't injuries keeping him off the field, and neither was it lack of talent—the outfielder hit .333 in his career. When Donlin didn't play, it most often was his own choice.

Donlin's lack of playing time didn't cost him fame in his own time. He was then a star in a larger-than-life way that transcended baseball. He was a New York playboy 65 years before Broadway Joe. He was an actor of some acclaim. He was a dater of starlets and a drinker and a rogue. But fame of this sort is fleeting. There is no Hall of Fame for drinkers, and even if there were, no one who'd visit would be sober enough to read the plaques. For all his talent and charisma, Donlin's best shot at fame was baseball, and he gave that chance away.

Mike Donlin reached the majors with St. Louis in July 1899. He was arrogant and unproven, a combination sure to rub crusty veteran teammates like Jesse "The Crab" Burkett the wrong way. But it wasn't long before Donlin showed that his bat was as big as his mouth, and soon he was a crucial part of the St. Louis lineup—at least during the early innings. Often at odds with umps, Donlin had a habit of getting thrown out before contests reached their conclusions. He hit .323 that year, and .326 the next, finishing two homers short of the league lead in 1900. In 1901, Donlin—along with his friend and manager John McGraw—jumped to Baltimore in the fledgling American League. Donlin's .340 average was second to Nap Lajoie in that year's AL batting race.

Just as Donlin seemed poised for stardom, his career took the first of its many odd turns. And not for the last time, the odd turn would involve an actress. Shortly before the start of the 1902 season, a drunken Donlin followed actress Mamie Fields down the street making what later would be described as inappropriate comments. When Ms. Fields' date protested Donlin's behavior, Donlin punched him. When Ms. Fields protested the punch, Donlin punched her too. Donlin was arrested and sentenced to six months in jail. By the time he was released from jail, he'd also been released by the Orioles.

Donlin resurfaced back in the National League with Cincinnati for 34 games at the end of the 1902 season. In 1903, he hit .351 for the Reds, and his average was at .356 in the middle of 1904 when the team suspended him for repeated drunkenness. Cincinnati gave up on the talented hitter and traded him to the New York Giants that August.

THE MORE SENSIBLE APPROACH TO LEAVING BASEBALL

Leave the game by choice? Many more ballplayers lean toward the retirement philosophy of Hall of Fame pitcher Early Wynn: "Somebody will have to come and tear the uniform off me," Wynn said late in his career. "And the guy who comes better have help."

Playing in New York made Mike Donlin famous. In 1905, Donlin and future Hall of Fame pitcher Christy Mathewson led the Giants to the pennant. Donlin was third in the league in batting, tied for third in homers, and first in runs scored. But Donlin missed all but 37 games of 1906 with a broken ankle—the one time in his career that an injury was to blame for keeping him on the sidelines for an extended stretch. The ankle was healthy by 1907, but Donlin held out all season for more money. He finally made it back on the field in 1908. Despite a layoff of nearly two years, Donlin was as good as ever. He also was as popular as ever.

"Donlin's first appearance was the signal for one of the greatest ovations I ever witnessed," wrote teammate Marty McHale a decade later. "The prodigal son had returned to the fold, and the crowd was there to pay tribute to one of the best loved ball players that ever ruined a pitcher's reputation." Donlin won the game 3–2 with a two-run homer in the bottom of the 9th. He ended the season behind only Honus Wagner in batting average and RBIs in the National League, and tied for fourth in homers. The Giants lost the 1908 pennant by one game to the Cubs in one of the most celebrated pennant races in history. Donlin was once again near the pinnacle of the sport . . . and he wouldn't play again until 1911.

The ballplayer recently had wed well-known vaudeville actress Mabel Hite. The relationship at first seemed a positive development for Donlin's baseball career. Now a married man, he'd sworn off drinking and generally cleaned up his behavior. But after touring the vaudeville circuit with Hite in the off-season, Donlin decided to leave baseball and pursue a career as an actor. "Human nature is a queer piece of goods," wrote Hite in late 1908. "I have talked with lots of baseball men who wanted to be actors, and then many big actors have told me that the one bright dream of their lives was to be a diamond hero. So it goes."

The acting efforts of star athletes typically fall somewhere between the laughable and the nausea-inducing, but Donlin's performances seem to have been the exception. Newspaper reports suggest he was a charming and even talented actor. For two years, Donlin and his wife toured the country to good reviews and great box-office receipts. But like most things in Donlin's life, it wouldn't last. By 1911, the crowds had stopped flocking to their act and Donlin returned to baseball. This time his comeback wouldn't go as smoothly. After two seasons away from the field, Donlin's foot speed was gone, and most agreed his play lacked its previous spark. He was shipped to the Boston Braves after just 12 games back in New York. Worse news lay ahead. Donlin's wife was diagnosed with cancer and died the following year at the age of 27. By all accounts she had been the great love of Donlin's life.

Donlin seemed lost without his wife, unable to settle on a career. He hit .316 for the Pirates in 1912, then returned to the stage in 1913. He was back in baseball for one last stab at the majors in 1914, then returned to the theater once more. He gave minor league managing a shot in 1917, but that didn't last long. By the late teens, Donlin had married another actress and returned to the stage for good. The couple later moved to Hollywood to work in film.

Show-biz periodical *Variety* noted with distinct surprise that the former ballplayer "could pass as a film lead on ability alone." Donlin never did become a lead actor, but he would have small roles in a large number of films, working alongside the likes of John Barrymore, Buster Keaton, Jimmy Cagney, and Cary Grant. Donlin even served as assistant director on a number of baseball movies. By the late 1920s, Donlin was experiencing serious health problems, and in 1927 his movie friends staged a benefit show to raise the money required to send him to the Mayo Clinic for a heart operation. Donlin lived another six years before dying in his sleep of a heart attack at age 56.

Donlin was a respectable actor, but not a great one. He was a great ballplayer, but not, to history, a famous one. Donlin's obituary in the *New York Sun* called him "the Babe Ruth of his day." But the talented outfielder played in just 1,049 games, the equivalent of less than seven full modern seasons. As talented and charismatic as he was, Donlin would be remembered only in his own times. One gets the feeling that the loss is ours. "If some of our present day ball players have 'color,'" wrote McHale, "Mike Donlin must have been a rainbow."

CAMPBELL GETS A PARTING GIFT

In 1912, the Boston Braves swapped aging Mike Donlin to Pittsburgh even-up for outfielder Vin Campbell. Campbell, like Donlin, was an outfielder who'd put up some great batting averages, but who often seemed uninterested in his baseball career. Campbell hit .326 for Pittsburgh as a rookie in 1910. He followed that up by hitting .312 in limited play in 1911. With Boston in 1912, Campbell hit a solid .296. But he wasn't happy on the last-place club, wasn't happy to be making less money than he had the year before in Pittsburgh, and reportedly was no fan of manager Johnny Kling. So Campbell took a page from the Mike Donlin playbook and sat out the entire 1913 season.

In 1914, Campbell jumped to the new Federal League. He hit .318 that year, then .310 in 1915. But the Federal League folded after the 1915 season. Campbell, then just 27, never played again. He left a career batting average of .310. Some theorized that Campbell was blackballed from baseball due to his reputation as a malcontent and contract jumper. But reports from the time indicate that Campbell turned down an offer to join Cincinnati.

While Campbell had stopped playing baseball, his association with the game wasn't yet over. The outfielder took the former owners of the defunct Federal League Newark Peppers to court, arguing that he had a multi-year contract and thus was owed his salary for 1916 whether the Federal League existed in 1916 or not. In early 1918, the courts ruled in Campbell's favor, awarding him $5,957.40.

LITTLE EVA AND HIS WOMAN

Bill Lange had speed, power, popularity, good looks, and a .330 career batting average—all the ingredients a ballplayer needs for fame. Unfortunately, the 1890s Chicago center fielder also had a crush on a girl from the snooty side of town. As a result, he's remembered today for little beyond his distinctly unflattering nickname, Little Eva. (Apparently some thought his stride lacked masculinity.)

By the end of the 1899 season, Lange had hit .319 or better for six consecutive seasons. He was one of the best baserunners and defensive outfielders of his era. He was only 28, and should have had many more fine seasons ahead of him.

Instead, he left baseball for a woman. Lange had proposed to the daughter of a wealthy San Francisco real estate magnate. Depending on which story you believe, either his new wife or his new father-in-law insisted that Lange give up baseball for a more socially acceptable line of work, and Lange agreed. Chicago reportedly offered Lange the then-sizable sum of $10,000 to remain in baseball, but Lange said money wasn't the issue.

For a 19th-century player to be famous today, it's a virtual necessity that he be in the Hall of Fame. Without a plaque, players from the game's early days tend to be forgotten. The minimum major league service time required for induction in the Hall of Fame is ten years. Lange had played just seven seasons before walking away from the game. He had traded his legacy for a woman. It would turn out to be a bad trade. The woman divorced him just a short time later. Despite the end of the marriage, Lange never returned to baseball.

Lange may have been disappointed at the way things played out, but he did okay in the end. Thanks in part to the start his former father-in-law had given him in business, Lange became successful in real estate. He spent close to half a century as one of San Francisco's leading citizens. Lange died of a heart attack in 1950.

GO WEST, YOUNG PITCHER

Few successful players have ever walked away from the big leagues as abruptly as Henry Schmidt. The right-hander went 22–13 in his rookie year of 1903, but when Brooklyn sent him his 1904 contract, the 22-game winner returned it unsigned. Attached was a note reading, "I do not like living in the East and will not report." He never pitched in the majors again.

In truth, Schmidt seems unlikely to have gone on to great fame even had he stayed in the majors. The former Pacific Coast League pitcher already was 30 years old by the end of his first season in the bigs, quite late to be making a start. And Schmidt was far from brilliant in the Pacific Coast League after jilting Brooklyn. He was released by the Oakland Oaks just two years after his brief fling with major league stardom. The pitcher's wife reportedly created "quite a lively little scene" with the club's president when she learned her husband had been dropped from the squad. Schmidt's minor league career ended three years later. Oddly, the man who walked away from the majors because he said he didn't like to live in the east later took a job with a railroad based east of the Mississippi. He died at the age of 52 in Nashville.

TOO MUCH WEALTH FOR FAME

Arthur "Tillie" Shafer might have become one of the top infielders in the National League in the 1910s, if only he'd had more interest in playing the game. The former Santa Clara College star, signed by the Giants in 1909 on the recommendation of Fred Snodgrass, had blazing speed, a splendid throwing arm, and the best batting eye in the game according to the *New York Evening Journal*. He hit little in brief trials in 1909 and 1910, but was slated to get regular playing time for New York in 1911 . . . until he failed to report. Shafer had spent the off-season in Japan coaching college baseball teams. When he finally returned to the U.S., he decided to stay with his ailing mother in Los Angeles rather than rejoin the Giants. (Some reports held that Shafer's mother insisted her son remain at home.) The Giants made the World Series that year without him, but lost to the Philadelphia A's in six games. Giant shortstop Art Fletcher hit just .130 in the Series. Shafer could have had those 1911 World Series starts had he been with the club.

Shafer returned to the Giants in 1912, and that year his talent finally started to translate into production. Though again just a part-time player, he hit .288 and received considerable acclaim for his defense. Yet after the season Shafer announced he was retiring. "I have positively decided to get out of the game," Shafer told the press. "[Giant manager John] McGraw has not enough money in his treasury to tempt me to alter my present plans. I have had enough of the game and think that I will tour Europe this year."

The tour of Europe hints at part of the reason for Shafer's recalcitrance: he came from a wealthy family and didn't need baseball's money. The Giants were able to convince Shafer to return in 1913, and in his first season as a regular he hit .287, stole 32 bases, and did a fine job on the infield. "Temperamental Tillie" was just 24 years old and very well might have developed into a star. Instead he announced his retirement once again, and this time he made it stick, though both New York and the new Federal League bid heavily for his services. The president of the Giants even traveled cross-country to campaign for the infielder's return. "I have satisfied every ambition in a baseball way; now I want to forget I was ever in it," Shafer said. "It is an episode in my life that I am trying hard to forget. I have plenty of money and I'm not dependant upon the $7,500 a year from the Giants."

Shafer offered many reasons for his desire to leave baseball during his time with New York. He said he didn't like the life of a ballplayer. He said he didn't like the eastern climate. He said he didn't like the fact he'd played 15 games in the outfield in 1913, taking playing time away from perhaps his only friend on the club, Fred Snodgrass. Shafer even complained that as one of the few attractive young bachelors on the popular Giants, "I get way too many perfumed notes." "The oldest base ball inhabitants assert there is no record of any player ever retiring from the game because he received perfumed notes," wrote one paper in response to this last complaint. "It was suggested by one base ball man here that Shafer engage a guardian to protect him from admirers."

Shafer's wealth and breeding reportedly caused him problems among his fellow ballplayers. Teammates and opponents considered Shafer a soft, effeminate, spoiled Mama's boy. It certainly didn't help that he'd had been stuck with the less-than-masculine nickname "Tillie," reportedly by his own teammate, veteran outfielder Cy Seymour. According to *Baseball Magazine*, only the intervention of McGraw on Shafer's behalf kept razzing under control.

Shafer might have been too soft for baseball, but he apparently wasn't too soft for war. He joined the Navy after leaving baseball and trained to fly a "hydro-airplane" during World War I. In 1918, the papers noted that the man who once refused to suit up for the Giants now was playing for the Navy Training Station team in San Diego. In late December of that year *The Sporting News* ran what that paper called its "annual story that Tillie has been invited to come back."

"The former third baseman of the Polo Grounds is being sought once more by manager McGraw," said the article. But Shafer never would return. After the war he found success in real estate and as part owner of a large fruit distributor. Only years later would he come to regret abandoning his baseball career. "I shouldn't have broken and run that way," a 43-year-old Shafer told *Baseball Magazine* in 1933. "I've been sorry ever since . . . But I hadn't learned enough about life when I came up with the Giants."

Shafer lived until 1962—long enough to see the team that he had so often refused to join in New York join *him* in California.

Tony Cuccinello

PART IV
MISSED MILESTONES

Securing a prominent spot in the record books or winning a major award virtually ensures a player's place in history. Earl Webb had just four full seasons in the majors, but he hit a record 67 doubles in one of them, so he's remembered. Zoilo Versalles hit just .242 in his career, but he won the 1965 American League MVP Award, so he's remembered, too. Such accomplishments mean careers will come up in conversation.

This aspect of fame has a flip side, however. When one's place in history depends on one's place in the record books, narrowly missing a milestone can mean completely missing fame. How many people remember that Al Cowens and Glenn Davis each finished second in the voting for an MVP award . . . that is, aside from Cowens and Davis themselves? Such close calls don't make you famous. At best, they make you the answer to a trivia question.

15

LOSING THE
NUMBERS GAME

I n the words of the Roman poet Horace, "we are just statistics." Horace Clarke, a career .256 hitter, might have different feelings on the matter, but the hard truth is that in baseball, the numbers on the scoreboard aren't the only ones that count. There also are the numbers on the back of one's bubblegum card, the batting averages and ERAs that often define a ballplayer.

These numbers can be unforgiving. One pitcher becomes a 20-game winner, another ends the year with 19. One hitter leads the league in batting, another is robbed by a diving catch in his final trip to the plate and falls to second. The difference between their seasons might be miniscule—statistically, a matter of chance—but it also is a matter of record. There is no silver medal. Numbers can carry a ballplayer to fame—but each time they do, they leave someone else behind.

.000087 AWAY

A major league regular might get 500 to 600 at-bats in the course of a season. Turn just one hit into an out for such a player, and his batting average for the year will drop by nearly two points—a .302 hitter will become a .300 hitter, for example. Two points might not sound like much, but batting titles have been decided by less. Considerably less. Four major leaguers lost batting titles by less than *half* a point in the 20th century. Three of those narrow losers—Bill Terry in 1931, Ted

Williams in 1949, and Carl Yastrzemski in 1970—went on to become Hall of Famers, so it's fair to say the batting title that slipped away cost them no great fame. But for the fourth narrow loser—the man who lost the closest big league batting race of all—the batting title represented his last, best shot at glory.

Tony Cuccinello had had a nice career. By the end of 1944, the infielder had played 14 seasons in the majors and had even been named to two All-Star teams as a reserve. But All-Star teams or no, Cuccinello was no star, certainly not by the mid-1940s. He wasn't fast, didn't have much of an arm, lacked power, and had a batting average that was, well, average. There had been a time, long before, when it appeared that Cuccinello's hitting might be something more than mediocre. He'd hit .312 and .315 in his first two big league seasons, back in the early 1930s with the Reds. But he'd never returned to those levels, though he had occasionally come close. "I hit .300 and over with the Reds, but somehow I've never been able to do it since," Cuccinello said in 1935. "I really don't know why . . . I haven't seemed to improve myself."

Cuccinello hit just .226 in 1940, a poor enough showing to drop him right out of the league. He spent 1941 as a player/manager in the minors, his major league days apparently over. "It's disappointing [that] I haven't made a great record as a hitter," Cuccinello once said. "But that's merely because I am not a great hitter. I might as well admit it and get it over with."

It would take a world war to resurrect Cuccinello's career. By 1942, the military draft had drained enough top talent out of the majors that there was once again room for the aging infielder. He resurfaced as a backup with the Braves that year, and hit .202 in 40 games. Cuccinello split 1943 between the Braves and White Sox, but hit only .230 and appeared in just 47 games all told. In 1944, he played a mere 38 games with Chicago and hit .262. Cuccinello looked for all the world like a marginal major leaguer playing out the string, his career batting average a pedestrian .278, his recent batting averages considerably worse. Once Cuccinello had been useful as a spare infielder, but at this point he lacked the range to play anywhere but third. Playing third for the White Sox in 1943 and 1944 wasn't going to get Cuccinello much action—Chicago had promising young Ralph Hodgin at the hot corner. But by 1945, Hodgin had been drafted into the Army. The 37-year-old Cuccinello would get to be a starter one last time. The White Sox hoped the old vet had one more decent season in him.

What happened in 1945 surprised even Cuccinello. By early May, his average was over .380. He couldn't keep up that pace, but still led the American League batting race as the season reached late September. "If I told you I had come up with a new stance or a new grip, or was doing something else I wasn't a year ago, I'd be kidding you," he said late that season. "No, it's just that balls are dropping in for me this year . . . No reason for it. Just plain luck."

It was, of course, an atypical season. In 1945, most of the game's top hitters were fighting

the war, not fighting Cuccinello for the batting crown. Nonetheless, Cuccinello wasn't just on the verge of winning a batting race, he was on the verge of writing his name into the record books as the oldest batting champion ever. He was about to become arguably the biggest baseball story of the year. "America's fourth war season has brought some odd developments in major league ball," wrote one publication, "but none stranger than . . . Tony Cuccinello—apparently washed up as a big leaguer in 1941—leading the American League hit parade."

The batting race wasn't over yet. With one day left in the regular season, Yankee second baseman Snuffy Stirnweiss had closed to within two points of Cuccinello, who'd led virtually all year. Stirnweiss' Yankees were finishing their season at home against Boston. Cuccinello's White Sox were scheduled to play a doubleheader at home against the Indians.

Stirnweiss got his first break that day before his game had even begun—Boston named Randy Heflin, a rookie with a 4–9 record, as starter. The Yankee infielder took advantage of the weak pitching, coming through with a hit in his first at-bat. Suddenly it seemed that Cuccinello's batting title was anything but assured. If Stirnweiss managed a hit in his second trip to the plate, things would really tighten up. But he hit a simple groundball to third. Boston third baseman Johnny Tobin booted it and was given an error, but errors count as outs when it comes to figuring batting averages. Cuccinello's lead in the batting race seemed safe . . . for a moment. Though the play initially had been ruled an error, an extremely charitable hometown scorer reversed his decision and credited Stirnweiss with a single. Now all Stirnweiss needed was one more hit in his remaining trips to the plate and he would have the lead in the batting race, pending Cuccinello's performance that day. Stirnweiss got the hit he needed in the 8th, off Otis Clark, a Boston righty working the last of the 12 games he'd pitch in his major league career.

If Cuccinello wanted the batting crown, he'd have to improve *his* average during Chicago's final-day doubleheader. But Cuccinello didn't get a hit that day. He didn't even get an at-bat. The doubleheader was rained out. Snuffy Stirnweiss won the batting title though he hadn't led the batting race until the last day of the season. "If the scorer hadn't changed [his ruling on that Stirnweiss grounder]," noted Cuccinello, "I would have won it."

LOSING IN A WALK

In 2003, Todd Helton staged a late-season charge at the National League batting crown. He hit in 20 of his last 21 games, and by the final day of the season was within striking distance of league leader Albert Pujols of the Cardinals. All Helton needed for the title was a hit in his final at-bat. Instead he was intentionally walked, despite the fact that the game had no meaning to league standings. Helton's final average was .35849, Pujols', .35871. Bruce Bochy, manager of the Padres team that issued the walk, later explained that he hadn't realized the batting title was on the line. "Obviously," said Helton, "I wasn't too pleased with that last at-bat."

It's hard to feel too sorry for Helton, though, considering that his batting numbers were inflated by playing home games in Coors Field. Pujols probably deserved the title anyway.

Stirnweiss' final margin of victory was .000087, the equivalent of just one hit in more than 11,000 at-bats. Though it remains the closest batting race loss in major league history, Cuccinello was savvy enough to know that the margin of loss was unimportant. "[Stirnweiss is] in the record book," he would later say. "Nobody remembers the guy who finished second."

As it turned out, that rained-out doubleheader hadn't just cost Cuccinello his chance to try for the batting title. It had cost him his last games in the majors. With the war over and younger players returning, the White Sox released the third baseman ten days after Christmas. Though Cuccinello nearly had won the batting title the season before, no one picked him up. He spent much of 1946 as the unemployed father of a seriously ill newborn child. But it wasn't long before Cuccinello returned to the big leagues as a coach. He remained in the game until 1969, one year after his Detroit Tigers won the World Series. It was the first title in Cuccinello's nearly 40 years in the majors. He died in 1995 at age 87.

> ### 3,000 MINUS 13 EQUALS A 29-YEAR WAIT
>
> Sam Rice retired in 1934 just 13 hits shy of 3,000, a number now considered among the most important of the game's statistical plateaus. "There wasn't much emphasis on 3,000 hits when I quit," Rice later explained. "And to tell the truth, I didn't know how many hits I had."
>
> Indeed, articles written about Rice's retirement at the time didn't mention his proximity to 3,000. But those 13 missing hits might have cost him. Despite a .322 career average, Rice wouldn't make the Hall of Fame until 1963, nearly three decades after the end of his career. "If I had hung around for one more season . . . and made 3,000 hits," complained the outspoken former outfielder, by the 1960s an elderly farm owner, "my election would have been just about automatic."

THE .299 CLUB

"To think you're a .300 hitter and end up at .237 in your last season, then find yourself looking at a lifetime .298 average," Mickey Mantle wrote in his autobiography, "it made me want to cry." But Mantle had no reason to cry where fame was concerned. Whether he hit .298 or

.300, Mantle remains one of the game's legends. Most ballplayers don't have this luxury. Coming up just short of .300 can mean coming up just short of lasting recognition as one of the game's elite hitters. This is a bit unfair, since rationally the difference between a .299 average and a .300 average is no more significant than the difference between .300 and .301, but that's round numbers for you. No one dreams of winning $999,999 in the lottery. "Someone who hits .300 looks back on the guy who [came up just short] and says, 'tough luck, buddy,'" explained Hall of Famer Warren Spahn. ".300 is the magic figure for batters. It pays off in salary and reputation. And those are the two things that keep a ballplayer in business."

A total of 11 hitters have retired with more than a thousand hits and career averages that round to .299.

Three of these men, Frank Demaree, Carl Furillo, and Bake McBride, would have been .300 hitters with just one more hit. (Technically, they would have been .2995 hitters, but since batting averages are inevitably rounded off at three digits, that's all it takes.)

Demaree, Furillo, and McBride are a mixed group. The one theme running through their baseball lives, if there is any theme at all, is that none of their careers ended particularly well.

THE .299 CLUB[*]

Frank Demaree	.29947
Carl Furillo	.29947
Bake McBride	.29925
Hardy Richardson	.29918
Rico Carty	.29914
Jack Doyle	.29906
Frank McCormick	.29897
Sammy West	.29896
Harry Rice	.29893
Dante Bichette	.29870
Charley Jones	.29862

[*]Minimum one thousand hits

• Frank Demaree. Cubs outfielder Demaree hit .325 in 1935, his second season spent mainly in the majors, .350 the next year, and above .300 in every season save one through 1940. But batting averages declined throughout baseball in the 1940s, and Demaree's declined considerably further than most. From 1941 through 1944, the end of his big league career, the two-time All-Star was reduced to the role of journeyman outfielder. He played for four teams in those four years, got into an average of only 45 games a season, and hit just .237. Demaree had 51 at-bats 1944. It was in the 51st—the final at-bat of the final year of his career—that Demaree's once stellar career batting average dipped below the .300 mark.

Without that .300 average, there was little reason to remember Demaree. The clean-cut Californian wasn't known for power or defense. He played in four World Series, but was on the losing side in each. He was a quiet sort, never one to get quoted much in the papers—no surprise, perhaps, considering both his parents were deaf. Even where Demaree was interesting, he was boring: The outfielder reportedly won several speed-typing championships. On the one hand, possessing such formidable speed-typing skills likely makes Demaree unique in major league history. On the other, typing is a pretty dull skill at any speed.

Demaree scouted for the White Sox after his playing days and managed a year in the minors. In the 1950s, he made his living in the movies. But while other former athletes go to Hollywood to become stars, Demaree worked behind the scenes at Universal Studios. He died of an intestinal hemorrhage at age 48.

• Carl Furillo. Furillo was one of the "Boys of Summer," the Brooklyn Dodgers of the 1950s. The Dodgers of that era have maintained a place in the hearts of Brooklyn natives, mostly since there weren't any new Brooklyn Dodgers to replace them after the team left for California in 1958. So Furillo, a rifle-armed outfielder, hasn't been completely forgotten. But if falling one hit short of .300 didn't cost Furillo his recognition, it was at least somewhat appropriate for a man said to be convinced the world was against him.

A leg injury late in the 1959 season slowed the aging outfielder by a step or two in early 1960. He had just two hits in ten at-bats that April when the Dodgers let him go. Furillo sued, claiming the team wasn't allowed to release him while he was injured. He won the suit and recovered his back pay—but never again played in the majors. Furillo couldn't even find a job in the minors and later claimed he'd been blackballed because of the lawsuit. Whatever the reason, his inability to get back to the majors cost him his chance to get back to .300. That two-for-ten 1960 performance had pushed him just below the magic mark.

Furillo owned a partial interest in a deli for a time after his playing days, and later took a job with Otis Elevators, installing elevator doors at the World Trade Center. He died in 1989.

• Bake McBride. McBride was National League Rookie of the Year in 1974, an All-Star in 1976, and a .300 hitter in each of the first five years of his career, albeit with little power. He was one of baseball's brightest young stars.

Then the knee problems started.

In 1976, McBride's left knee required surgery. In 1981, *both* knees went under the knife. McBride's game had been based on speed, but now he didn't even have a leg he could refer to as "my good leg." The outfielder blamed the artificial turf he played on as a Cardinal and Phillie for his knee pain. In 1982, at age 33, he finally got a chance to play on a grass home field in Cleveland, but by then it was too late. McBride played sparingly for two seasons with the Indians to close out his career. Thanks to injuries, McBride had just six seasons in which he played one hundred games. He hit .291 in his final year, not bad considering he could hardly run. But that was just low enough to shrink his lifetime batting average from .29975 before the season, which rounds up to .300, down to .29925, which doesn't.

Six years after McBride left the majors, he got one last chance to play ball professionally, in the ill-fated Senior League, the Florida-based baseball league for old-timers. "Bake McBride could still hit," wrote sportswriter Peter Golenbock, "but it wasn't clear that he could still walk."

Golenbock was right—McBride could still hit. Despite his bad knees, the man who'd come up one hit short of .300 in his major league career went 29 for 98 in the Senior League.

If you do the math, 29 for 98 works out to a batting average of .296. Bake McBride had come up exactly one hit short of .300 once again.

DANTE'S PURGATORY

Dante Bichette might hold the mark for narrowly missing key marks. He recently walked away from the game with a career batting average of .299, a career slugging average of .499 and 274 career home runs, only 26 short of 300. True, had Bichette not spent much of his career in that hitter's paradise known as Coors Field, his numbers would have been nowhere near as impressive, but history has a way of ignoring such details.

Phillie outfielder Chuck Klein's numbers aren't all that much better than Bichette's—.320 batting average, .543 slugging percentage, exactly 300 homers. And like Bichette, Klein played most of his career in a great hitter's park (the Baker Bowl) and a great hitter's era (the 1930s). Yet in 1980, decades after his career was over, Klein was elected to the Hall of Fame. As a .300 batter, .500 slugger, and 300 home run hitter, Bichette might have someday been grouped among the game's greats, deservedly or not. At .299, .499, and 274, it seems more likely that he'll be grouped among the game's pretty goods.

FAME OF 400 FALLS TO SHAME OF .248

If there is one seemingly certain route to glory in baseball, it's being the greatest power hitter in the game. Starting with Babe Ruth, 15 consecutive players who reigned as the active career home run leader reached the Hall of Fame. But the run of Hall of Famers that started with Ruth appears to have ended in 1989, with the retirement of Mike Schmidt. When Schmidt left the game, the active player who'd hit the most career homers was Darrell Evans. Despite his 414 home runs and all-around excellent career, no one's ever seemed particularly anxious to put Darrell Evans in the Hall of Fame. And since it is called the Hall of *Fame*, perhaps they have a point. Evans isn't all that famous. But why isn't he?

Perhaps Evans can blame Hank Aaron for his lack of fame. Evans' first big season was 1973, when he slugged 41 homers. The man hitting behind him in the Braves batting order most of that year was Hank Aaron. That season Aaron was stalking Ruth's record of 714 homers, and stealing the limelight from Evans in the process. "It is conceivable the Braves' third baseman will lead the National League in home runs," wrote one reporter that year, "and nobody would notice."

Or perhaps Evans can blame Candlestick Park for his lack of fame.

The slugger was shipped off to the Giants in the middle of the 1976 season. Candlestick Park's swirling winds and distant fences were blamed for sapping much of Evans' power in his seven and a half years in San Francisco. Evans had averaged close to 30 home runs a year in his last three full seasons in Atlanta. He hit more than 20 homers only once with the Giants.

Or perhaps Evans can blame Mike Schmidt for his lack of fame. The two men played the same position—third base—mainly in the same league and during the same years. Darrell Evans was in many ways a great player, but he was no Mike Schmidt—Schmidt very well might be the best third baseman in history. Thanks in no small part to Schmidt, Evans made the All-Star game only twice. And though Evans was regarded as an excellent fielder, he never won the Gold Glove—Schmidt won nine straight in the late 1970s and early 1980s.

Or perhaps Evans can blame Dwight Evans for his lack of fame. Baseball's two D. Evanses had remarkably similar careers. Darrell played 21 seasons starting in 1969; Dwight played 20 seasons starting in 1972. Darrell had 8,973 at-bats and 414 home runs, Dwight had 8,996 and 385. Each man led a league in homers once. Each was from California. You can't be famous if no one remembers which Evans you are. "[Dwight and I] kind of played the same way and were kind of perceived the same way," Darrell once said. "We always wanted to make the All-Star team at the same time, so we could change uniforms and see if anyone really noticed."

Or perhaps Evans can blame Dave Kingman for his lack of fame—specifically, his lack of a place in the Hall of Fame. When Evans retired, every player who'd hit at least 400 home runs was in the Hall—every player, that is, except Kingman, who'd retired with 442 in 1986. Everyone agreed that Kingman didn't belong in the Hall of Fame despite his 400 homers, which meant 400 was no longer one of those magic numbers that seems to guarantee a place in Cooperstown, like 300 wins for a pitcher. If not for Kingman, Evans would have been the *only* 400 man left out of the Hall, and surely there would have been greater inclination among voters to put him in. Instead, Evans received eight votes from the Hall's nearly 500 voters in 1995 and was dropped from the ballot after one year. Evans wasn't surprised. "When my name gets on [the Hall of Fame ballot]," he told a reporter in 1989, "people are probably going to say, 'Who is that guy?'"

Or perhaps Evans can blame 15 at-bats in October, 1984, for his lack of fame. In his 21 major league seasons, Evans reached the World Series just once. His Tigers beat the Padres in five, but Evans—alone among the Tiger's regulars—failed to produce at the plate. He managed just one lone hit, for a .067 average.

Or perhaps Evans can blame the lack of attention paid to the base on balls for his lack of fame. Evans walked 1,605 times in his career—that's good for tenth on the all-time list as of 2003. He led the National League in walks in 1973 and 1974, even though the dangerous Hank Aaron often was hitting behind him. In 1976, Evans set a National League record by walking in 15 consecutive games. You can bet that had the fans on the edge of their seats.

Yet in the end, Evans has no one to blame but himself for his lack of fame. He hit .208 and .207 in his final two seasons, pulling his batting average below .250 to its unfortunate final resting place, .248. Rightly or wrongly, batting averages above .300 tend to be associated with the words "great

DARRELL EVANS *IS* FAMOUS . . . JUST NOT IN OUR UNIVERSE

According to an article in *USA Today*, Darrell Evans and his wife, LaDonna, claimed to have seen an object 30 feet wide and triangular in shape hovering silently over a neighbor's house one night in the summer of 1982. The object, which apparently featured festive multi-colored lights, departed before Darrell could retrieve his camera. When the Evanses told their story, some delicately suggested that perhaps the couple had been looking at an airplane—there was an airport only a short distance away. But Darrell and LaDonna were convinced they'd been visited by a UFO. "My wife was a stewardess," Darrell told the press. "So she knows what an airplane looks like." Oh.

It turned out that Evans' alien visitors were intergalactic batting coaches. He'd been slumping early that season, but "soon after [we saw the UFO], things turned around," Evans said. "It definitely helped my career."

"I believe there is something out there," he continued. "They've evolved beyond war; they've come through it and they want to come and show us how. I hope it happens." In the meantime, they'll just help baseball players get out of hitting slumps. It's good to know E.T. has his priorities straight.

hitter," batting averages short of .200 with the words "non-hitter." Evans' .248 leaves him south of the tipping point of .250. The number .248 was no doubt very much on the minds of the Hall of Fame voters who overwhelmingly decided Evans didn't belong in Cooperstown.

It's possible that some day Evans' career will be held in higher esteem. Thanks in part to Oakland general manager Billy Beane and his ilk, baseball fans are starting to pay more attention to stats like on-base percentage. Maybe those reviewing Evans' career ten years from now will put less weight on his .248 batting average, and more on his fine .361 career on-base percentage. Yet it seems more likely that Evans' fame will fade

A BAD ERA FOR A GOOD ERA

An ERA above 4.00 is a bit like a batting average below .250. In the eyes of many, the number alone is enough to prove the player wasn't great. Wes Ferrell's career ERA is 4.04, but he might very well have been great, or something close to it. Ferrell simply pitched at the wrong time for impressive pitching stats.

The vast majority of Ferrell's major league innings were thrown between 1929 and 1938, one of the greatest hitter's eras in history. His seemingly unimpressive 4.04 career ERA is considerably more impressive when one considers that the AL as a whole had an average ERA of 4.54 in those years. And Ferrell was at the additional disadvantage of pitching most of his career in Cleveland's League Park and Boston's Fenway Park, both somewhat hitter-friendly venues.

Ferrell won over 20 games in each of his first four full seasons, 1929 through 1933. Arm problems then robbed him of his fastball, yet he still won a league-leading 25 in 1935 and followed it with another 20-win season in 1936. But the arm troubles grew worse, and after drifting around baseball for parts of five more seasons, then managing in the minors, he went home to North Carolina to live the life of a gentleman farmer. Well, a farmer, anyway. Some might argue that Ferrell's temper was a bit too hot and his language a bit too coarse to call him a gentleman.

Ferrell's career record was an impressive 193–128, but today he's mainly remembered as one of the best hitting pitchers in baseball history and as the brother of Hall of Fame catcher Rick Ferrell. One can't help but think the Hall picked the wrong Ferrell. Not only was Wes one of the top pitchers of his day, he was a better hitter than his Hall of Famer brother. Wes' .280 average was just .001 less than Rick's, and Wes had significantly more power.

over time. With homers flying out of ballparks at record rates in recent seasons, Evans' total of 414 round-trippers will seem less impressive in the future. Already Rafael Palmeiro and Fred McGriff have stormed past 414. More very-good-but-not-great modern sluggers are sure to follow.

WRIGHT WRONGED

Lots of men have lost out on fame by losing a batting race. One man, Taft Wright, found a whole new way to fall short of glory. He *won* the 1938 batting race, only to see the official batting crown given to someone else instead.

In 1938, baseball rules required that a player appear in at least one hundred games to qualify for the batting title. Senators rookie outfielder Wright did this—barely. Fighting with the more established George Case, Sammy West, and Al Simmons for playing time in the Washington outfield, Wright got into exactly one hundred games, many of them as a pinch hitter. He had only 263 at-bats, but took full advantage of the chances he was given, hitting .350. That was tops in the league, but apparently being the best wasn't enough. American League president Will Harridge ruled that even though Wright met the official qualifications for the batting crown, his 263 at-bats weren't sufficient. The batting title would go to Jimmie Foxx, who'd hit .349, one point less than Wright, in more than twice as many at-bats.

That doesn't seem entirely fair, but then baseball never was entirely fair to Wright. He hadn't reached the major leagues until age 28, held back in part because he'd started as a pitcher and in part because his roly-poly build didn't look very athletic. "When I arrived at the Washington training camp," Wright later said, "I discovered there was no place for a fat man with a major league club."

After hitting .350 in part-time play in '38, Wright hit .309 as an everyday player in 1939. Traded to the White Sox the next year, he hit .337 in 1940, then .332 in 1941. In '41, Wright drove in runs in 13 consecutive games, an AL record—but that year Joe DiMaggio collected hits in a record 56 straight, and no one paid much attention to Wright's streak. Wright's potent bat should have won him fame. Instead, he was the target of ridicule. Fans, opponents, teammates, and sportswriters made fun of his weight, his North Carolina drawl, his straight-from-the-tobacco-farm wardrobe, and his perceived low intelligence. At first Wright took the ribbing in good humor. But when it didn't let up, it reportedly began to get to him. "Taft was made a kind of unwilling straight man," wrote the *Washington Times Herald*. "Life became rather unbearable for him."

In 1942, Wright's .333 batting average would have been good enough for second in the American League, behind only Ted Williams, but again Wright hadn't played enough to qualify—he'd been drafted into the military just 85 games into the season. "Taffy" Wright spent the next three and a half years in the war.

He was 34 years old when he returned, and he wasn't the same. Complaining that he'd lost his baseball muscles, Wright hit .275, quite a comedown for a man who'd been a .328 career hitter before World War II intervened. He rebounded in 1947, and for a time in mid-September trailed Ted Williams by only four points in the batting race. But Wright tailed off to finish at .324, fourth in the league. "I sure am going to wear out them pitchers in 1948," Wright promised after the 1947 season.

He didn't. The aging Wright hit just .279 in 1948, then .235 in limited action with the A's in 1949. He retired to his North Carolina farm, then to Orlando, Florida, where he owned a bar that was popular with local sports fans. Wright died in 1981.

PATIENCE GETS PUNISHED

Ted Williams lost the 1954 batting title by taking too many walks. The rules then in place required that hitters record at least 2.6 at-bats per team game to be eligible for the title. Williams hit a league-best .345, but had just 386 at-bats, 15 short of the 401 necessary. He'd missed some games to injury that year, but still would have managed the requisite number of at-bats with ease if not for one thing—he walked a league-leading 136 times, and walks don't count as at-bats. Bobby Avila and his .341 average were awarded the title.

The same thing happened to Williams in 1955, when he hit .356, but lost the batting title to Al Kaline's .340. That year injuries held Williams to just 98 games, however, so it's tougher to make an argument that he was robbed.

The batting title eligibility rule was altered in 1957 to require 3.1 plate appearances per game, walks included.

Taft Wright had had just three full seasons and parts of two others to make a name for himself before the war interrupted his career. He might have succeeded, too, except his one batting title was overturned. Today, few fans remember his name.

LITTLE RESPECT

It's possible that 1910 Boston Brave infielder Pete Burg lost his place in the record books to a Bill Veeck promotional stunt. On August 19, 1951, Veeck famously sent 3'7" Eddie Gaedel up to hit in the 1st inning of a St. Louis Browns game. Gaedel drew a walk and immediately was removed for a pinch runner, ending his stay in the majors. Thanks to that one plate appearance, Gaedel is a permanent part of baseball lore. But his presence in the record books means that the *next* shortest man in the history of the majors has been deprived of his place in history. That hardly seems fair, considering that this next shortest man had to overcome long odds to become a big league-quality ballplayer despite small size. All Gaedel did to earn *his* fame was not grow.

According to many record books, Pete Burg, listed at just 5'1", is the second shortest ballplayer in the game's history. Tragically, Burg's time in the majors was, yes, short. He played just 12 games at third for the Braves, and one at, inevitably, shortstop. But he managed to hit .326 in 46 at-bats when he got his chance, which might have earned him at least a (sorry) small measure of recognition had Gaedel not usurped his glory. Perhaps Burg's, uh, shortcomings, were in the field, where he committed eight errors in those 13 games.

The only trouble with this short story is it might be a big mistake. Some baseball researchers believe that the Pete Burg who played briefly for the Braves was a different Pete Burg from the minor leaguer who stood just 5'1". That would be a shame, because if Burg *isn't* the shortest non-Gaedel major leaguer, we might never know which of the ten or so men listed at 5'3" was the smallest of the small. Unless someone took the trouble to apply calipers to this veritable Lilliput of players, the shortest man to earn his way to the bigs seems doomed to be forgotten.

RAINED OUT

Poorly timed storms denied a pair of power-hitters their best shots at a day in the sun . . .

• Cliff Johnson. On August 25, 1975, a rainout cost Houston Astro slugger Johnson a chance at the record for home runs in consecutive games. Johnson already had homered in five consecutive contests when he went deep off Bob Gibson in the top of the 11th inning to give Houston a 4–3 lead over the Cardinals, seemingly extending his power streak to six. Unfortunately for Johnson, a downpour stopped play with two outs in the bottom of the 11th. When the game couldn't be resumed for the final out, it reverted to a 3–3 ten-inning tie. Officially, everything that took place in the eleventh—including Johnson's homer—never took place at all. "I've never seen this happen in the 35 years I've been in baseball," said umpire Ed Sudol. "A rainout with one out to go."

Johnson's home run streak was officially over—despite the fact that he'd hit a home run. "That's the way it goes," said Johnson. "At least the rain will help the farmers."

The major league record for homers in consecutive games is eight, so there was no guarantee that Johnson would have reached it, even had that homer counted. Still, there was a cruel irony to the situation. As an Astro, Johnson was required to play his home games in the spacious Astrodome, where many well-hit balls that would have been homers anywhere else stayed in the park. Now in a *road* game, he hit a home run that was wiped out because he *wasn't* playing in the Astrodome, where the roof made rainouts impossible.

Oddly, it was the second time Johnson had hit a home run that didn't count during his hot streak. He'd also connected in an exhibition game against Houston's Des Moines affiliate.

With no home run streak, Johnson instead is remembered as a somewhat enigmatic slugger and as the man who injured Yankee closer Goose Gossage's thumb in a 1979 shower fight, perhaps costing the Yankees their fourth straight pennant. "I'm not like people think," Johnson said in 1979. "I'm not trouble. I'm not looking to hurt anybody. I can't believe all that has happened this season. I'm going to be remembered for all the wrong reasons."

Johnson was right. He would be remembered for the wrong reasons, specifically for causing trouble. He was shipped off to Cleveland that June, starting a stretch that would take him to six teams in seven years.

• Bobby Bonds. The term 40/40 club has received considerable attention in recent years. Only three major leaguers—Jose Canseco, Alex Rodriguez, and *Barry* Bonds—have accumulated the 40 steals *and* 40 homers in one season required for membership. The 40/40 club is so exclusive that hip-hop star Jay-Z borrowed the term 40/40 Club as the name for his own Manhattan nightclub.

Bobby Bonds might have become the first man to enter baseball's 40/40 club . . . if rainouts hadn't washed away two of his homers in 1973. Bonds ended the season with 43 steals and 39 home runs. On several occasions in his remaining years in the majors, Bonds predicted that he would reach the 40/40 plateau that had so narrowly eluded him in '73. He never did. With no 40/40 season, Bobby Bonds instead is remembered as a somewhat enigmatic slugger, and as the father of Barry Bonds, who did reach 40/40. Like Johnson, Bonds drifted around baseball after his washed-away chance at statistical notability, playing for eight teams in his final eight years in baseball.

Johnson and Bonds both are remembered for their stormy careers—yet if not for storms, they might be remembered for something else as well.

THE MAN WHO MEANT TO SINK THE CLIPPER

Johnny Babich wasn't a good enough pitcher to set any records worth remembering. But there *is* a chance that he once very nearly prevented a much better player from setting one of the most famous records of all time. Had he done so, it seems certain that Babich would have secured lasting infamy.

In 1941, A's pitcher Babich boasted that he was going to end Joe DiMaggio's famed hitting streak. Ordinarily such talk from a pitcher with a losing record would be chalked up to pure bluster. But Babich also explained *how* he planned to do it: He'd just retire Joe DiMaggio in his first trip to the plate, then walk him every other time up. An 0–1 day would end DiMaggio's streak as well as an 0–5.

By the time Babich and DiMaggio met on June 28, Joe D.'s hitting steak had captured the nation's attention. It was at 39 games, just two short of George Sisler's modern record of 41, five shy of Willie Keeler's all-time record of 44. If Babich carried out his plan, he surely would have become one of the game's great villains. The pitcher took care of the tough part—he retired DiMaggio in his first trip to the plate, though only after DiMaggio had scorched a ball just inches outside the left-field foul line. All that was left was to walk him three or four times. When DiMaggio came to the plate for his second at-bat in the 3rd inning, Babich started him with three pitches well off the plate, and it seemed the A's hurler intended to do as he'd said. But Joltin' Joe proved no easier to walk than he was to retire. He reached a ball outside the strike zone and shot it back through the middle. It was a clean single, and with DiMaggio hustling all the way, it turned into a double. New York pounded Babich all game, and he was pulled for a pinch-hitter in the 7th. DiMaggio's streak would roll on all the way to 56.

Did Babich really intend to walk DiMaggio in his remaining trips to the plate? There's no way to know for sure. Few men would intentionally set themselves up for the abuse the perpetrator of such a plot surely would endure. But then most men didn't hold a grudge against the Yankees the way Babich did. The pitcher had wasted several years of his career buried in the Yankee farm system, before being drafted away by the second-division Philadelphia A's. Ever since, Babich had seemed intent on sticking it to New York. In 1940, Babich's record was 14–13—yet he was 5–0 against the Yanks, allowing just 37 hits and 12 runs in 6 starts. New York lost the pennant by two games that year, and Johnny Babich was said to have taken pleasure in causing their downfall. "Babich?" Yankee manager Joe McCarthy reportedly moaned after one of those five wins. "Who in hell ever heard of Babich?"

Babich also might have considered Joe DiMaggio a personal rival, noted Richard Ben Cramer in his book *Joe DiMaggio: The Hero's Life.* DiMaggio had put together a 61-game hitting streak in the Pacific Coast League back in 1933. The pitcher who arguably came the closest to stopping it before then was none other than Johnny Babich. Babich had held the young DiMaggio hitless until the 8th, but Joe's triple in that frame kept his streak alive *and* beat Babich 1–0.

In his short major league career, Babich would compile an unimpressive record of 30–45, and an ERA of 4.93. He walked 220 batters in 592 innings. Three more walks and he might have been remembered forever.

THERE'S NO FAME BASED ON THE BASE ON BALLS

Certain stats carry significantly more weight in baseball circles than others, sometimes for reasons that don't seem entirely rational. Setting records or leading leagues in unpopular categories won't make you famous.

The walk is a prime example. They say a walk is as good as a hit, but they don't seem to mean it. Only eight ballplayers have more career walks than Eddie Yost—Rickey Henderson, Babe Ruth, Ted Williams, Barry

ANOTHER STREAK, ANOTHER BRUSH WITH INFAMY

Fifty-five years after A's pitcher Johnny Babich took his shot at ending Joe DiMaggio's hitting streak, White Sox pitcher Roberto Hernandez nearly became infamous for stopping a streak of a different sort—and he wasn't even playing in a game when he did it. Hernandez and his fellow 1996 American League All-Stars had just posed for a team picture when Hernandez slipped, swinging his arms backward to catch his balance. One of his flailing arm broke the nose of an All-Star teammate—Oriole shortstop Cal Ripken, Jr.

The freak injury threatened to end Ripken's record-setting consecutive-games-played streak. Hernandez avoided infamy when the nose was re-set without difficulty, and Ripken played on.

Bonds, Joe Morgan, Carl Yastrzemski, Mickey Mantle, and Mel Ott. That's pretty good company, considering six of the eight breezed into the Hall of Fame and the other two soon will do the same. Yet Yost never received a single Hall of Fame vote. True, the Senator third baseman probably doesn't belong in the Hall of Fame, but if the walk got *any* respect, surely someone would have given him a vote. It's not like it takes all that much to get one vote. Steve Yerkes once got a vote . . . Pep Young once got a vote . . . and Yerkes and Young can't claim to be the greatest in the game's history at anything. Yost, on the other hand, just might have been the greatest worker of walks who ever walked the Earth. Sure, eight men walked more often, but hitters like Ruth, Bonds, and Williams often walked because pitchers were afraid to pitch to them. No one was afraid to pitch to Ed Yost. The third baseman only once managed more than 14 homers in a season. When he walked, it was because he earned it.

Eight times Yost worked more than one hundred walks in a year. Six times he led the American League in walks. Four times he had more walks in a season than he had hits—and five additional times he was within ten walks of doing so. Yost became known as "The Walking Man," or "Mr. Wait." "Every time I look up," complained Yankee manager Casey Stengel, "that feller is on base."

Had the intelligent, handsome Yost played for Casey's Yankees or indeed any top team, the value of his great eye, patient style, and bat control might have been more widely appreciated. But he spent virtually his entire career with the uncompetitive Washington Senators. "We never even had a .500 season," Yost said after he'd left the game. "I look back and wish I had at least gotten to a World Series."

Yost retired with a .254 lifetime average and 139 home runs, but those numbers fail to show his true offensive contribution. The next year he began a long career as a major league coach. But coaching, like walking, is not a great way to gain fame. Yost had been in the majors more than a quarter century as a coach or player when the headline of an article in the *Wall Street Journal* asked a telling question. "Who," it wondered, "is Eddie Yost?"

Ferris Fain's fame fell victim to the walk's low status as well. Fain's willingness to work a walk is the main reason his career on-base percentage is a spectacular .425 despite his comparatively prosaic .290

career batting average. That on-base percentage is eighth among retired predominantly 20th-century players behind only Ted Williams, Babe Ruth, Lou Gehrig, Rogers Hornsby, Ty Cobb, Jimmie Foxx, and Tris Speaker. It's hard to find a better group of hitters—yet few would consider Fain an elite player, since his best skill was the quietest skill: dropping one's bat and trotting to first. Fain *averaged* more than 100 walks a season in his career, and thanks to those walks, he reached base more than 40 percent of the time in every one of his major league seasons—even 1953, when he hit just .256.

Like Yost, Fain never received a single Hall of Fame vote. But in Fain's case, lack of longevity was part of the problem. A ballplayer must appear in at least ten major league seasons to be eligible for the Hall; Fain played only nine. Thanks to World War II, Fain was nearly 26 when he reached the big leagues in 1947, and thanks to knee injuries, he was only 34 when he left. Seven full seasons and parts of two more wasn't enough time to build much of a legacy, except perhaps a legacy as an injury-prone hell-raiser. In 1951, Fain broke his foot when he kicked first base in anger after grounding out. In 1952, he broke his hand in a nightclub brawl. In 1953, he broke his hand again in another bar fight. In 1954, he hurt his knee in a home plate collision with Red Sox catcher Sammy White—perhaps just to prove he could get injured while actually playing baseball. None of Fain's off-the-field escapades affected his career much, but he never seemed to fully recover from that leg injury. Perhaps he should have stuck to punching drunks.

Fain returned to the Pacific Coast League as a coach and pinch-hitter in 1956, then became a building contractor in California. He continued to get into trouble after his playing days, serving time in his late 60s for growing sizable amounts of marijuana. Perhaps if Fain had received more fame for his playing career he could have supplemented his ballplayer's pension through autograph shows instead of drug production. But as *The Sporting News* noted after one of his arrests, "Ferris Roy Fain is not exactly a household name in modern-day baseball."

Fain died in 2001 at the age of 80.

In 1887, for one season and one season alone in baseball history, walks officially counted as hits. Perhaps they were on to something that year. Ever since, players like Yost and Fain who specialize in walks haven't received their due.

RE-JOYCE

"Scappy Bill" Joyce was in some ways the Ferris Fain of the 19th century. While Fain's .425 on-base percentage is highest among *20th-century* retired players not in the Hall of Fame, Joyce's .435 on-base percentage is highest among *all* players not in the Hall, and sixth overall. Like Fain, Scrappy Bill was, well, scrappy—never a man to back down from a fight. Like Fain, Joyce had leg injuries that cost him playing time. And like Fain, Joyce's major league career was over just nine years after it began. In Joyce's case, the central issue was money—Joyce sat out the entire 1893 season in a salary dispute and left the majors for good after 1898, when his team tried to impose heavy fines on its players to cut payroll costs.

The Fain/Joyce comparison isn't perfect, though. Joyce had considerably more power than Fain relative to his times, once leading the National League with 13 home runs. Joyce played third, Fain first. And if Joyce had a marijuana farm in his backyard, he at least had the good sense not to get caught.

ONE STRIKE YOU'RE OUT

Matt Williams was one of baseball's top third basemen in the 1990s. He was a five-time All-Star, a four-time Gold Glove winner, and he led the National League with 122 RBIs in 1990 and 43 home runs in 1994. It's those 43 home runs that are the story. On its surface, the number doesn't seem all that impressive; certainly not enough for lasting fame considering the astronomical home run totals men like Mark McGwire and Barry Bonds have posted since. What makes Williams' 43 notable is the season in which he hit them. He did it in 1994, the year that a strike shut down major league baseball after Williams' Giants had played only 115 games. In virtually any other year, Williams would have had 47 more games in which to chase the home run record. Unfortunately, he picked a bad year to have a great year.

Matt Williams was not a glamorous ballplayer. He was a modest, laid-back, family-oriented, prematurely bald slugger who'd never hit more than 39 home runs in a season until '94. Only once to that point had he ended a season with a batting average above .277. And the one time he'd played in the

World Series, he'd hit poorly in his Giants' earthquake-interrupted sweep at the hands of the A's. Williams was a very good player, but not a great player—and certainly not a player who appeared destined for great fame.

Yet in 1994, it was Matt Williams who took arguably the first serious run at Roger Maris' celebrated 61 home run season in the third of a century since the record had been set. In the years between 1961 and 1994, the best single-season home run total was 52, by Willie Mays in 1965 and George Foster in 1977. Now Williams had 43, and it was still the first half of August. The rate at which Williams had hit home runs in the first 115 games of the year put him on pace to hit 61 in the full 162—exactly the number required to tie the record. (Actually it put him on pace to hit 60.6, but since you can't hit six-tenths of a home run, it seems reasonably fair to round up.) Then on August 12 the strike hit. Days turned into weeks with few signs of progress. By September it was clear the lost games couldn't be replayed. Williams' chance for fame was gone, and soon the postseason was gone as well. For the first time since 1904, there would be no World Series. The lost Series, not Williams' lost run at 61, would come to symbolize the season—Matt Williams had been deprived even of his chance to be famous for being deprived of his chance to be famous.

"There's no reason to drive yourself nuts over something you can't control," said Williams in October 1994, when it was clear his opportunity to get the record was gone. "I really don't feel anything . . . I may hit more home runs next year, or I may not hit as many."

He didn't hit as many. Didn't even came close, and never again challenged Maris' home run record. Instead the record would fall to the likes of McGwire and Bonds a few years later. Matt Williams had one chance at fame. Like the Mighty Casey, he was struck out—but in Williams' case, it took only one strike to do it.

OUT OF ROUND

There's nothing like reaching a nice round number to get a power hitter to that next level of fame. Join the 500-home-run club and you're a legend. Make the 400 club and your status as a leading power hitter is secure. The 300 club? That one's getting a bit crowded these days, with membership climbing into the triple digits. Still, it's probably enough to ensure a steady stream of autograph requests for the rest of your life.

Retiring just short of one of these home run plateaus seems an awful waste of an opportunity for increased fame. The closest anyone's come to 500 without breaking the tape is Lou Gehrig with 493. Considering his tragic fatal illness, perhaps we can forgive the Iron Horse for bowing out.

Al Kaline came the closest to 400 without reaching the mark, retiring with 399 (not to mention a batting average of .297, just .003 below .300). But Kaline was a Detroit institution and certain Hall of Famer even if he did quit one homer short of exclusive company.

Dale Murphy's legacy was in far greater doubt when he retired with 398 home runs in 1993. It seems particularly odd for a player in such a stat-conscious era to walk away at such a time. But in truth, it wasn't entirely Murphy's choice to make. His club, the Colorado Rockies, wanted to make a roster move and had hinted at his release.

The slugging Mormon outfielder had been a star in his younger days with the Atlanta Braves, but went into a rapid decline in his early 30s. In 1992, knee surgery limited Murphy to 18 games and two homers. He landed with the expansion Rockies the following year, but didn't manage a single homer in his 26 games. When you can't hit a homer in Colorado, it's a pretty good sign it's time to hang them up. "I really wanted to [hit 400]," Murphy said later. "Probably more than I let on."

Though Murphy was a seven-time All-Star and two-time MVP, wire stories about his retirement began, "Just two homers shy of 400. . . ." It does not appear likely he'll make the Hall of Fame.

16

HONOR DOTH FORGET MEN'S NAMES

E ach winter, baseball keeps itself busy by handing out trophies to the top players of the season just completed. The most valuable player in each league is honored, as is the best pitcher, the best rookie, and a host of others. It's a bit like the Oscars, except that baseball distributes its awards one at a time over a period of months. The Oscars only seem to take that long.

Winning a major award adds to the stature of a ballplayer. Achieving baseball's ultimate honor—a plaque in the Hall of Fame—does so all the more. Over the years, a few men have found creative ways to miss out on such glory.

ROOKIE OF A YEAR TOO SOON

Del Ennis was a fine ballplayer, but he didn't leave us much reason to remember his name. The 1940s and 1950s Phillies outfielder hit over .300 a few times in his career, but he never led the league in batting, and his career .284 average barely warrants a second glance. Ennis hit 30 home runs a couple times, but never led the league there either, and his 288 career homers don't exactly jump off the page. He made the World Series with the Phillies in 1950, but there hit just .143 as the Yanks whizzed right past Philadelphia's "Whiz Kids." Ennis made the All-Star team three times, but was never really a big star, overshadowed by Richie Ashburn in his own outfield. Like many Phillie players, Ennis had a love/hate relationship with the Philadelphia fans. Despite his years of solid if unspectacular play, he often was the target of booing. "Those people don't realize what they've got going for them [in Ennis]," said Cubs catcher Walker Cooper.

Ennis never won an MVP, and he certainly didn't draw much support for the Hall of Fame, topping out at just short of 1 percent of the vote in 1966. But by all rights Del Ennis should have at least one honor on which to hang his hat. In April 1946, Delmer Ennis returned from more than two years in the Navy, stepped right into the Phillie lineup, and hit .313 with 17 home runs to win *The Sporting News'* inaugural Rookie of the Year Award.

Yet that accomplishment essentially has been forgotten. The Baseball Writers' Association started their own Rookie of the Year Award the following year, with Jackie Robinson taking home the initial trophy. Since the Writers' Association honor now is considered the "official" Rookie of the Year Award, Ennis' *Sporting News* trophy has been dropped from most record books, his name not appearing on lists of past rookie winners.

Today the Rookie of the Year Award is known as the "Jackie Robinson Award," after its first official winner. One suspects it's unlikely that we'd be calling it the Del Ennis Award today even if Ennis were considered the first man to win. But at the very least, Ennis' 1946 victory deserves to be remembered.

After 11 strong years in Philadelphia, Ennis spent the final three years of his career with the Cardinals, White Sox, and Reds. He retired with little fanfare in 1959 and returned to suburban Philadelphia to run his bowling alley, just another player whose time had passed. Ennis died in 1996.

THE HALL OF FAME'S CLOSEST CALL WITH FAME

Usually when someone narrowly misses making the Hall of Fame, it just means he has to wait a little longer. Orlando Cepeda fell seven votes short of election in 1994, but made the Hall in 1999. Jim Bunning missed by four votes in 1988, but made it in 1996. Nellie Fox came up an excruciating two votes short of the 297 needed in 1985, but he got in in 1997.

Nick Young might have lost his place in the Hall of Fame to the

THE CHICAGO ROOKIE OF THE YEAR CURSE

The Sporting News Rookie of the Year Award that Del Ennis won in 1946 was the most significant Rookie of the Year honor prior to the Baseball Writers' award, but it wasn't the *only* previous Rookie of the Year Award. The Chicago Chapter of the Baseball Writers' Association of America gave out their own prize between 1940 and 1946.

Indians shortstop Lou Boudreau won the initial award in 1940 and went on to a Hall of Fame career. But the 1941 through 1946 winners all had careers marked by tragedy and failure. Dodger outfielder Pete Reiser won in 1941, but saw his career shortened by frequent injuries (see page 158). Cardinal pitcher Johnny Beazley won in 1942, but hurt his arm in World War II (see page 179). Yankee third baseman Billy Johnson won in 1943, but lost the next two years to the war and had only two quality seasons upon his return. Braves pitcher Bill Voiselle took the award in 1944, but that would be his only season with more wins than losses (see page 298). Red Sox pitcher Boo Ferriss was honored in 1945, but after winning 46 games in his first two seasons, he'd have arm trouble and win only 19 more in his career. In 1946, the Chicago writers selected not Del Ennis, but first baseman Eddie Waitkus—perhaps because Waitkus played for the hometown Cubs. In 1949, Waitkus was shot and nearly killed in a Chicago hotel room (see page 299).

In 1947, the national Baseball Writers' Association started their own Rookie of the Year Award, and the Chicago writers stopped awarding theirs. Talented young ballplayers everywhere no doubt breathed a sigh of relief.

ultimate narrow margin—simple luck of the draw. But unlike Cepeda, Bunning, or Fox, Young probably never will be inducted.

Nicholas E. Young was a prominent player once—a prominent cricket player. He did play some baseball as well, but it was as an executive, not an athlete, that the Civil War vet made his mark on the game. In 1871, it was Young, a Treasury Department clerk and founding member of the Washington Olympics, who suggested that the nation's professional baseball clubs get together for a meeting. That meeting, held on March 17 in a room above Collier's Restaurant at the corner of Broadway and 10th in New York City, led to the formation of the world's first professional baseball league, the National Association of Professional Baseball Players. James Kerns, a U.S. Marshall and member of the Philadelphia Athletics, was selected as the Association's president. Young was given a lesser role.

"I was honored with the then thankless position of secretary," Young joked in 1906. "With the special privilege of buying my own stationary and postage stamps." It might not have been the most glamorous job, but the assignment seemed appropriate for Young. The government clerk was friendly and well-liked, but also modest and unassuming—a secretary by nature, not leadership material.

Young remained in the role of secretary until the National Association's demise in 1875. When the National League was formed to replace it in 1876, Young again was named secretary. According to Dr. Harold Seymour's seminal history of the game, *Baseball: The Early Years,* the National League selected its first executives by picking cards out of a hat. Each of the teams that was to join the league had one card. Hartford's card came out first, so that team's representative, Morgan Bulkeley, became the National League's first president. Bulkeley, son of the founder of Aetna Insurance, served as president of the National League for just one year, and was an absentee figurehead of a president at that. Yet decades later, Bulkeley was enshrined in the Hall of Fame simply because he'd been the first president of the NL. If Bulkeley truly was selected simply because his card was the first out of a hat, then Nick Young, Washington's representative, missed being immortalized in the Hall of Fame by exactly one draw of the cards. (Some baseball researchers have suggested that the card-from-a-hat tale was a mere cover story concocted by Chicago White Stockings owner Bill Hulbert to keep bickering over the choice of league president to a minimum. After all, try to pick the best man for a job, and everyone will pull for their own candidate; let fate decide, and people tend to live with the result.)

Bulkeley didn't even bother to attend the league meetings during his year as president, but he later served a more active role as president of Aetna Insurance, then as mayor of Hartford, governor of Connecticut, and U.S. Senator. Bulkeley even received some support for the Republican Vice Presidential nomination under William McKinley in 1896.

As for Young, he finally got a chance to be National League President in 1885. The teams still didn't think of him as a true top man, they'd simply decided they wanted a leader who'd do as he was told, not one who was trying to lead all the time. "Uncle Nick" Young was well liked during his presidency, but served mainly as an administrator, not a shaper of policy. Young remained National League president into the early years of the 20th century, when intra-league tensions forced his resignation. He returned to the Treasury Department, though he continued to attend ball-games in Washington whenever he got a chance. Young became seriously ill in the early 1910s, went blind in 1914, and died two years later.

Young had played crucial roles in the formation of arguably the two most influential leagues in baseball history, and was one of the longest-serving presidents in the history of the National League, yet

THE LONG WAIT

The first Hall Of Fame election was held in 1936. Five players were enshrined that year, all stars of the early 20th century. The intention had been to honor 19th-century greats as well, but the committee put in charge of selecting old-timers couldn't manage the necessary 75 percent support for any player—Cap Anson and Buck Ewing fared best, at 51 percent. The stars of the early days would have to wait.

In the years that followed, most of the 19th-century players who received significant support in that first vote were elected to the Hall. In fact, of the 13 old-timers who got at least eight of the possible 78 votes in that 1936 election, 12 are now Hall of Famers. The lone exception: Herman Long, who finished eighth in 1936 with 15.5 votes, ahead of such well-known future Hall of Famers as George Wright, Amos Rusie, Al Spalding, Hughie Jennings, and Monte Ward.

As the years went by, support for Long among Hall of Fame voters only declined. Long's candidacy was based on defense—he was considered the top fielding shortstop of the 1890s—and defensive players generally depend on testimonials from those who saw them play to establish their greatness. Those who could vouch for Long died off as time passed, and eventually his skills were forgotten. The speedy German speaker couldn't even hang onto his nickname. He'd once been known as "The Flying Dutchman." Honus Wagner had long since taken over the title.

The hot-tempered Long managed in the minors after his major league playing career ended in 1904, and there were rumors he was in the running for a job piloting Boston's National League team. But Long's "love of drink" ended his managing career, and he contracted tuberculosis a short time later. The illness ravaged Long's health and depleted his financial resources. He died in 1909 at age 49, reportedly broke and alone.

he's largely forgotten. In 1939, a *Boston Globe* columnist stumped for the election of Young and fellow baseball pioneer Harry Wright into the Hall of Fame as key early organizers of professional baseball. Wright was elected in 1953. Young in all likelihood never will be enshrined. But if the stories are true, he was once just a card away.

A BANG-BANG PLAY SHOOTS DOWN A TRIPLE CROWN

The Triple Crown isn't an award, exactly. It's merely a collection of offensive accomplishments. It is, however, an extremely prestigious collection of accomplishments. Only 11 major leaguers won a Triple Crown in the 20th century (that is, led a league in batting average, homers, and RBIs in the same year). All eleven are in the Hall of Fame—Nap Lajoie, Ty Cobb, Rogers Hornsby, Jimmie Foxx, Chuck Klein, Lou Gehrig, Joe Medwick, Ted Williams, Mickey Mantle, Frank Robinson, and Carl Yastrzemski. A 12th man, Al Rosen, once came within inches of adding his name to the list. Unlike the other 11, Al Rosen is not a Hall of Famer. Missing the Triple Crown cost him his one chance to place his name among the greats of the game.

Rosen's major league career got off to a bit of a late start. World War II and college slowed his progress, and when he finally reached the top of the Cleveland Indians' farm system in the late 1940s, he found his path to the big leagues blocked by Indian All-Star Ken Keltner at third, and, in 1949, solid hitter Mickey Vernon at first. Keltner faded in 1949 though, and the 26-year-old Rosen finally got his chance to take over at the hot corner for Cleveland. He hit .287 with 116 RBIs and a league-leading 37 home runs in 1950, and backed it up with two more solid seasons in '51 and '52. But entering 1953, no one would have considered Al Rosen a Triple Crown threat—not even with the American League's best hitter, Ted Williams, off flying jets in Korea. Rosen hadn't managed more than

> ### ANOTHER LOST CROWN
>
> Al Rosen wasn't the only man to lose a Triple Crown by a narrow margin. In 1949, Ted Williams missed a Triple Crown when he lost the batting title to George Kell, .3429 to .3427. But Williams won the Triple Crown on two other occasions and today is considered one of the great hitters in baseball history, so his close call in 1949 didn't cost him much in terms of fame.

28 homers or 105 RBIs since his rookie year. He'd hit a career-best .302 in 1952, but even that had been 25 points short of the batting title.

Yet with one day left in the 1953 season, Rosen had run away with the American League RBI title and maintained a slim lead over Philadelphia outfielder Gus Zernial for the home run title. Rosen's pursuit of an unexpected Triple Crown came down to the batting race. Heading into the last game, Rosen's average was .333. That would have been enough to lead the league the year before, but in 1953, it left him .003 behind Senator first baseman Mickey Vernon's .336. It wasn't the first time Vernon had stood in Rosen's way. Just four years earlier, Vernon's solid play at first base for the Indians was one reason Rosen had remained stuck in the minors.

With everything riding on his final game of the season, Rosen singled in the first, then doubled in the third, pushing his average up to .3356. That rounded up to .336, but it still wasn't enough to catch Vernon. Rosen grounded into a force in the 5th, eliciting groans from the crowd of 9,579 who'd turned out for the otherwise-meaningless game to root for a Triple Crown. Rosen bunted for a single in the 7th, and his average climbed to .3361. But it *still* wasn't enough. The stadium announcer was keeping everyone posted on the news from Washington: Mickey Vernon had lifted *his* average to .3377. It was still possible for Al Rosen to win the Triple Crown, but two things had to happen—Rosen had to get one more hit, and Vernon had to make one more out.

When the Indians reached the 9th, it wasn't even certain that Rosen would get another at-bat. He was due up fourth in the inning, meaning someone had to reach base. That someone turned out to be Indians backup catcher Joe Ginsberg, who worked a one-out walk. Cleveland pitcher Art Houtteman, up next, intentionally struck out to avoid grounding into a game-ending double play. Rosen was due up after the pitcher's spot in the order—fortunately, Cleveland manager Al Lopez had inserted Rosen in the leadoff slot that day, correctly forecasting that the third baseman might need every at-bat he could get to catch Vernon. On the mound for Detroit was rookie pitcher Al Aber.

Aber might very well have been rooting for Rosen to get his hit. When the year began, the men had been teammates in Cleveland. Aber had been dealt to Detroit in June, a trade that netted the Indians both Houtteman and Ginsberg, among others. Though Rosen had played only a few years in the majors by 1953, he was a team leader whom Indian rookies like Aber tended to admire. Now Rosen needed a hit for the Triple Crown, and Aber was in a position to help. Only the pressure of the moment appeared to overwhelm the pitcher—he couldn't get the ball over the plate. Aber's first three pitches were nowhere near the strike zone. Usually a walk is a positive result for a hitter. In this case, a walk would cost Rosen his shot at the Triple Crown. The fourth pitch was a ball, too, but Rosen understood the situation and swung anyway, fouling it off. Three more bad pitches followed, and a desperate Rosen fouled them off as well. When Rosen stepped to the plate that inning, he no doubt was hoping for a hit. By this point he must have been hoping for nothing more than a pitch he could reach. Aber's eighth pitch wasn't much better than the first seven, but Rosen had to swing. He chopped a high, slow hopper towards third and started running.

The ball was charged by Tiger third baseman Gerry Priddy, who'd been playing Rosen deep—so deep, in fact, that some later speculated he was trying to offer his fellow third baseman a no-risk bunt single. Now it seemed Rosen's chopper might serve the same purpose. Priddy once had been among the better defensive infielders in the game, but by 1953 he was well past his prime, and this was no sure out. Priddy fielded and fired to first. Priddy would be out of the majors by the next year; this would be the last play of his career.

Waiting for the throw at first was Fred Hutchinson. Hutch had been with the Tigers since 1939 . . . as a pitcher, and recently as the team's player/manager. The sight of him anywhere but on the mound was an oddity. Hutchinson would play a grand total of one game in the field in his ten-year career, and this was it. He'd pitched in only three games all year, and with the season drawing to a close must have realized that this would be his final game as an active player. No doubt he didn't want to spend it on the bench.

Rosen and the ball arrived at first virtually the same time. Hutchinson reached for the throw. Rosen leaped for the bag. The crowd roared, certain he had his hit.

Umpire Hank Soar called Rosen out. "I thought I might have had him," Hutchinson said after the game. "But I wouldn't have argued if he had been called safe."

Over at third, Priddy wasn't so sure. "I though he was safe," he said.

But Rosen knew otherwise. "The umpire was right," he said. "He could have called me safe, but in my heart I'd have known I was out and I wouldn't have wanted to win it that way. . . . It was my own fault. I tried to leap for the base and I missed it. I didn't brush my spikes against it until I was almost past it."

The news arrived from Washington a short time later. Vernon had made an out in his last at-bat. The bang-bang play at first had indeed cost Rosen the Triple Crown. "I feel very bad about losing it after coming so close," said Rosen. "I gave it a battle. I gave it all I had."

Though his playing career was over, Fred Hutchinson continued to manage in the majors for more than a decade. In 1961 he took the Cincinnati Reds to an unexpected National League pennant, winning the Manager of the Year Award in the process. After the 1963 season, Hutchinson was diagnosed with terminal lung cancer, but decided to manage Cincinnati in 1964 anyway. The Reds, a fifth-place team the year before, fought valiantly to win the pennant for their dying manager, but fell just short. Cincinnati ended the year in second, a single game behind St. Louis. Hutchinson died that November. In 1965, the Reds slid back to fourth place.

Gerry Priddy returned to the minors after 1953 to play and manage a few more years. He'd later try his hand as a professional golfer with little success. In 1973, Priddy was arrested and charged with attempted extortion for threatening to set off a bomb on a ship. He was convicted and given a nine-month sentence. Priddy died in 1980.

Al Aber remained in the majors through 1957 as a left-handed relief pitcher. His career record would come to just 24–25. After baseball, Aber worked as a salesman for a housewares company in the Cleveland area, and died in 1993.

Al Rosen had another fine season in 1954, hitting .300 with 24 home runs and 102 RBIs. He didn't come close to winning any of the legs of the Triple Crown, but that year the Indians finally did topple the Yankees, winning 111 games to claim the pennant. Cleveland was swept by the Giants in the Series.

In 1955, Rosen's batting average dropped to .244, his homers to 21. Most blamed a neck injury he'd sustained in a serious car accident the previous off-season, though some thought the third baseman's prolonged contract battle that year also had thrown him off kilter. When Rosen hit just .267 with 15 homers in 1956 and started to hear boos from the Cleveland fans, he decided he'd had enough and retired at age 32. It was an abrupt and unglamorous end to what had not so long before been a excellent career.

Within a few years, Rosen was vice president of a brokerage firm in Cleveland and reportedly doing quite well financially. But in the late 1970s, he returned to baseball, serving as general manager and in related front-office capacities for the Yankees, Astros, and Giants. Rosen had a mixed reputation as an executive. He was considered one of the game's better judges of talent, but he also was known as a soft touch for agents—perhaps a response to his own sometimes-painful contract negotiations. In the book *Lords of the Realm*, John Helyar refers to Rosen as "the Typhoid Mary of GMs," a man whose overly generous contracts drove up salary expectations throughout baseball.

Thus Rosen seems unlikely to go down in history as one of baseball's greatest executives. Neither will he go down as one of its greatest players. The other 11 men who won the Triple Crown are in Cooperstown. Rosen, who came just inches short, never received even a single Hall of Fame vote.

A TRIPLE CROWN DETHRONED

At one time it was believed that Cubs third baseman Heinie Zimmerman won a Triple Crown in 1912—some reference books still give him credit for this achievement. But long after Zimmerman's career ended, it was discovered that his true RBI total that year was 99, not 103 as long had been believed. The adjustment left Zimmerman's total behind Honus Wagner's 102 and Bill Sweeney's 100.

On the subject of Bill Sweeney—one of the two men whose RBI total exceeded Zimmerman's in 1912—someone should find out what they were feeding him that year. The Braves infielder hit .314 with 63 RBIs in 1911, then .344 with 100 RBIs in 1912. He even managed a 31-game hitting streak. Yet in no other season in the infielder's eight-year career did his average exceed .267 or his RBIs reach beyond 47. One source credits a switch to a heavier bat for his dramatic improvement in those two exceptional seasons, but that doesn't seem to explain why Sweeney went right back to being mediocre after his two years as a star. Did his bat lose weight? Sweeney's major league career was over at 28, the ultimate two-year wonder.

As for Zimmerman, his career ended in 1919 at age 32, when he was banned from baseball for attempting to fix games.

17

SLAPPED IN THE FACE WHILE FLIRTING WITH PERFECTION

Throwing a perfect game doesn't necessarily make a pitcher a baseball legend—how many statues of Charlie Robertson do you come across? But with only 16 such games in all of major league history, a perfect game does go a long way to ensuring that a pitcher's name is remembered. Unfortunately, perfection is devilishly difficult to achieve. For every hurler who has completed a perfect game, there are many more who fell just one pitch short.

TOM BROWNING ALMOST ACHIEVES DOUBLE PERFECTION

Tom Browning of the Cincinnati Reds pitched a perfect game on September 16, 1988, and remains suitably well-known for it. What makes Browning's story one of opportunity lost is that on July 4, 1989, he nearly did it again. No pitcher ever has thrown two perfect games. Doing so surely would have made Browning the first name mentioned whenever the subject of perfect games is raised. Browning, far from the greatest pitcher ever to toe the rubber, was as surprised as anyone by his brush with history. "I never anticipated doing it the first time," he said. "So there's no way to anticipate doing it the second time."

Pitching in Philadelphia's oppressive Independence Day heat, Browning took his attempt for repeat perfection to the 9th, just three outs from glory. Leading off for the Phillies that inning was Dickie Thon, already 0-for-2 on the day. Thon once had been an extremely promising shortstop, but that was back before his career was derailed by a beanball in 1984 (see page 148). For the past five years he'd mostly been a marginal platoon player. Browning got one strike on Thon, but he wouldn't get a second. Thon stroked a clean double into the right-center field gap on the 0–1 pitch. It would turn out to be one of many hits for the shortstop in the second half of the 1989 season, as he launched into a tremendous three-month run that, for a time, hinted at a return of Thon's once considerable talents. His revival would prove fleeting, but that hardly mattered to Tom Browning. In one swing, the pitcher's pursuit of history *was* history "I was exhausted in the humidity," admitted Browning after the game, "out of gas."

It wasn't the first time fame had eluded Browning. In 1985, he'd become the first rookie to win 20 games since Bob Grim in 1954. But Mets pitcher Dwight Gooden won 24 that year, and Browning's team-mate Pete Rose eclipsed Ty Cobb's all-time hit record, so no one paid Browning much notice. He didn't even win the National League Rookie of the Year, finishing second to Cardinal outfielder Vince Coleman.

Browning never did quite live up to his rookie promise, but through the early 1990s he seemed well on his way to a respectable career, averaging more than 14 wins a season for the next six years, and making headlines with his perfect game. Browning won a game in Cincinnati's 1990 upset World Series sweep of the A's, and even made the All-Star team for the first time in 1991 at age 31. But his career slid downhill quickly from there. Browning injured his left knee in 1992 and missed half the season. He broke a finger on his pitching hand in 1993 and was out again. Then on May 9, 1994, Browning snapped a bone in his upper arm as he delivered a 6th-inning fastball to Padres infielder Archi Cianfrocco. "It was one big, excruciating moment of pain," Browning told reporters. "'Why the hell did this happen to me?' did cross my mind."

Browning tried to return in 1995 with the Royals, but after two starts and two losses his career was over. Thanks to one perfect game his career would be remembered—but thanks to a second that came up three outs short, he wouldn't be a legend.

JIM BARR'S FORGOTTEN PERFECTION

In 1972, Giant rookie righty Jim Barr put together the longest string of perfect pitching in major league history . . . and no one much noticed.

Barr's August 23 start against the defending World Champion Pittsburgh Pirates didn't look particularly promising in the early innings. He allowed a pair of singles in the second, then walked pitcher Bob Moose to lead off the third. When a young pitcher like Barr—career record just 5–8—walks the opposing pitcher, it's generally not a great omen. But something unexpected happened after the walk: nothing happened. Not a hit, not a walk, not an error for the rest of the game. Barr retired the final 21 batters he faced, ending his 8–0 victory with a strikeout of future Hall of Famer Roberto Clemente. It was a fine victory, but it wasn't a perfect game, or even a no-hitter, so the game received no special attention in the press. Even Barr didn't consider it anything particularly noteworthy. "I do

ONE STRIKE AWAY

Three pitchers have been within one strike of a perfect game and failed to finish the job:

• On September 2, 1972, Milt Pappas of the Cubs lost his perfect game when he walked Padre pinch hitter Larry Stahl on a full count with two down in the 9th. Pappas still got his no-hitter.

• Ron Robinson of the Reds lost his perfect game when Expo pinch hitter Wallace Johnson singled on a 2–2 pitch with two out in the 9th on May 2, 1988. Tim Raines followed with a homer, and Robinson had lost his shutout as well. "I'm never going to live that down," Robinson said later. "It's one of those things you've got to live with the rest of your life."

• Mike Mussina of the Yankees lost his perfect game when Red Sox pinch hitter Carl Everett singled on a 1–2 pitch with two out in the 9th on September 2, 2001. It was the closest of Mussina's several brushes with perfection. He'd already lost perfect games with four outs to go and with two outs to go.

remember thinking in the 8th or 9th inning they hadn't had many baserunners," the pitcher said years later.

Barr's next start came in St. Louis on August 29. The young pitcher picked up right where he'd left off: by retiring a future Hall of Famer, this time Lou Brock, who flew out to left. Barr had a perfect game until Bernie Carbo doubled with two out in the 7th, though Barr later said he didn't realize it at the time. The Cardinals added singles in the 8th and 9th, but Barr held on to win, 3–0.

Again Jim Barr hadn't pitched a perfect game, again he hadn't pitched a no-hitter—but between the two games he *had* retired 41 consecutive batters, the longest such stretch of pitching perfection in major league history. Yet no one cared.

Barr's two-day string of greatness was exactly the wrong format for fame. When a player has *one* day of greatness, throwing a perfect game or hitting four home runs in a single contest, the fans in the stadium know what's happening—they've seen the whole thing with their own eyes. When a player puts together a *long-term* string of greatness, like Joe DiMaggio's 56-game hitting streak, the fans know what's happening because the story receives ever-increasing attention in the press. But a two-day stretch of greatness? It's doubtful many of the 9,003 in Busch Stadium that day even knew Barr was chasing a record. Barr himself didn't even know until Cardinals broadcaster Jack Buck told him before a post-game interview.

Those 41 consecutive outs would have been the only truly noteworthy achievement of Barr's major league career, had anyone bothered to note it. The former University of Southern California star was a competent performer for the Giants and Angels, but rarely much more. He won between eight and 15 games a season during the eight years that followed, often losing more than he won. Arm injuries brought Barr's career to an early end; his career record 101–112.

After his playing days, Barr moved into the relatively anonymous role of pitching coach at Sacramento State College. In 2003, the *San Francisco Chronicle* noted that Barr is best known to today's sports fans as the father of Emmy and Betsy Barr, WUSA women's professional soccer players.

The WUSA folded before the end of that season.

A PAINFUL WAY TO LOSE PERFECTION

Of all the ways there are to lose a perfect game, errors seem particularly unjust. These pitchers made the pitches and earned the outs—but thanks to their fielders, they failed to get the fame . . .

- Walter Johnson. Washington second baseman Bucky Harris'

error on July 1, 1920, certainly didn't cost Johnson fame—he's considered one of the greatest pitchers in the game's history. But it did cost Johnson what would have been his only perfect game. Johnson had to settle for his only no-hitter instead. Losing the perfect game turned out to be the least of The Big Train's misfortunes that day. He developed a sore arm after the start, resulting in an un-Walter-Johnson-like 8–10 record and 3.13 ERA in 1920. Until that year, Johnson hadn't won fewer than 20 since 1909, nor had he posted an ERA above 2.30. After that year, Johnson wouldn't win 20 or deliver an ERA below 2.99 again until 1924.

• Bill McCahan. Walter Johnson might not have needed any more fame, but A's rookie pitcher McCahan could have used some in 1947. He was already 26, old for a rookie, his climb to the majors delayed by his years at Duke University and a stint as an Army test pilot during World War II.

On September 3, 1947, Ferris Fain's poor flip to McCahan on what should have been a routine 3–1 putout allowed Senators outfielder Stan Spence to reach first as Washington's only baserunner that day. McCahan got the no-hitter, but it was the third no-hitter thrown that season, nothing very special in the grand scheme of things. A perfect game would have been the major's first since 1922, and certainly would have put the rookie pitcher on the map. "It was my fault," admitted Fain after the game. "I threw the ball while I was still pivoting, and it was a full five feet wide of the bag."

McCahan went 10–5 for the surprisingly competitive A's that year and was considered a real prospect, but his record fell to 4–7 in 1948, his ERA rising from 3.32 to 5.71. The consensus at the time was that McCahan's struggles were the result of his newly sculpted physique, his formerly fluid motion now said to resemble the efforts of a shot putter. If this indeed was the problem, then the A's had no one to blame but themselves. In prior years, McCahan had played professional basketball in the off-season. When the A's forbade him from doing so after the 1947 season, fearing injury, McCahan took a job rolling one-hundred-pound oil drums, which resulted in his new-found brawn.

McCahan's major league career was over after just 20 innings in 1949. The son of a movie cowboy returned to the minors as a player, coach, and manager, before leaving baseball in the mid-1950s. The canny McCahan then spent 23 years at General Dynamics, heading the F-16 mockup project. He died of cancer in 1986 at age 65.

• Dick Bosman. The sometimes-hotheaded Bosman wasn't mad about the error that turned his potential July 19, 1974, perfect game against the powerful Oakland A's into a mere no-hitter. He couldn't be. He'd committed the miscue himself. "This is the culmination of everything I've worked for and dreamed about," the Indian pitcher said of his no-hitter. "I almost feel like I'm dreaming."

Throughout his 11 years in baseball, Bosman didn't get as much credit as he perhaps deserved for his talents. Stuck on bad Washington Senator, Texas Ranger, and Cleveland Indian teams for most of his career, he never won more than 16 games in a season—though he was talented enough to lead the AL with a 2.19 ERA in 1969. Bosman finally got to pitch for a contender in 1975 when he joined the Oakland team he'd recently no-hit. But despite a solid record in Oakland, he was released just before the 1977 season, ending his pitching career.

Bosman coached at George Mason University and worked at a car dealership briefly after his playing days (cars were a passion; he'd once nearly won the National Drag Racing Championships). He later became a well-regarded major league pitching coach.

• Jerry Reuss. Like Dick Bosman, Reuss claimed to be perfectly happy on June 27, 1980, even though an error had cost him a perfect game. Despite the error, Reuss had achieved his long-standing goal of throwing a no-hitter. Twice before in his career, Reuss had taken a no-hitter into the 9th. On both occasions, he'd not only lost the no-hitter, but lost the game as well. "If I ever get to the 9th inning again with a no-hitter," Reuss vowed after his second failed attempt in 1972, "I'm going to get it."

A lot would happen to Jerry Reuss before he'd make good on

that promise. His record would soar as high as 18–11 in 1975, and fall as low as 7–14 in 1979. But in 1980, Reuss rediscovered his former fine form, and in late June got his no-hitter—though a wild throw by Dodger shortstop Bill Russell stood between him and perfection.

Reuss won the Comeback Player of the Year Award that season, and won a World Series with the Dodgers the next. In 1982, he again would miss a perfect game by one batter, this time the first batter. Eddie Milner led off the game with a double, then Reuss retired 27 in a row. Reuss pitched 22 seasons in all, retiring in 1990 with a 220–191 record. He later worked as a sportscaster. His hobby, he'd say in 1997, was collecting action photos of himself. It's nice to see ballplayers find worthwhile pursuits after leaving the game.

• Terry Mulholland. Journeyman left-hander Mulholland was an unlikely candidate to pitch a perfect game. But then he was an unlikely candidate to pitch a no-hitter, too, so he wasn't about to complain about the error that cost him pitching's ultimate one-day accomplishment. In the 7th inning of the Phillies' August 15, 1990, game against the Giants, a throw from Philadelphia third baseman Charlie Hayes pulled John Kruk off the bag at first, allowing San Francisco outfielder Rick Parker to reach base. He was the only Giant baserunner of the day. (Ever the team player, Kruk lobbied unsuccessfully to have the error charged to him instead.) Hayes redeemed himself by making a nice catch on the game's final play to preserve the no-hitter. "That would have been nice," said Kruk afterward. "A perfect game."

Though he didn't have perfection, Mulholland did have the first no-hitter by a Phillies pitcher at home since 1898. It must have been particularly gratifying for Mulholland that his masterpiece came against San Francisco, the team that had traded him away the year before. (Hayes, the man who made the error, also came to Philadelphia in that trade. Parker, the Giant who reached base on Hayes' error, was one of the players Philadelphia sent to San Francisco in return.)

Mulholland would never again come close to making

pitching history, but he did put together a long career as one of those soft-tossing lefties who seems to catch on somewhere every year. "I'm not Nolan Ryan. I'm not knocking on the door for the Cy Young Award," he said after his near-perfect game. "I'm just Terry Mulholland."

PERFECTION STOPPED BY AGREEMENT

Four major league pitchers have failed to earn official perfect games despite throwing complete games without allowing a baserunner. The problem: their complete games didn't go nine innings. In three of these cases—Rube Vickers in 1907, Dean Chance in 1967, and David Palmer in 1984—rain or darkness stopped the contest after only five innings. Five perfect innings is barely half a normal game, not really enough to get excited about. But the fourth pitcher, Ed Karger of the Cardinals, threw a respectable seven perfect innings against Boston before his game was halted. It wasn't rain or darkness that concluded the proceedings; the game was "stopped by agreement." Early in the century, it wasn't uncommon for teams to agree beforehand to forego the final two innings of the second game of a doubleheader. On August 11, 1907, such an agreement cost Karger his shot at official perfection.

"St. Louisans who saw Karger shut out the visitors in seven innings without allowing one to reach base regretted that the second game did not go the regulation number of innings," wrote *The Sporting News*, "for they were satisfied that the southpaw would have equaled the world's record for a perfect game." As of 1907, there had been just one perfect game thrown since 1880, and it had been pitched by the great Cy Young. Nine perfect innings surely would have made Karger's name.

Karger's record was just 15–19 in 1907, but considering his club went 52–101, it was an admirable showing, and *The Sporting News* was quite complimentary of his talents. Yet that season would be the only one in which Karger got 30 starts. He pitched for four teams in his six years in the majors and compiled a career mark of just 48–67. Alcohol might have been part of his problem. When Pittsburgh manager Fred Clarke sold the pitcher to St. Louis, he commented that Karger "liked his beer."

Perhaps Ed Karger is fortunate that that 1907 game was called after seven. Perhaps he would have allowed a baserunner in the final two innings and wouldn't have had even an "unofficial" perfect game on his resume. Still, it seems a shame he didn't get a chance to try for the real thing.

AN EVEN MORE PAINFUL WAY TO LOSE PERFECTION

Infield hits are a bit like errors. Typically they mean the pitcher has done his job and prevented solid contact, only the hitter caught a break and reached base anyway. But losing a perfect game to an infield hit is even worse than losing one to an error—with an infield hit, you don't even get the no-hitter as a consolation prize.

On September 7, 1955, speedy Cub outfielder Frankie Baumholtz cost Pittsburgh pitcher Bob Friend a perfect game when he legged out a 4th-inning roller in the direction of shortstop Johnny O'Brien. It was a bang-bang play at first. "A small matter of about 12 inches separated Friend from taking his place among the immortals," wrote the *Pittsburgh Press*. "A right handed batter would have been out."

Amazingly, it happened to Friend again a decade later, though this time he lost just a no-hitter, not a perfect game. On July 23, 1965, *another* 4th-inning infield roller toward short off the bat of *another* speedy left-hand-hitting Cub outfielder was all that stood between Friend and at least a small place in history. This time it was Cub outfielder Don Landrum who barely beat a throw from Pirate shortstop Gene Alley. "What's all the fuss?" Friend quipped to the crowd of reporters surrounding his locker after the game. "A one hitter? Why I pitch one-hitters every ten years right here at Wrigley Field."

According to the *Pittsburgh Press*, most of the assembled scribes didn't realize that the pitcher wasn't kidding. This second near-miss came in Friend's 15th and final season with the Pirates. After one more year split between the Yankees and Mets, his career was over, his record an unspectacular 197–230 due in part to his generally weak Pirate teams. Friend never did pitch a no-hitter, much less a perfect game. He did have a successful career after baseball, however, as an executive in banking and insurance, then as a popular Republican politician in the Pittsburgh area.

In the late 1980s, big Phillies left-hander Don Carman seemed to be channeling the spirit of Bob Friend—which would have been quite a trick, considering Friend was still alive. On September 29, 1987, the only thing that stood between Carman and a perfect game was a speedy outfielder beating out a 4th-inning infield grounder toward short. In this case, the outfielder in question was Met Mookie Wilson, the shortstop, Steve Jeltz. "As much as I wanted him to be out, I could see him crossing the bag just ahead of the throw," said Carman after the game. "Steve made a great play. But I knew as soon as he hit the ball that, with his speed, it was a hit."

Barely one year earlier, on August 20, 1986, Carman had taken a perfect game to the 9th against the Giants. San Francisco catcher Bob Brenly opened the bottom of the final frame with a long line drive to the gap in left center. Phils center fielder Milt Thompson was in position to make a running catch, but the ball glanced off the base of his glove. It was ruled a hit. "I thought I had a bead on it," said Thompson. "But the sun and wind confused me. When I put my glasses down, I lost it. I feel real bad."

Like Friend before him, Carman never would get a no-hitter or a perfect game—in fact, he managed only three career shutouts. He retired in 1992 with a record of just 53–54.

POSSIBLY THE MOST PAINFUL WAY TO LOSE PERFECTION

On June 23, 1994, A's pitcher Bobby Witt missed a perfect game when first-base umpire Gary Cederstrom called Kansas City shortstop Greg Gagne safe on a ground ball to first in the 6th inning. Replays showed that Gagne actually should have been called out. He was the Royals' only baserunner. Witt just missed greatness again in his next start, throwing a two-hitter.

Despite such flashes of brilliance, the former University of Oklahoma ace never harnessed his control. He drifted around the majors, pitching for eight teams in a 16-year career and three times leading his league in walks.

Though Witt didn't get his perfect game, more than a few fans would come to think that he did, confusing his near miss with the successful perfect game thrown by equally mediocre American League pitcher Mike Witt, no relation, in 1984.

EFFICIENCY COUNTS FOR NOTHING

It wasn't a perfect game in the conventional sense of the term. But in its own way, it aproached perfection as perhaps none had before. On August 10, 1944, Braves pitcher Red Barrett—displaying precisely the sort of economy the war department asked of Americans during those difficult years—required just 58 pitches to beat the Cincinnati Reds 2–0.

Pitch counts aren't available from every contest in major league history, but as far as is known, this is the fewest number of pitches ever used to win a nine-inning game. That might not make it a perfect game in the conventional sense, but it seems like it ought to count for something. After all, coming up with an efficient way to make a car is what made Henry Ford famous. Using an efficient number of strokes to play 18 holes is what's made Tiger Woods famous. Unfortunately for Barrett, it doesn't work that way in baseball. The greatest games are considered those with the most strikeouts or fewest baserunners, not those requiring the least effort to reach the desired result.

Newspapers gave Barrett's low pitch count little if any mention. *The Sporting News* didn't bring up pitch count at all in their game summary—though they were suitably impressed by the succinct 1 hour 15 minute game time. (To answer the obvious question, no, neither team had a train to catch.)

Barrett was known in his day as an infuriatingly inconsistent pitcher who would breeze through some games and have trouble recording an out in others. His greatest success came not in 1944, the year of his 58-pitch masterpiece, but in 1945, when he went 23–12 to lead the National League in wins.

Despite that league-leading season, Barrett proved better at avoiding fame that achieving it. He was selected for the All-Star team once, in 1945, but that year the game was called off to limit unnecessary wartime travel. Twice Barrett would fall one hit short of a perfect game. His career record was an uninspired 69–69. Barrett appeared in the 1948 World Series, but pitched less than four total innings in a losing cause, as his Braves fell to Cleveland. The only Barrett who'd get noticed that October was Red's wife. According to a United Press story, Mrs. Charles Barrett was selected "most chic World Series wife" by the Cambridge Press Club and presented with a $1,000 hat.

Thus, despite Red Barrett's 58-pitch masterpiece of efficiency, despite his 23-win season, and despite his brushes with perfect games, one leaves a synopsis of Barrett's career thinking just two things:

1. A *$1,000* hat?
2. Did Red report it on his income taxes?

Bill Sherdel was the Red Barrett of relief pitching. In the bottom of the 2nd inning of a July 30, 1924, game against the Phils, Cardinal lefty Sherdel took over for starter Leo Dickerman and provided perhaps the most efficient relief effort in history: he threw one pitch and recorded three outs. Pinch hitter Johnny Mokan popped up his attempted bunt, and Cards first baseman Jim Bottomley started the triplet killing, a phrase that somehow sounds considerably more violent than "twin killing."

This would be a better story if Sherdel mowed down the Phillies the rest of the way. Instead he allowed four runs, but his Cardinals still rallied for a 9–8 win. Sherdel, like Barrett, received no great acclaim for his efficiency, and in fact isn't especially well remembered for anything he did in his career. (As far as can be determined, his wife never won any hats of particular note.) "Wee Willie" Sherdel's changeup and sweeping curveball did earn him the title "The Slow Ball King of the Big Leagues" in his day, but it wasn't an enduring fame. Great slowballs aren't remembered like great fastballs.

Sherdel came up just short of World Series glory, too. He pitched well in two starts against the Yanks in the 1926 Series, and in one of his two starts against Ruth and company in the 1928 Series, but thanks to poor run support and shoddy Cardinal defense, he never earned a postseason win. "I have a clean record in the World Series—I didn't win once," joked the always upbeat Sherdel late in his life. "But I think I pitched nice ball."

Sherdel had some health problems in his old age, and lost a leg to poor circulation in 1961. (Coincidentally, Sherdel was listed immediately after one-legged pitcher Bert Shepard in *The Baseball Encyclopedia* until the 1990s.) When Bill Sherdel died in 1968, his obituary didn't mention his historically efficient relief appearance.

18

NO NO-HITTER MEANS NO-NAME PITCHER

The major leagues average close to two no-hitters per year, so they're really not rare enough to confer lasting fame on the pitchers who throw them. But if the circumstances surrounding a no-hitter are just right—a particularly important game, a particularly compelling story—it might make a pitcher's name.

For example, Bill Bevens would have been famous if he'd finished his 1947 near no-hitter. It was, after all, the World Series. But the unheralded Yankee pitcher lost the no-hitter and the game with two outs in the 9th inning on a double by Dodger pinch hitter Cookie Lavagetto. According to Bevens, the Yankee scouting report said to pitch Lavagetto high and outside—but it turned out that's just where Lavagetto liked 'em. Bevens would never start another game in the majors. Though he'd failed to finish his no-hitter, Bevens' effort was such a noble failure on such a grand stage that his name would enter baseball lore to a certain extent. "It's what people remember me for," Bevens said 40 years later, "although they would have remembered me more if I'd gotten that no-hitter."

Other pitchers of near no-hitters have been even less fortunate. Most often, losing a potentially memorable no-hitter means losing one's place in history entirely.

QUANTITY COUNTS

Throwing one no-hitter might not be a guaranteed path to fame, but throwing lots of them sure seems to work. Only Nolan Ryan (seven no-hitters), Sandy Koufax (four), and Bob Feller (three) pitched more than two official 20th-century major league no-hitters. All three of these Hall of Famers derive some—though certainly not all—of their considerable fame from their multiple masterpieces.

Perhaps no man came closer to joining this three-no-hitter club than Jim Maloney, who by some definitions *did* pitch three no-hitters—only to have one of them declared officially void more than a quarter century after the game was played. On June 14, 1965, the hard-throwing Reds right-hander no-hit the New York Mets for nine innings. Unfortunately for Maloney, Cincinnati couldn't manage a run either, and the contest went to extra innings. Maloney shut the Mets down in the 10th, but faltered in the 11th, allowing a solo home run to outfielder Johnny Lewis. The long ball cost him not only the no-hitter, but also the game. "I don't feel so badly about losing," joked Maloney to teammate Roger Craig after the extra-inning loss. "What hurt was flipping my hat so many times for the ovations."

Maloney had pitched nine no-hit innings and more besides, so some chose to consider this a no-hitter. Others didn't, on the grounds that he did eventually give up a hit.

Remarkably, the same thing nearly happened to Maloney again a little over two months later. On August 19, 1965, Maloney threw another nine-inning no-hitter and didn't even let the Cubs hit a ball to the outfield until the 8th. Yet once again he found himself in a 0–0 extra-inning game. Fortunately, Reds shortstop Leo Cardenas got Maloney the run he needed in the 10th, homering off the foul pole, and Maloney earned a no-hitter that was beyond debate. Only 13 times before in baseball history had *any* pitcher taken a no-hitter to extra innings. Maloney had turned the trick twice in a single season.

Four years later, on April 30, 1969, Maloney collected a more conventional nine-inning no hitter against the Houston Astros. But by this time Maloney's list of no-hitters paled in comparison to his list of no-hitter misses. In addition to that 11-inning loss, Maloney had thrown five one-hitters and combined on a sixth with reliever Clay Carroll. Twice in his career Maloney had to leave no-hit bids after suffering injuries, the second of these a perfect game in the 7th inning. All this, and Maloney was still in his twenties. Future no-hitters seemed certain. But the man whom Sandy Koufax called the hardest thrower in the National League was pitching on borrowed time. Maloney had had a chronically sore arm since his second season in the big leagues. On days the arm felt good, a no-hitter was always a possibility. On days it felt bad, Reds fielders had to remain on their toes. "It hurts most of the time, now," Maloney admitted in 1969.

The arm hurt so much that in one game against the Mets that year, the famously tough Maloney asked to come out. The Reds lost, and the next day manager Dave Bristol reportedly told his pitchers that in the future they'd just have to pitch through their pain. (That sort of thinking might help explain why four potentially great Reds pitchers— Maloney, Don Gullett, Gary Nolan, and Wayne Simpson—all saw their careers derailed by arm injuries in the late 1960s and 1970s.) Some of Maloney's teammates reportedly resented that he was no longer carrying the club.

Maloney's ever-growing arm troubles were joined in April 1970 by leg troubles, when he tore his Achilles tendon running the bases. Maloney had compiled an impressive 134–81 record with Cincinnati, most of it while pitching through pain, but the Reds apparently felt they didn't owe the 30-year-old pitcher anything. They traded him away that off-season. In a strictly commercial sense, the Reds made the right move— Maloney never won another game in the majors. But then,

REPLACING MALONEY

When Jim Maloney blew out his Achilles in the 3rd inning of an April 16, 1970, game against the Dodgers, he was replaced by a young pitcher named Don Gullett. Gullett threw five innings of three-hit shutout ball to earn his first win in the majors. As it happened, Gullett was destined to replace Maloney not just in that game, but as Cincinnati's ace, compiling a 91–44 record in seven seasons with the Reds. But by the late 1970s, Gullett had followed in Maloney's footsteps another way as well—he blew out his arm, ending his career before he turned 30.

neither did Greg Garrett, the pitcher the Reds got in return, so maybe there is something to all this karma stuff you hear so much about.

Maloney tried managing in the minors after his early retirement and later ran an auto dealership. Occasionally he was referred to as one of the select group of pitchers who'd thrown more than two no-hitters, but on September 4, 1991, baseball's ominously named "Committee for Statistical Accuracy," ruled that no-hitters lost in extra innings weren't official no-hitters. Two decades after he'd left baseball, Maloney had been deprived of the greatest claim to fame of his once-promising career.

On May 1, 1969, one day after Jim Maloney of the Reds no-hit Houston, Don Wilson of Houston no-hit the Reds. The no-hitter was the second of the hard-throwing Astro's career, and he was just 24 years old. Nolan Ryan, another hard-throwing Astro, wouldn't get his second no-hitter until he was 26.

Like Ryan, Wilson was known for strikeouts as well as no-hitters. On July 14, 1968, Wilson struck out 18 Reds, tying the then major league record for a nine-inning game and tying the record for most consecutive strikeouts, eight, in the process. But while Ryan's fastball remained famously swift for decades, Wilson hurt his arm in late 1969 and could no longer get by on his heat. It might have been the end of his career, but unlike so many other sore-armed former fastball pitchers, Wilson successfully substituted guile for gas. The Astros hurler didn't just survive his sore arm, he improved—Wilson's winning percentage went up after 1969, his ERA down. Still, Don Wilson wasn't one of the best-known pitchers in baseball. His record was never outstanding, since he was stuck on mediocre Astros teams. He made the All-Star team just once.

On September 4, 1974, Wilson appeared on the verge of becoming considerably more famous. He'd dominated the Cincinnati Reds all day, and was three outs away from his third career no-hitter. That would have put him in some very select company. Wilson wouldn't get the no-hitter, but it wasn't the Reds who stopped him. It was his own manager, Preston Gomez. Despite the no-hitter, the Astros were trailing 2–1, the result of a 5th-inning error. So Gomez did what he'd always done when trailing late in the game. He sent up a pinch hitter for his pitcher.

There are those who will argue that Gomez made the correct move, that a manager must put team success ahead of individual accomplishment. But certainly circumstances must be taken into account. The circumstances here were that it was the last month of the season, and the Astros were far out of contention. Winning or losing the game meant little. The circumstances also suggested that going to a pinch hitter wasn't all that big of an advantage. Don Wilson hit .206 that year, Tommy Helms, the man sent up in his place, hit .279. Gomez in effect had ended Wilson's no-hit bid for an added one-in-13 shot at a hit. As it turned out, he'd ended it for nothing. Helms grounded out, and relief pitcher Mike Cosgrove gave up a hit in the 9th, costing Wilson a share of a combined no-hitter. Wilson took the loss, dragging his record for the season below .500, where it would remain for the rest of the year.

THE FIRST NO-HIT MASTER

Larry Corcoran pitched three no-hitters—but he did so in the early 1880s, a time when no-hitters weren't considered much more notable than any other shutout. It's a shame his no-hitters weren't more celebrated, because Corcoran's short career deserves to be remembered. Between 1880 and 1884, the 120-pound flame-thrower was one of the top pitchers in the National League, winning 170 games and losing just 83 for Chicago. But Corcoran hurt his shoulder in early 1885, ending his days as an effective major leaguer when he was just 25.

Corcoran spent the next few years pitching ineffectively in the majors and later in the minors. He switched to umpiring in 1890, but soon contracted Bright's Disease, a kidney inflammation, and died in 1891 at the age of 32. He left a wife and four children.

Don Wilson had a reputation as a man who didn't get along with managers, so reporters were expecting fireworks in the clubhouse. They wouldn't get them. "I respect [Gomez] more than ever tonight," said Wilson when he finally agreed to talk to the press. "He wants to win and I want to win as much as he does. When people start putting personal goals ahead of the team, you'll never have a winner.

"I could scream and say, 'Look at what the manager did to me.' The third no-hitter would have meant a lot because I would have been doing something no other man pitching today has done. But I still have enough confidence in myself that I believe I might get another one."

A little over three weeks later, on September 28, 1974, Wilson nearly did just that, holding the Braves to two hits. It was his last start of the season. It also was the last start of his life. On January 5, 1975, Wilson was found slumped on the front seat of his car in the garage of his Houston home, dead of carbon monoxide poisoning. The car had idled for hours, the garage door shut. Carbon monoxide had filled the garage, then seeped through the ceiling into the home above, hospitalizing Wilson's wife and daughter and killing his five-year-old son, Alexander.

Wilson's death eventually was ruled a suicide, though the pitcher was not known to have any significant personal, psychological, family, financial, or baseball-related problems. Former roommate Curt Blefary, by this point a New Jersey sheriff, cast doubt on the suicide explanation, calling Wilson a level-headed guy with a stable marriage and good off-season job with the Heinz Corporation. The autopsy found that Wilson had a high level of alcohol in his blood, so others have suggested that perhaps he simply passed out in his car after having had a few too many. Whatever the explanation, Wilson was dead at 29.

DOUBLING UP

Throwing two no-hitters can bring even more fame than throwing three—*if* you throw them in consecutive starts. Johnny Vander Meer enjoys remarkable celebrity for a pitcher with a career record below .500 who's been retired more than half a century. The Reds lefty owes his stardom to two games he pitched for an otherwise forgotten fourth-place team. On June 11 and June 15, 1938, Vander Meer pitched no-hitters in back-to-back outings. Ever since then, any time any pitcher throws a no-hitter, baseball's unwritten rules require that Vander Meer's name be mentioned at least once each inning in the pitcher's next start until a hit is allowed. "You always hear 'Can you pitch two in a row like Johnny Vander Meer?'" said Sandy Koufax, author of four no-hitters. "I never even came close to that . . . Unless you call the second inning close."

Vander Meer remains the only man in baseball history to throw consecutive no-hitters—though two others came tantalizingly close.

GOMEZ GOES TO THE PEN

When Don Wilson's September 1974 no-hit bid against Cincinnati reached the late innings, Reds pitcher Don Gullett asked teammate Clay Kirby whether he thought Astros manager Preston Gomez would pinch-hit for Wilson. "I guarantee he will," answered Kirby.

He had good reason to think so. Four years earlier, on July 21, 1970, Kirby, then a Padre, no-hit the reigning World Champion Mets through eight but trailed 1–0. His manager in San Diego, none other than Preston Gomez, pulled *him* for a pinch hitter that day, just as he later would Wilson. The strategy worked no better on that occasion, as pinch hitter Cito Gaston struck out, San Diego's relief pitcher gave up a hit, and the Padres lost. Chants of "Gomez must go" filled Jack Murphy Stadium. That game, too, was irrelevant to the standings. The Padres would finish their second season at 63–99, 39 games off the pace. Kirby, a fine pitcher with a lousy record thanks to poor support from his expansion teammates, certainly deserved better. "What happened is over with," said Kirby after the game. "There's nothing I can do about it. I came close, that's all."

He would come close again. On September 13, 1971, Kirby held Houston without a hit until there was one out in the 8th, only to lose both the no-hitter and the game. In Kirby's very next start, he took a perfect game into the 8th, but Willie McCovey launched a wind-assisted home run. Kirby never successfully pitched a no-hitter, and for his career was just 75–104—though the poor record had more to do with the lack of talent around him on those early Padres teams than it did with a lack of talent on his part. After leaving baseball, Kirby had greater success as a securities broker, but died of a heart attack at the age of 43.

As for Preston Gomez, he was unapologetic about costing Wilson and Kirby their shots at no-hitters. In fact, he once said he'd do the same thing a *third* time if a similar situation presented itself. He should have said *fourth*. Back in 1962, he'd yanked Phil Ortega from a potential minor league no-hitter in Spokane. Spokane would finish eighth that year in the Pacific Coast League. (Gomez's teams had a habit of finishing in the back of the pack.) It was an otherwise meaningless minor league game.

On September 11, 1923, 15 years *before* Vander Meer, Red Sox right-hander Howard Ehmke took the mound against New York for his first start after throwing a no-hitter. He immediately allowed a single to Yankee outfielder Whitey Witt, the first batter he faced. That should have ended any talk of a double no-hitter right there—except that Witt's hit was a simple chopper down the third base line that Boston third baseman Howard Shanks, a converted outfielder, allowed to bounce off his chest. Official scorer Fred Lieb ruled the play a single and couldn't be persuaded to change it to an error even when Ehmke set down the next 27 hitters in order. *Baseball Magazine* took a petition to the American League president asking that the call be overturned, but Lieb's ruling stood. "If that wasn't an error," said Tom Connally, who umpired that game, "I never saw one."

"This was, in retrospect, perhaps the saddest decision I ever made," admitted Lieb a half century later. "It *was* a doubtful call on my part."

Perhaps it was fate catching up with Ehmke—while that one-hitter probably should have been a no-hitter, the no-hitter he'd thrown four days earlier probably should have been a two-hitter. In the 7th inning of that earlier outing, A's pitcher Slim Harriss appeared to have a double . . . but was called out for missing first base. Then in the 8th, a misplayed line drive was first ruled a hit and only later was changed to an error by an official scorer far more charitable than Lieb.

He'd missed out on double-no-hitter fame, but six years later, Ehmke would get his moment of enduring glory. The 35-year-old pitcher, now barely hanging on to to a major league job, was named the surprise starter in game one of the 1929 World Series. A's manager Connie Mack thought the right-handed side-armer would fare well against the Cubs' largely right-handed-hitting lineup. He was right. Ehmke's assortment of off-speed pitches held the Cubs to one run, and the A's were on their way to a five-game Series win. It would be the last win of Ehmke's major league career. To this day, Ehmke's name often is invoked when a manager names a surprise starter in a big game.

In 1947, nine years after Vander Meer threw his famed double no-hitter, 24-year-old Ewell Blackwell took a stab at matching the feat. The Cincinnati Reds pitcher was called "The Whip" for his lanky 6'5" frame and distinctive side-arm delivery, and he was called the most prom-ising new talent in baseball by press and players alike. *The New York*

Herald Tribune said Blackwell was "the greatest young star on the rise in the post-war era of major leagues" and "almost universally acclaimed by National League batters as the best hurler in the circuit."

Blackwell no-hit the Braves on June 18, 1947, and in his next start on June 22, nearly did the same to the Dodgers. With one down in the 9th, Brooklyn second baseman Eddie Stanky squibbed a broken-bat bouncer back through the middle. Blackwell dropped down to one knee to field it, but it skipped over the pitcher's left foot, sneaked past the shortstop, and trickled into center field. Blackwell retired the next hitter, then allowed another soft single—this one a Texas Leaguer to Jackie Robinson—before finishing off his shutout. Had he fielded that Stanky squib for an out, Robinson wouldn't have come to the plate and the no-hitter would in all likelihood have occurred. "I should have shoved [Stanky's squib] into my pocket," Blackwell chastised himself after the game.

The pitcher's teammates were understandably sympathetic in the clubhouse after Blackwell failed to follow his no-hitter with another no-hitter. "I knew you were just a flash in the pan," said first baseman Bert Haas. "And you proved it letting them get two hits."

It's good to have friends.

Another of Blackwell's Reds teammates didn't crack jokes. "I was pulling for you all the way," said Johnny Vander Meer, still with Cincinnati nearly a decade after he so famously turned two. "I know you were," said Blackwell, who'd seen Vander Meer on the top step of the dugout in the 9th, waiting to rush out to congratulate him. "And thanks."

Even without the back-to-back no-hitters, Blackwell seemed destined for greatness. That year he led the National League in wins and strikeouts and was second in ERA and winning percentage. He started the All-Star game and pitched three innings of shutout ball, striking out Ted Williams in the process. He was the best young pitcher in baseball. The suitably impressed Dodgers said he was the next Dizzy Dean.

It would be the Blackwell's only great year. A shoulder injury in his final pre-season start and kidney problems held him to a 7–9 record in 1948. The troublesome kidney was removed in January 1949, and Blackwell's record the following season was just 5–5 as he struggled to return from surgery. In 1950, Blackwell managed a 17–15 record and an ERA a shade below 3.00—even though he'd made another trip to the operating room, this time to have his appendix removed. Lackluster records of 16–15 and 4–12 followed. "I've had my share of bad luck," Balckwell said in 1952. "But I believe things will even up from now on."

They didn't. After short stints with the Yankees and Kansas City A's, Blackwell was out of the majors at age 32. His career record was just 82–78. Without his marvelous 1947 season, his record would have been 60–70.

LOST PITCHERS, LOST GAMES, LOST NO-HITTERS

In 1989, the New York Yankees paid the then-sizable sum of $3.6 million to sign mediocre Padres free-agent pitcher Andy Hawkins to a three-year deal. Then they wondered why he was so mediocre. Hawkins' 1989 record was 15–15, with a 4.80 ERA. For the first two months of 1990, Hawkins could only dream of such mediocrity—his record was 1–4, his ERA a hefty 8.01—and booing Hawkins became a favorite sport of Yankee fans.

On June 5, Hawkins gave up five runs in a third of an inning. Manager Bucky Dent was fired after the game, and three days later Hawkins was given a choice: accept a demotion to the minors or be released. Hawkins chose release. But before the release became official, Yankee pitcher Mike Witt injured his elbow, leaving the club a pitcher short. Hawkins was back on the team and—eventually—back in the rotation. On July 1, he took the mound in Chicago and pitched the game of his life, holding the White Sox without

STEIB'S THREE FAILED STABS

On September 24, 1988, Blue Jay pitcher Dave Stieb had a no-hitter with two outs in the 9th inning and two strikes on the batter, Indian second baseman Julio Franco. Franco singled. In Stieb's very next start on September 30, 1988, he again had a no-hitter with two outs in the 9th and again had two strikes on the batter, Oriole pinch-hitter Jim Traber. Traber singled. A year later, on August 4, 1989, Stieb had a perfect game with two outs in the 9th. Yankee outfielder Roberto Kelly doubled. One year after that, on September 2, 1990, Steib once again had a no-hitter with two out in the 9th. This time Cleveland second baseman Jerry Browne lined out to right. Steib finally had his masterpiece.

a hit. The no-hitter might have restored Hawkins' shattered confidence if not for one thing: He lost. With two outs in the 8th, the White Sox turned three errors and two walks into a 4–0 win. "Everybody congratulated me," said Hawkins after the game. "But I gave up four runs and lost. I'm stunned that I threw a no-hitter, and I'm stunned that I got beat. I'll have to sleep on this."

He woke to find he'd made the front page of *The New York Times*. "No-Hitter, But With No Glory," read the headline. Still, the performance seemed to energize Hawkins. For the first time the New York fans were on his side, sympathizing with the painful loss. Hawkins was nearly as good in his next outing five days later, shutting out the Twins on three hits, all singles, through nine—but once again it wasn't enough. The Yankees failed to score for Hawkins and the game went into extra innings. Hawkins shut the Twins out through ten, then eleven. Finally with two outs in the 12th he cracked, allowing two runs on a pair of walks and a pair of singles. It was the longest outing by a Yankee pitcher since 1976. It was another stellar performance. It was another loss. Hawkins' record for the season fell to 1–6.

Remarkably, it wasn't even Hawkins' most impressive game of the year against the Twins. The hard-luck pitcher had retired every Twin he'd faced in a game back in May . . . only to have the contest rained out in the 4th, less than an inning shy of becoming an official game. Also remarkably, Hawkins' next start after the 12-inning loss *would* be a no-hitter. It just wouldn't be his. On July 12, Hawkins' teammates not only couldn't get him a run, they couldn't get him a hit. The Yankees were no-hit by Melido Perez in a rain-shortened six-inning affair. That game marked the end of Hawkins' string of stellar starts. The pitcher gave up eight runs on seven hits in 4⅓ innings. He must have wondered why the rain couldn't have waited till the 6th when *he* was shutting down the Twins back in May.

Hawkins finished the season at 5–12, then started 1991 0–2 before the Yankees finally did release him. He was picked up by Oakland, but it would be Hawkins' final season in the majors. His career was over at 31, his record 84–91. Also in 1991, major league baseball ruled that a pitcher must throw at least nine innings for his no-hitter to be official. Hawkins had only pitched eight innings in his no-hitter—since the hometown White Sox led after eight, they'd had no need to hit in the bottom of the 9th. Hawkins' already dubious moment of glory in a Yankee uniform was wiped from the record books entirely.

On April 12, 1992, Red Sox pitcher Matt Young followed in Andy Hawkins' unfortunate footsteps. Like Hawkins, he pitched a no-hitter but lost. Like Hawkins, he did so in a road game, so he didn't get to pitch the bottom of the 9th, and his no-hitter didn't count. Like Hawkins, Young was a mediocre pitcher recently signed to a big contract by a team with unforgiving fans. And like Hawkins, his no-hitter might have gone some way to rebuilding his reputation after a shaky start with his new club. "In my book it's a no-hitter," Young said of his eight-inning effort. "I wanted to go out and pitch the 9th inning, they just wouldn't let me."

Matt Young hung on for one more season with Cleveland—the team that had beaten him in his no-hit bid—before disappearing from baseball. His record was just 55–95. Some years later, Matt Young and his wife heard on their car radio that Hideo Nomo had thrown a no-hitter for Boston. The broadcaster called it the team's first no-hitter since 1965. "It sure didn't take them long," Young commented to his wife, "to forget about my no-hitter."

Would pitching no-hitters have made Hawkins and Young famous? Probably not in any lasting way. They would have been just two no-hitters among the 17 thrown between 1990 and 1992. But perhaps no-hitters could have helped these ill-fated pitchers turn the tide on their failing careers, or at least added something positive to their legacies. Instead, when Hawkins and Young are thought of at all, it's as overpaid free-agent disasters.

UP AGAINST GREATNESS

On September 9, 1965, a sore-armed journeyman left-hander went toe to toe with greatness and nearly made history. The Dodgers were hosting the Chicago Cubs that day. Sandy Koufax was on the mound for Los Angeles, on his way to a 26–8 record, the Cy Young Award, and a World Series ring. Bob Hendley was on the mound for the Cubs, just happy to be in the majors. The 26-year-old Hendley was playing for his third big league team in the past two seasons. He was in his fifth year overall, and had never had a winning record.

For four innings, Koufax didn't allow a baserunner—but neither did Hendley. Hendley blinked first, walking Dodger outfielder Lou Johnson in the 5th. The Dodgers sacrificed Johnson to second, and he came around to score when Cubs rookie catcher Chris Krug's throw sailed into left on Johnson's attempted steal of third. Hendley was down 1–0, but he still hadn't allowed a hit—until the 7th, when Johnson doubled on a Hendley changeup.

It would be the only hit Hendley allowed—but he wouldn't get the win. That day Koufax threw his fourth and final career no-hitter, this one a perfect game, and Hendley was saddled with a 1–0 loss. If not for the Lou Johnson double, the game would have gone into baseball lore, and Hendley would have gone with it. He would have been the man who matched no-hitters with Koufax, and no one would have held it against him that he'd lost. Instead, Hendley shared with Koufax the records for fewest hits in a complete nine-inning game and fewest baserunners in a game. That's not enough to be remembered.

Five days later, Hendley earned a measure of revenge. Again matched up with Koufax, Hendley beat the Dodgers 2–1. This time Hendley allowed four hits. A four-hitter won't make anyone famous, but under the circumstances it must have felt pretty good.

Hendley remained in the majors for two more years, starting now and then, but more often throwing in relief. It was an undistinguished career made heroic by the fact that Hendley had been pitching with elbow pain for the durationof his tenure in the majors. Some days the pain was a mere annoyance, others he could hardly straighten out his arm. After the 1967 season, Hendley, now a Met, decided to take a chance on surgery. "I'm 48–52 in the big leagues—all with the bad arm," he said. "I don't know what I would have done if I had been sound. I would like to have pitched seven years with a sound arm to know."

Hendley returned to the minors in 1968 for post-surgery rehab. He pitched well that year, but was one of the last players cut from the Mets before the start of the 1969 regular season. Hendley never made it back to the majors. He soon left baseball and became a circuit court bailiff in Illinois.

Two men have had the only hit in five major league one-hitters. Spoiling no-hitters isn't going to make you famous, but it does deny fame to others, which has a value of its own—in a bitter, petty sort of way.

• Cesar Tovar. Tovar was all that stood in the way of no-hitters by Barry Moore, Dave McNally, Mike Cuellar, Dick Bosman, and Catfish Hunter. Before heading to the plate to face McNally in the 9th inning of that pitcher's no-hit bid, Tovar correctly predicted to his teammates he'd end the no-hitter. McNally's post-game comment: "Tovar is pesky as hell."

The pesky utility player didn't just stand in the way of notable accomplishments by pitchers, either. In 1967, Carl Yastrzemski won the Triple Crown. Tovar hit .267 with six homers. Yet Tovar drew a first-place MVP vote from *Minneapolis Star* writer Max Nichols, costing Yastrzemski his unanimous victory.

After his playing career, Tovar returned to his native Venezuela and worked as a scout.

• Eddie Milner. Milner's victims included Dickie Noles, Jerry Reuss, Chuck Rainey, Len Barker, and Alejandro Pena. (Barker and Pena were removed from their games before the end, the one-hitters completed by other pitchers.) Pitchers were never safe from Milner. His hit off Reuss led off the game, his hit off Rainey came with two out in the 9th.

The speedy Milner hit .253 in his nine-year career before drug problems brought his career to an end.

A NEARLY MEMORABLE DEBUT

In 1967, Billy Rohr of the Boston Red Sox nearly became the first pitcher of the modern era to throw a no-hitter in his first game—and he did so under conditions that would have guaranteed that he'd be remembered.

It was the New York Yankees' 1967 home opener, and future Hall of Famer Whitey Ford was on the mound for New York. Rohr got the start for Boston, making his major league debut. Whitey Ford versus some kid making his debut on opening day in Yankee Stadium? It looked like one of those intentional mismatches college football teams arrange for homecoming weekend to ensure the alumni get a win—Michigan versus Leon's Barber College, that sort of thing.

Only this time the barbers clipped the Yankees.

Billy Rohr had been too nervous to sleep the night before the game, but once he stepped on the mound he was cool and collected. Rohr didn't allow a hit through five innings. In the 6th, Yankee outfielder Bill Robinson hit an apparent single back through the middle—but the ball deflected off Rohr's leg to Joey Foy at third, who threw to first for the out. For a moment Rohr thought his leg was too badly hurt for him to continue, but he walked off the pain and told Sox manager Dick Williams he could stay in the game.

"I nearly took him out," said Dick Williams later. "I was afraid he might hurt his arm by favoring his sore leg." An inning later, Boston catcher Russ Gibson told Williams that Rohr's stuff had *improved* since he got hurt. Mickey Mantle pinch-hit in the 8th, but Rohr got him to pop up. Tom Tresh flew to deep left to lead off the 9th, but Carl Yastrzemski made a terrific diving catch to keep the no-hitter alive. Joe Pepitone flew out next, leaving Rohr just one out away from a no-hitter over Boston's long-time rival, New York. The Red Sox and Yankees had been fighting it out in the American League for more than 60 years, but the fight had been a tad one-sided in the Yankees' favor for the past 47 or so. For Boston fans, a no-hitter against the hated Yanks might have been even more memorable than a no-hitter in a debut. Rohr was one out away from accomplishing both.

Yankee catcher Elston Howard was up next. Rohr worked the count

> ### FIRST START, BUT NOT FIRST GAME
> No modern pitcher has thrown a no-hitter in his first major league *game*, but it has been done in a pitcher's first major league *start*. In 1953, colorful St. Louis Browns right-hander Bobo Holloman threw a no-hitter in his first start. Doing so made him probably the best-remembered career 3–7 pitcher in history. In 1991, Wilson Alvarez threw a no-hitter in the first game of his rookie season with the White Sox. It would have been his first game in the majors, except that two years before Alvarez had made an appearance for the Rangers without recording an out.

to 1–2, and his fourth pitch seemed to catch the corner—but the umpire called it a ball. Two pitches later the count was full. Rohr hung a 3–2 curve, and Howard hit a clean single to right center. The no-hit bid was over. "I would have liked to have had the no-hitter," Rohr said. "But that's the way it is. Howard gets paid to hit."

Though it was Rohr's first game in the majors, he'd been through this before. Rohr had had a no-hitter broken up with two out in the 9th one year earlier in the minors. His opponent that day was the Toledo Mud Hens—then the International League affiliate of the New York Yankees.

Rohr's next start for the Sox in 1967 would be less dramatic, but just as effective. He cruised to a 6–1 victory, again over the Yankees. The success wouldn't last. After a few less-impressive outings and a stint in the Army Reserves, manager Dick Williams proclaimed that Rohr wasn't tough enough to pitch in the majors, and took away his spot in the rotation.

The 1967 season developed into something special for the Red Sox. Though the club had gone just 72–90 in 1966, they captured the '67 American League pennant. But like Rohr that day in April, the Sox came up just short of glory, losing the World Series in seven games. The Sox fell back to fourth place in 1968, but by then it didn't matter to Rohr, who was no longer with the club. He spent part of 1968 with Cleveland, then was out of the majors for good, his big league career over at age 23. Rohr's lifetime record was 3–3, his ERA 5.64. Without

MORE ROHR

Billy Rohr wasn't the only tall left-handed pitcher named Rohr to arrive in the majors in 1967. Les Rohr, no relation, was that season beginning an equally disappointing baseball career with the New York Mets. The English-born Les had been the *second* player selected in the first-ever major league amateur draft in 1965, narrowly missing becoming—if not actually famous—then at least the answer to a trivia question about who was drafted first. (Correct answer: Rick Monday.) Les Rohr put together a career record of 2–3 in parts of three seasons with the Mets. In his final major league appearance, he threw 1⅓ innings in the Miracle Mets 1969 championship season, allowing three earned runs.

the no-hitter, there was little reason to remember his name, except for what might have been that April day in New York.

Like so many stories of failed athletes, Rohr's tale does not have a pleasant ending. The former pitcher—perhaps meaning to take revenge on the world for his unsuccessful baseball career—became a lawyer.

Bobby Matthews

PART V
WHAT'S IN A NAME?

Name recognition might not be fame, exactly, but it's a sizable step in that direction. Most baseball fans remember the name Jack Murphy as the first two-thirds of Jack Murphy Stadium, former home of the Padres, though many might not know that the real-life Murphy was a local sports editor. And virtually every sports fan is familiar with the name Spalding thanks to the sporting goods company, even if more than a few don't know that the real-life Albert Spalding was a star pitcher in the 19th century.

Reach the big leagues, and you're more or less guaranteed at least a few years of name recognition. Have an extended career, and you can expect to hear "Oh yeah, I think I remember you," for the rest of your life.

Yet names of even successful players can get lost in the shuffle. Some are simply too common to be remembered. It's just as well that the six John Smiths in baseball's record books weren't all that good, because considering their name, they were destined to be forgotten whatever their talents—that is, except for John Francis Smith, a 19th-century pitcher with a career 57–78 record. He had the good fortune to be known not as John Smith, but by the far-more-memorable if notably inaccurate nickname Phenom-enal Smith. That handle alone guaranteed this John Smith greater name recognition than his fellow John Smiths. Giant outfielder James Lamar "Dusty" Rhodes had a point when he said, "You have to have a nickname to be remembered."

Others players contributed important innovations to baseball, yet are not widely known. Their names did not become tied to their ideas. Al Spalding had the good sense to name his sporting goods empire after himself, but he's an exception. Cleveland Indians manager Lou Boudreau's plight is more typical. When he shifted his infield around to the right to combat Ted Williams' pull hitting, some called it the "Boudreau Shift." But when other teams began copying the maneuver, it entered baseball history as the "Williams Shift" instead, any glory going to the victim, rather than the innovator. (In fairness, other managers had used similar shifts on other pull hitters long before Boudreau.)

The sad fact is, not every major leaguer name is des-tined to endure. "I'm a household name," noted Paul Householder, a relatively obscure 1980s outfielder, "but not a household word."

19

FORGETTABLE
NAMES TO
REMEMBER

T hey did their part. Some were talented players who had great careers that deserved to be remembered. Others, by luck or foresight, had their names attached to some element of baseball that once seemed destined to serve as their legacy, the way a .200 batting average became the legacy of shortstop Mario Mendoza, inspiration for the so-called "Mendoza line." Yet for various reasons their names are not widely known today.

LEWIS' FAME TAKES A CLIFF DIVE

In the 1910s, Duffy Lewis, Tris Speaker, and Harry Hooper formed the Boston Red Sox famed "Golden Outfield." Hooper was known for his speed, Speaker for his bat, and all three for their defensive abilities. Left fielder Lewis might have been the least talented of the trio, but for a while it seemed that his name was the one that would remain most familiar to future baseball fans.

It isn't easy to gain lasting name recognition for left field defense, but Lewis nearly pulled it off, thanks to a unique feature of his home grounds. When Fenway Park was built in 1912, a ten-foot-high grassy incline was installed in front of the left field wall, not unlike the outfield incline that once existed in Crosley Field in Cincinnati or the one recently included in Houston's new park. Lewis was the acknowledged master of playing Fenway's hill. "I'd go out to the ballpark mornings and have somebody hit the ball again and again out to the wall," he said. "I experimented with every angle of approach up the cliff until I learned to play the slope correctly."

The outfielder's skill with the hill was such that the lump of dirt itself came to be known as "Duffy's Cliff." And though Lewis last played with the Red Sox in 1917, the slope's sobriquet stuck. It seems likely it still would be known as Duffy's Cliff today, if not for the trifling fact that it no longer exists. The hill was largely removed when Thomas Yawkey bought the Sox in 1934 and was completely phased out in the years that followed. Perhaps it's for the best. One shudders at the thought of some of the less-than-graceful Red Sox left fielders of recent years trying to run up a hill and catch a baseball at the same time. But from Lewis' perspective, removing that dirt removed the best reason to remember his name. His career lasted just ten seasons and part of an eleventh, and his .284 lifetime average and 38 home runs were nothing spectacular. Harry Hooper and Tris Speaker are in the Hall of Fame. Duffy Lewis, the third member of the Golden Outfield, never came close.

Lewis managed in the minors after his playing days, then joined the Braves—first as a coach, then as traveling secretary from 1936 through 1961. He finally retired to New Hampshire at 73 and died in 1979 at the age of 91. Unlike so many parks of Lewis' era, Fenway remains in use. The only part they've torn down is the part that might have made Duffy Lewis' name famous.

WITNESS TO FAME

As a Red Sox outfielder, Duffy Lewis saw Babe Ruth hit his first major league home run in 1915. As a Braves coach, he saw Ruth hit his last in 1935. As the Braves' traveling secretary, Lewis *might* have seen Hank Aaron's first home run in 1954. Lewis was in the stadium that day, but he'd later admit that he couldn't remember if he'd witnessed the home run or not—no one realized its significance at the time. "Who ever thought," Lewis asked, "he'd catch Babe?"

HELEN DAUVRAY LOSES HER CUP

In 1892, Lord Stanley of Preston, Governor General of Canada, cemented his name into sports history by agreeing to supply the ice hockey trophy later known as the Stanley Cup. More than a century later, the Stanley Cup enjoys better name recognition in the United States than does the current Prime Minister of Canada. For all most Americans know, the Stanley Cup might *be* the current Prime Minister of Canada. If Stanley's name could become a household word based on its association with an ice hockey trophy, imagine the fame one could derive in the U.S. by linking his or her name to a baseball trophy.

In the 1880s, Helen Dauvray, real name Helen Gibson, was a well-known Broadway actress and enthusiastic baseball fan. So enthusiastic, in fact, that she married John Montgomery Ward, the New York Giants' star shortstop. And so enthusiastic that in 1887, she commissioned a $500 sterling silver trophy to honor the winner of the World Series. (The World Series back then matched the National League and the American Association pennant winners; the American League was not yet in existence.) The cup was to pass from one year's champ to the next, much as the Stanley Cup later would.

Some saw this as a blatant attempt by Dauvray to increase her name recognition for the sake of her acting career. And considering that Dauvray had her trophy prominently inscribed "The Dauvray Cup, Presented by Miss Helen Dauvray," perhaps those critics had a point. But if it was a publicity stunt, it was a successful one—more successful, anyway, than Dauvray's marriage to Ward, which didn't last all that much longer than Joe and Marilyn's union would a half century later. In the years that followed, the Dauvray Cup became perhaps professional baseball's biggest prize. In 1887, the trophy was captured by Detroit, in 1888 and 1889 by Ward's Giants, and in 1890 by Brooklyn. Each year, thanks to her Cup, Dauvray's name made the sports page in addition to the theater page.

The first snag came in 1891. The Dauvray Cup was supposed to go to the winner of the World Series between the National League and the American Association. But the Series wasn't played in 1891, and by 1892, the American Association was out of business. It was brought down in no small part by competition with the Players' League, an ill-fated circuit spearheaded by Dauvray's former husband, John Montgomery Ward. With no World Series, the Dauvray Cup lost a bit of its luster. But it still had a role in the sport, awarded instead to the National League pennant winner. In 1891, 1892, and 1893, that winner was Boston. The Beantown three-peat brought an odd rule in the Dauvray Cup's bylaws into play. According to Dauvray's instructions, her Cup belonged permanently to the team that won it three straight times.

If not for this unusual rule, the Dauvray Cup could have remained baseball's biggest prize. When the modern World Series began a decade later, the Dauvray Cup might well have been awarded to the victor. Instead, both the Cup and Helen Dauvray's name were lost to baseball history. In the case of the Cup, the loss was literal. The Dauvray Cup's present whereabouts are unknown. It could still be out there somewhere, standing on a dusty shelf or hidden away in an attic, waiting to be discovered. But the trophy's chance to provide Dauvray with lasting fame ended one hundred years ago, when the modern World Series began without the Dauvray Cup as its prize.

Dauvray remarried in 1896, this time to a Navy Admiral, and continued her acting career. She was a well-known actress in her day, but her day was a day in which actors worked on stage, not film. The fame of stage actors isn't preserved for future generations. When Dauvray died in 1923, her fame was already fading.

THE TEMPLE CUP

After the Dauvray Cup was permanently awarded to Boston, the president of the National League's Pittsburgh team, William Temple, had a cup of his own made to replace it. But the Temple Cup wasn't just given to the National League pennant winner. Instead, it went to the winner of a postseason series between the two top teams in the National League. Since the whole point of the regular season is to determine which of a league's teams is best, the first-versus-second concept never caught on and the Temple Cup was retired in 1897. The trophy is now in the Hall of Fame in Cooperstown.

LOWDERMILK LOSES ITS MEANING

Grover Lowdermilk narrowly missed baseball fame twice in his life. One of these lost chances was the passing of his place in the sport's lexicon. According to *The New Dickson Baseball Dictionary*, Lowdermilk's last name once was an eponym for wildness. In the 1910s and 1920s, you apparently could refer to a pitcher who couldn't get the ball over the plate as "a Lowdermilk," and baseball fans would nod in agreement. That might not have been the most positive way to enter America's vocabulary, but other ballplayers have done worse. Lou Gehrig's name became linked with the disease that killed him. All wildness killed was Lowdermilk's career.

"I had a lot of trouble with my control," Lowdermilk conceded long after his playing days. It was an admission more on-target than his pitches. The lanky right-hander walked 376 batters in 590 major league innings, which helps explain why his record was just 23–39 in his six-team, nine-season career, despite a good curve, a tricky delivery, and a fastball said to be as fast or faster than that of Walter Johnson. "Lowdermilk ought to be one of the greatest pitchers in the business," wrote umpire Billy Evans in 1918. "Inability to get the ball over the plate has been Lowdermilk's fatal fault."

Unfortunately for Lowdermilk's lasting name recognition, however, the expression "Lowdermilk" eventually fell into disuse.

Despite the relatively brief, unsuccessful nature of his career, it wouldn't be Lowdermilk's only missed shot at celebrity. The pitcher went 5–5 for the 1919 Chicago White Sox, the team that became known to history as the Black Sox when seven Chicago players threw the World Series to the Cincinnati Reds. (An eighth, Buck Weaver, knew about the fix but apparently didn't take part.) Chicago manager Kid Gleason had strong suspicions that the fix was in well before the Series was over, but with few options he gave star pitchers Eddie Cicotte and Lefty Williams three starts apiece anyway. Cicotte and Williams were both in bed with the gamblers, and Chicago dropped five of those six games. Had Gleason gone with honesty over quality, Grover Lowdermilk might well have been the man given some of these starts. Of course there's no guarantee that Lowdermilk would have won—he surrendered two hits, a walk, and a hit batter in the one inning he did pitch in the Series. But he likely

SPIT OUT

The whole Black Sox scandal might have turned out differently had Chicago's future Hall of Fame spitballer Red Faber not been out with an injury that October. With Faber and Dickie Kerr starting, Chicago might have won the Series even with crooked pitchers Eddie Cicotte and Lefty Williams trying to lose. On the other hand, it's possible Faber would have been drawn into the plot and banned from baseball with the rest, and it's also possible that with so many pitchers available, the fix wouldn't have been attempted at all.

Faber remained in the big leagues until 1933, spending his entire 20-year major league career with the White Sox. He compiled a career record of 254–213. Faber's post-1920 record no doubt would have been considerably more impressive had not so many of his best White Sox teammates been banned from the game following the scandal, turning the once-great Chicago club into a second division outfit.

would be remembered, either as the pitcher who saved the Series from scandal, or as the pitcher so wild that he looked like he was trying to throw the Series even if he really wasn't.

The majors finally gave up on the hard-throwing Lowdermilk in 1920. It was a career marked by near-misses with fame and not-so-near-misses with the strike zone. The often temperamental pitcher remained in the minors through 1922, then became a coal miner. He died in 1968 at the age of 83.

HALL OF FAME GAMES, EVERYDAY NAMES

Pete Rose by any other name would have had a swing as sweet. But would he be remembered as well a century from now if his name was Pete Smith or Pete Jones or Pete Johnson? Well, yes, he probably would. Rose felled a big enough record and caused a big enough stink that baseball fans likely would remember him even if he hadn't gone to the trouble of having any last name at all. But what of the Smiths and Joneses and Johnsons who had great careers but didn't give us anything as memorable as an all-time hit record or a gambling scandal to remember them by?

If you earn a place in the Hall of Fame, it more or less follows that you deserve to be famous. But that isn't always how things work out. Consider blandly named one-time superstars Joe Kelley, Fred Clarke, and George Davis. Hall of Famers all, but how much fame do they really enjoy today? A glimmer of name recognition, perhaps. Those up on their baseball history might even be able to identify their teams and positions. But surely Kelley, Clarke, and Davis enjoy nowhere near the enduring fame of more memorably monikered turn-of-the-century stars like Wee Willie Keeler, Big Ed Delahanty, Hughie Jennings, Nap Lajoie, or Sliding Billy Hamilton.

"Fate tried to conceal him by naming him Smith," Supreme Court Justice Oliver Wendell Holmes once wrote of Samuel F. Smith, author of "My Country 'Tis of Thee." One wonders if fate didn't have more luck concealing Kelley, Clarke, and Davis.

• Joe Kelley. Joe Kelley falls well short even of fellow old-time Hall of Fame Kellys Mike "King" Kelly and George "Highpockets" Kelly in the name recognition department, if only because those Kellys had cool nicknames. Joe, the left fielder of the powerful Baltimore Orioles teams of the 1890s, was apparently called "the Kingpin of the Orioles" from time to time, but as nicknames go, that's not exactly catchy. Yet Joe Kelley was unquestionably a better player than George Kelly, the first baseman for the great Giants' teams of the 1920s, and he was not all that much less talented than the great King Kelly, who played mostly outfield and catcher for the Chicago and Boston teams of the 1880s.

Perhaps the most telling comparison isn't with these other Kellys at all, but with Wee Willie Keeler, who played with Joe Kelley in the outfield on those great Baltimore teams. The undersized Keeler is widely remembered even today, a century after his career, for his .341 lifetime batting average and general ability to hit 'em where they ain't. But the handsome, cocky Kelley was considered Keeler's equal as a place hitter at the time. And while Kelley's .317 career batting average falls short of Keeler's .341, Kelley's on-base percentage tops Keeler's .402 to .388. Kelley also hit for substantially more power than his diminutive outfieldmate, compiling a career slugging percentage of .451 to Keeler's .415. Both Kelley and Keeler were considered very strong defensive players.

It's not as though Joe Kelley was a colorless performer, either. His temper was just as quick as that of teammate John McGraw. And his vanity was legendary—Kelley had the unique habit of carrying a small mirror inside his cap while he was on the field. Yet while Keeler is remembered, Kelley for the most part is not. Could part of the problem have been that one was known rather lyrically as Wee Willie Keeler, the other rather mundanely as Joe Kelley?

Kelley managed in the minors after leaving the big leagues in 1908 and did some scouting. He later landed a series of cushy government jobs thanks to his well-connected father-in-law. Kelley died in 1943 and wasn't elected to the Hall of Fame until 1971. Wee Willie Keeler had been enshrined since 1939.

• Fred Clarke. It's been noted that Fred Clarke's baseball career was not unlike John McGraw's. So why isn't Clarke as noted today? McGraw remains one of the best-known names from his era. Despite his place in the Hall of Fame, Clarke enjoys very little fame.

Clarke and McGraw both starred as players in the 1890s and early 1900s. McGraw hit .334 to Clarke's .312, but Clarke had more than twice as many at-bats, and longevity ordinarily counts for a considerable amount where baseball fame is concerned. Of course the greatest part of McGraw's fame is rooted not in his batting average but in his managerial success. Yet here, too, Clarke held his own. Clarke had only moderate success in his first assignment, as the 24-year-old boy manager of a talent-bereft Louisville club. But once he moved to Pittsburgh in 1900, he was one of the most successful managers in the business. For the first 14 seasons of his tenure there, Clarke guided Pittsburgh to four first-place finishes, four seconds, three thirds, two fourths, and a fifth, winning 1,280 games.

McGraw's managerial career began in remarkably similar fashion. Like Clarke, McGraw was a boy manager—though he started in Baltimore at age 26, two years older than Clarke. Like Clarke, his early teams had no great success. But in McGraw's first 14 full years at the helm of the New York Giants, he led the team to five firsts, five seconds, one third, two fourths, and one eighth place finish, winning a total of 1,296 regular-season games. The difference between McGraw in New York and Clarke in Pittsburgh came to barely more than one win per year during those 14 seasons.

The more significant differences between their managerial careers were issues of length and placement. McGraw was in New York, a much better town for fame than Pittsburgh. And McGraw remained in charge of the Giants through the 1930s, while Clarke gave up managing in 1915 when most of his best players jumped to the rival Federal League. When the team fell out of contention and Pittsburgh owner Barney Dreyfuss tried to cut Clarke's salary, the manager decided he'd had enough and walked away from baseball. He didn't need the money. Throughout his career, Clarke had invested wisely, acquiring a wheat and cattle farm in Kansas and an interest in a coal mine. He already was regarded as one of the wealthiest players in the game by 1916, when he bought up the oil and gas rights to ranches around his land. In early 1917, it was reported that an oil strike had made Clarke a millionaire.

The clever Clarke even invented perhaps the first flip-down sunglasses for outfielders—although he discontinued this experiment after accidentally poking himself in the eye while trying to make a catch.

McGraw made the Hall of Fame in 1937, just the second year there *was* a Hall of Fame. Despite starring as both a player and a manager, Clarke wasn't added until 1945, and certainly isn't as well known these days. Certainly managing in a small market and leaving the game before McGraw had reduced Clarke's fame—but he still had long and successful careers as both player and manager. Others have become famous on less. Would Clarke be better known today if he, not contemporary William Clarke, had been known as Boileryard Clarke?

Clarke continued to pull for the Pirates throughout his remaining years. But by the end of the 1950s, Pittsburgh had won just one championship in the half century since Clarke led the team to its 1909 victory. "This year we are going to do it," he predicted in the last summer of his life. "I can feel it."

Clarke died on August 14, 1960. Two months later the Pirates shocked the New York Yankees by winning the World Series.

• George Davis. Between 1893, when 22-year-old George Davis joined the New York Giants, and 1901, the year he left to join the Chicago White Stockings, Davis hit .332 and was regarded as one of the best fielding shortstops in baseball. That combination of offense and defense should have made him one of the best-remembered names of his era. Instead, he's probably one of the sport's least-known greats.

Why isn't Davis more famous? Certainly it didn't help that his batting average tailed off after he left New York, in part because hitting batting averages throughout baseball declined in the first two decades of the 20th century. But Davis' lifetime .295 average is still very impressive for a slick-fielding shortstop with a 20-year career. Might the real problem have been that George Davis' name wasn't as memorable as his game? There have been at least 62 Davises in major league history, and well in excess of 300 Georges.

Davis couldn't seem to find direction in life when his playing career ended in 1909 at the age of 39. He spent one year as a minor league manager, two running a bowling alley in Manhattan, five coaching baseball at Amherst College, and at least a short time selling cars in St. Louis. But despite considerable effort by baseball historians, no one seems to know what Davis did between 1920 and 1934—it isn't easy to track a man's movements when he has such a common name. It is known that Davis entered Philadelphia General Hospital in 1934 and soon was transferred to the Philadelphia Hospital for Mental Diseases, apparently suffering through the later stages of syphilis. He spent the final six years of his life in the psychiatric hospital, dying there at the age of 70. His remains were buried, somewhat appropriately, in an unmarked grave. Davis finally was elected to the Hall of Fame in 1998, 89 years after playing his last game.

20

THAT NAME'S TAKEN

In 1998, Kareem Abdul-Jabbar, the leading scorer in NBA history, filed suit against Karim Abdul-Jabbar, Miami Dolphins running back, for alleged trademark infringement. The trademark in question was his name. Basketball's Kareem, it seems, was concerned that another athlete using his name—even an athlete in a different sport—would detract from the value of his own name. The suit was settled out of court.

The NBA's all-time leading scorer might have been concerned about the marketing value of his name, but football's Abdul-Jabbar is the one who should be concerned about his long-term fame. Thirty years from now when sports fans hear his name, they won't think of him—they'll think of an extremely tall man in funny goggles. Perhaps the horse racing people were on to something when they decided that each active steed should have a different name, and that the names of famous horses should be retired forever. Until other sports adopt a similar policy, there will be those who lose out on name recognition simply because they share their names with better-known athletes.

FRANK THOMAS AND THE OTHER FRANK THOMAS

Frank Thomas, outfielder of the 1950s and 1960s, was a pretty good player. The big slugger might not have been the most popular man in baseball, but he made some All-Star teams, hit plenty of home runs, and did and said lots of memorable things. All things considered, it seemed likely that baseball fans would remember his name. And they would—just not for him.

Frank *Joseph* Thomas has been consigned to live in the shadows of Frank *Edward* Thomas, White Sox first baseman and DH of the 1990s and 2000s. This new Frank Thomas made more All-Star teams than the first, hit more home runs, won two MVP awards, and generally made the baseball world forget that the name Frank Thomas once referred to anyone else.

There's no question the new Frank Thomas is an improvement on the first, but it's hard not to feel a bit sorry for the original Frank Thomas. Not only was he a noted hitter, he was a noted character. Thomas was called "Big Donkey" for his size and reputed lack of smarts. He was also, reportedly, called "Mary" for his unusual habit of playing stewardess on team flights. By many accounts, Thomas was called even worse things behind his back. "The small trouble with Frank Thomas is that nobody can stand him," wrote Dick Young of the *New York Daily News*. "He has the most abrasive personality in baseball."

The 37-year-old Thomas' career ended in 1967, 14 homers short of 300, 38 RBIs short of 1,000, and a season and a half short of a big bump in his baseball pension. By 1969, Thomas was playing in the

BASEBALL'S ONE TRUE ACE

By all rights, Ace Adams' name should be one of the most remembered in baseball—after all, what could be more appropriate than a pitcher named "Ace." Trouble is, the name Ace is *so* appropriate for a pitcher that it's been used as a nickname for any number of other hurlers, robbing Adams—who actually was christened Ace—of his name's distinctiveness. "People still think it's a nickname, but it's right there on my birth certificate," said Adams. "I tell people my daddy was a hell of a poker player."

In truth, the Giants All-Star relief pitcher of the 1940s was named after an Adams family friend.

Adams jumped to the renegade Mexican League in 1946, ending his major league career. Long after his pitching days were over, Adams finally got a bit of mileage out of his name—he opened Ace's Liquors and Ace's Oyster Bar in Albany, Georgia.

Greater Pittsburgh Slow-Pitch Softball League. His manager sat him against high-arc pitchers.

After struggling to find employment, Thomas finally landed a job as recruiter for a small Pittsburgh business school. He stayed 18 years, never missing a day of work. At the 1994 All-Star game in Pittsburgh, the first Frank Thomas met the man who already was well on his way to replacing him as *The* Frank Thomas in public consciousness. The older man expressed no bitterness toward the youngster usurping his name. "We had our picture taken together," said the first Frank Thomas. "He seemed like a nice kid."

BILL LEE AND THE OTHER BILL LEE

Baseball's two pitching Bill Lees in many ways had similar careers. Each played 14 seasons. Each made two trips to the postseason and threw well there, though neither came away with a postseason win. Each seemed poised for stardom in his late 20s, but faded quickly in his 30s, hampered by injury—failing eyesight for the first Bill Lee, a bum left shoulder for the second. The first Bill Lee, William Crutcher Lee, won more games, 169 to 119. But the second Bill Lee, William Francis Lee, had a better winning percentage, .569 to .518. Their ERAs were a very comparable 3.54 (first Bill Lee) and 3.62 (second Bill Lee).

Yet the second Bill Lee, the one who pitched for the Red Sox and Expos in the 1970s, now dramatically overshadows his forerunner, for

FRANK THOMAS, STEWARDESS

Of all the unique aspects of the original Frank Thomas' character, perhaps none was more distinctive than his habit of serving meals on team flights. "You haven't lived," wrote one reporter, "till you've heard Frank Thomas say, 'coffee, tea, or milk?'"

"Everybody would ask me why I was helping the stewardesses," the 6'3", 200-plus-pound Thomas said. "They'd make some nasty comment. But they didn't realize that they wouldn't eat nearly as soon if I hadn't helped out. Those stewardesses have other jobs, too, you know."

Thomas decided to give up stewardessing in the early 1960s. "I just feel like I've had enough of everybody's kidding," he explained. "They'll be sorry when they don't get fed as fast. They'll miss me. Oh, yes."

two reasons. First, he came second. All else being equal, it's the modern player who'll be remembered by modern fans. But there's also the matter of color—the second Bill Lee was known for saying and doing colorful things (see page 10). The same cannot be said for the first Bill Lee, who threw for the Cubs and assorted other National League teams in the 1930s and 1940s. "Lee has no color," wrote one sports publication in 1941. "Lee resents deeply the intrusion of all things colorful on the baseball scene. . . . Lee knows that he is not colorful. But he doesn't fully know what makes others colorful."

After his playing days, the second Bill Lee made a career of his colorfulness, writing books about his colorful life and colorful opinions, and generally capitalizing on his image as a baseball rebel. The first Bill Lee, on the other hand, became a bank director, slowly went blind, and died in 1977. The second Bill Lee received three votes for the Hall of Fame. That's not much, but it's three more than the first Bill Lee ever got.

FRANK BAKER, THE OTHER FRANK BAKER, AND A THIRD FRANK BAKER
Frank Baker, Cleveland outfielder in 1969 and 1971, never stood a chance. Frank Baker, infielder with the Yankees and Orioles in the early 1970s, had it even worse. Both men shared a name not only with a major league contemporary, but also with a long-since-retired Hall of Famer. The Hall of Fame Frank Baker was, of course, Frank "Home Run" Baker, the A's and Yanks third baseman so labeled for his pair of long balls in the 1911 World Series. The careers of the two Frank Bakers who followed proved that there's one thing worse than being a mediocre player who shares his name with a Hall of Famer: being a mediocre player who shares his name with a Hall of Famer who had a nickname you can't possibly live up to.

Cleveland outfielder Frank Baker first reached the majors in late July 1969, after missing the 1967 and 1968 seasons serving as an infantryman in Vietnam. He caused a brief stir, hitting .458 in his first week with the Indians. "Not since Rudy Regalado in 1954," wrote *The Sporting News* early that August, "have Cleveland baseball fans been so excited by a rookie as they are about Frank Baker."

Clearly Cleveland fans are too easily excited. Despite his auspicious start, Regalado would get only 253 major league at-bats and hit just .249. Frank Baker would fare no better, his major league career amounting to 353 at-bats and a .232 average. But the real problem for this Baker wasn't his low batting average, it was his low home run total—he hit only four in his career. When you're a ballplayer named Frank Baker, there's no avoiding the nickname "Home Run." When you don't go deep often, the name takes on a cruel irony. "A nickname," noted English writer William Hazlitt, "is the hardest stone that the devil can throw a man."

At least Cleveland's Frank Baker had *some* home-run power. The third Frank Baker, who like the Hall of Fame Frank Baker, played infield for the Yanks, had almost none. "For a while, he was merely Frank (Triples) Baker," cracked one writer after Baker finally managed the lone home run of his four-year career. "[When he hit the homer] five players stretched out on the bench, pretending they had passed out from the shock."

Neither of these later Frank Bakers were destined for fame. Frank Baker number two hit .232 over parts of two seasons. Frank Baker number three hit .191 over parts of four seasons. But they did make it to the major leagues and deserved at least a chance to earn themselves a bit of name recognition. Instead, all they got were home run jokes.

BILLY WILLIAMS AND THE OTHER BILLY WILLIAMS

They both played outfield in the 1960s, they both hit left-handed and threw right-handed, and they both spent a long time in professional baseball. But beyond that, it's pretty tough to confuse the careers of the two Billy Williamses. Billy Williams the Chicago Cub was a Hall of Famer outfielder who hit .290 and 426 home runs in 18 seasons in the majors. Billy Williams the Seattle Pilot played 18 seasons in the *minors* before earning a four-game stint with an expansion team as a 35-year-old rookie. He went 0 for 10 in the bigs.

It wasn't much of a major league career, certainly not the sort that's destined for fame. But considering how hard this *other* Billy Williams worked to reach the majors, it seems a shame he'll have to spend the rest of his life known as the *other* Billy Williams.

HIS NAME SHALL BE CALLED WONDERFUL

All outfielder Wonderful Terrific Monds III had to do to be remembered in baseball was play a single game in the big leagues. Being named Wonderful Terrific Monds III surely would have done the rest. But though Monds hit the home run that won the 1998 AA All-Star Game, he never reached the majors, held back in part by injury.

Wonderful's brother, the less-vaingloriously named Mario Monds, successfully reached the NFL, which goes to show you the importance of not putting too much pressure on a child to succeed.

Wonderful III's father, Wonderful, Jr., a former NFL player himself, wasn't wholly to blame for his son's name. According to the family story, it was Wonderful III's great-grandfather who set the dynasty in motion when he exclaimed, "Wonderful! Terrific!" upon the birth of his son.

One wonders how close we came to having a major league prospect named "F––– Yea" Monds.

BOB GIBSON AND THE OTHER BOB GIBSON

Right-handed pitcher Robert Louis Gibson might have had it even worse than the less-than-fabulous Baker boys. The man with whom *he* shared a name, Hall of Fame right-handed pitcher Bob Gibson, was still alive when the younger Gibson pitched. No doubt this second Gibson often was introduced as "major league pitcher Bob Gibson," only to see looks of confusion and disappointment on people's faces. And no doubt he had to endure taunts from the stands that he might be Bob Gibson, but he was sure no Bob Gibson.

The second right-handed pitcher Bob Gibson (third, if you find it necessary to count the one who appeared in four games in 1890, which, of course, you should) hung around the major leagues for five years in the mid-1980s, mostly with the Brewers. This Bob Gibson threw hard, like Bob Gibson, but he didn't have Bob Gibson's control, Bob Gibson's grit, or Bob Gibson's off-speed arsenal. The lesser Bob Gibson was out of the majors after one game with the Mets in 1987, his career record 12–18. He no doubt moved on to a life of insisting to people that he really was former major league pitcher Bob Gibson.

COZY DOLAN BESMIRCHES COZY DOLAN'S GOOD NAME

Patrick Henry "Cozy" Dolan might not have been a great baseball player, but considering that he gave his life to the sport, he had a right to expect that when his name *was* remembered, it would be remembered in a respectful or at least sympathetic manner.

Dolan reached the majors as a teenage pitcher in the 1890s, but by 1900 he was making his living as an outfielder. Heading into the 1907 season, Dolan had played for six teams in ten major league seasons and hit .269 with no particular power. He was an established everyday player, though certainly not a star. Had there been money in professional football in those days, Dolan, a talented halfback, likely would have found greater fame in that sport. Instead, the most memorable part of Dolan's athletic career would be the way it ended. Dolan contracted typhoid fever during the Boston Doves' spring exhibition swing though West Baden, Indiana. He died in a Louisville hospital on March 29, thereby providing future ballplayers with yet another reason to arrive late to spring training.

After a two-season major league Cozy Dolan dry spell, Albert J. "Cozy" Dolan, reached the majors in 1909. Like the original Cozy Dolan, this new version was no star, hitting a lifetime .252 as an outfielder/third baseman and playing for six teams in parts of seven seasons. Unlike the original Cozy Dolan, this one survived his playing career and became a coach. It was in that capacity that the second Cozy Dolan ruined the name Cozy Dolan for everyone.

Shortly before a game in the 1924 pennant race, New York Giant outfielder Jimmy O'Connell offered Philadelphia Phillies' shortstop Heinie Sand $500 to not bear down too hard. The game was meaningless for the Phils, but the Giants were locked in a tight pennant race with the Dodgers. Sand reported the attempted bribe, and O'Connell was called before Commissioner Kenesaw Mountain Landis. O'Connell confessed and named four co-conspirators who he said put him up to it. The list included three future Hall of Famers—Frankie Frisch, George Kelly, and Ross Youngs—and one decidedly non-Hall of Famer, Giant coach Cozy Dolan. The stars denied any wrongdoing, and Landis took no action against them. Dolan denied taking part as well, yet he was banned from baseball for life. (O'Connell also was banned. The outfielder was just 23 years old and had hit .317 that year in limited action.)

Dolan had damned himself with his own testimony before

Commissioner Landis. Time and again, Landis had inquired about some aspect of O'Connell's description of events, and time and again, Dolan answered "I can't remember." It was an odd thing to say, considering the whole thing had taken place just days before. How could he have forgotten? Dolan later would try to explain away his apparent evasions as a misunderstanding. "I did say I didn't remember to some [of Landis' questions]," Dolan said. "But I meant in each case that I didn't know anything about the business."

Few believed Dolan's explanation. The suspicious testimony and subsequent expulsion from baseball cost him his coaching career. In the process, it cost the *original* Cozy Dolan his place in the public memory, which was all the now-departed player had left. Later baseball fans wouldn't associate the name Cozy Dolan with the outfielder who died tragically in spring training. Those who knew the name at all would think instead of the coach banned from the sport for alleged game-fixing.

The Giants held off the Dodgers in the 1924 pennant race, apparently without the help of any fixed games. But thanks to O'Connell and Dolan, the World Series against the Senators was played under a cloud of scandal. American League president Ban Johnson thought the Series should be called off entirely, arguing the New York club "is tainted in the things it represents." In the end, the Series was played, with Johnson boycotting. The Senators won in the 12th inning of the seventh game for the only championship in team history.

Dolan later made some noise about suing Landis, but he never was allowed to return to baseball, leaving the name Cozy Dolan tarnished forever. Dolan became a court bailiff and died in 1958.

21

INNOVATORS

I t doesn't happen often, but every now and then a ballplayer has a good idea. A backup catcher isn't going to cure cancer, mind you, but he might have a thought that changes the way baseball is played—say, a new piece of equipment or a better way to defend the bunt. Yet by and large, baseball's innovators are forgotten over time, their names not bound to their notions.

PATERNITY ISSUES FOR THE FATHER OF BASEBALL

Abner Doubleday is famous for being the guy we were once told invented baseball, even if it was always pretty obvious that he didn't. Alexander Cartwright is famous for being the guy who replaced Doubleday as "The Father of Baseball" in the public consciousness. But recently baseball historians have come to question Cartwright's pre-eminent place in the game's development as well. The man who's been overlooked by history, some now say, is a New York physician named Daniel Lucius Adams.

"Doc" Adams didn't invent baseball any more than Doubleday or Cartwright, of course. No one invented baseball—the game evolved slowly over the years from earlier bat-and-ball games such as rounders. But Adams as much as anyone seems to deserve the credit for many of the ideas that landed Cartwright in the Hall of Fame.

According to Cartwright's Hall of Fame plaque, it was he who set the bases 90 feet apart, established the nine-inning game, and assigned nine players per side. It now seems likely that *all* of these ideas might be more accurately credited to Adams. Cartwright, a young bank clerk, was among those who founded New York's Knickerbocker Baseball Club in 1845. And as secretary and vice president of the club, he likely played a significant role in the decision to write down the club's rules of play, a key moment in baseball history. But it was Adams, a team-mate of Cartwright on that Knickerbocker team, who chaired the club's rules committee in 1848. And it was Adams who in May 1857 was elected "presiding officer" of the first convention of baseball players. In this capacity, Adams added the now familiar 90-foot basepaths and nine-inning game to the rule book—by this point Cartwright was long gone from the New York baseball scene. Adams also apparently lob-bied for only balls caught on the fly to count as outs though he was voted down in favor of a rule allowing outs on balls fielded on one hop as well. Baseball eventually would come around to Adams' thinking on this point, too.

Adams married in 1861 and had less to do with baseball thereafter. In 1865, he and his wife moved to Ridgefield, Connecticut, effectively ending his role in the history of baseball. But Adams never lost his love for the sport. He took part in a Knickerbocker reunion game in 1875— presumably the oldest of old-timers' games—and reportedly could still "astonish all the boys with his batting" in neighborhood games into his late 70s.

Adams became president of a local bank and served as a Con-necticut State Representative. He died of pneumonia in New Haven, Connecticut, in 1899 at the age of 84. Adams might have been the most important figure in the early shaping of baseball, yet his name remains virtually unknown.

MATHEWS' BAD BREAKS

As Hall of Fame pitching careers go, 21 wins against 22 losses isn't all that impressive. Yet that's the major league tally that 19th-century pitcher William Arthur "Candy" Cummings took to Cooperstown. In fairness, Cummings also posted a 124–72 mark during four seasons in the National Association, a circuit that predated the National League but generally is not considered "major league" these days. Still, there's little in Cummings' statistical record to suggest a place among the game's greats.

Cummings' fame rests entirely on the fact that he, to quote the words preserved in bronze on his Hall of Fame plaque, "pitched [the] first curve ball in baseball history." That makes Cummings perhaps the only ballplayer ever elected to the Hall of Fame on the basis of an innovation rather than career success (not counting those elected for their role as baseball executives). Cummings' plaque goes on to state he "ended [his] long career as [a] Hartford pitcher in [the] National League's first year[,] 1876." Actually, Cummings ended his career in 1877 with a lackluster 5–14 record in Cincinnati, which goes to show you that just because something is cast in bronze doesn't mean it's set in stone. What's more important than Cummings' 1877 stats, however, is the plaque's accuracy on the subject of that first curved ball. Does Cummings deserve the credit?

Any number of potential curveball inventors have been put forward over the years. But arguably the leading rival to Cummings' claim is another early pitcher named Bobby Mathews. "In his time," wrote *The Sporting News* in 1913, "[Mathews] divided with Arthur Cummings the honor of discovering the curve ball, although now that distinction is bestowed entirely on Cummings."

Cummings seems to have secured his status as the man who pitched the first curve in 1908 when he authored an article entitled, "How I

Pitched the First Curve." Mathews might well have responded with a counter-claim, except that he'd made the regrettable blunder of dying in 1898, reportedly of complications from syphilis.

Whether or not Mathews invented the curve, he generally was credited with being the first to use the pitch "scientifically," infuriating batters with unpredictable pitch sequences. Standing only 5′5½″ and weighing just 140 pounds, Mathews reportedly "depended on head work" and "outguessed the batter, hardly ever using the same delivery twice." He's credited with throwing the first "outcurve"—that is, a breaking pitch that moves away from a right-handed batter when thrown by a right-handed pitcher—and occasionally he's mentioned as a possible inventor of the spitball as well. Mathews was, in short, the original crafty junkballer.

THE FIRST WINNINGEST PITCHER

On May 4, 1871 Bobby Mathews shut out Cleveland's Forest City club for his Fort Wayne Kekiongas. It was the first game in the history of the National Association, the first professional baseball league, making Mathews the first pitcher to reach the one-win plateau.

If the National Association was today considered a major league, Mathews would come painfully close to being remembered even without getting his due as a breaking-ball innovator. Add Mathews' 132 wins in the National Association to his official major league tally of 166, and he'd have a total of 298 victories, just two short of the 300-win mark that's come to be seen as the benchmark for pitching greatness. (Some accountings give Mathews credit for only 131 wins in the National Association, leaving him three away.) So perhaps it's for the best that National Association stats don't count. It would be a shame to think that two wins cost Mathews his shot at fame. On the other hand, maybe some major league team would let him stage a comeback to get those last few victories. True, Mathews has been dead more than a century, but he was a crafty pitcher. He'd figure something out.

RUSS FORD INVENTS TOO GOOD A PITCH

In 1908, minor league right-hander Russell Ford discovered a pitch so effective that it made him a star—for a while. Ford was denied lasting fame as a pitching innovator when his pitch proved *so* effective that it was banned from the sport.

Atlanta got more than its share of rain in the spring of 1908. So much, in fact, that the Atlanta Crackers of the Southern Association couldn't just call off practice when the skies opened up or they wouldn't be ready when the season opened. So the team improvised, retreating under the stadium grandstand to stay dry and get what practice they could. Russ Ford, a promising young pitcher with Atlanta that year, was under those stands waiting out the rain with his fellow Crackers and getting some throwing in when he threw the ball that nearly ensured that his name would be remembered. The crucial pitch was a wild pitch. One of Ford's fastballs got away from him and struck a wooden post that supported the grandstand. His catcher retrieved the baseball, and Ford tried another fastball—only this time his pitch had a sharp break. When Ford examined the ball he noticed that it had been scuffed on one side when it grazed the grandstand support. The abrasion, he realized, must have caused the ball to move.

This was extremely valuable information, for two reasons. First, in

GOLDSMITH STAKES A CLAIM

Bobby Mathews died too soon to defend any claim he might have had on the invention of the curveball. Fred Goldsmith wasn't going to make that mistake. Goldsmith lived until 1939, arguing till the end that credit for the curve rightfully belonged to him. Goldsmith was a fine pitcher, but it's difficult to take his claims about inventing the curve too seriously. His evidence reportedly consisted of an old article about an exhibition of curveball pitching he put on in 1870. Since Cummings, Mathews, and others are thought to have thrown curveballs in the late 1860s, Goldsmith's "proof" proved little.

Goldsmith also did little for his credibility by claiming that in addition to the curve, he'd set the record for longest measured throw of a baseball, at just over 131 yards in 1876. The sportswriter to whom Goldsmith made this claim pointed out in his article that John Hatfield, a second baseman with the New York Mutuals, had thrown a ball slightly more than 133 yards in 1872.

1908 there was nothing in the rule book to prevent a pitcher from intentionally scuffing a ball in a game. (In fact, another now-illegal pitch, the spitball, was then both legal and in common use.) And second, as far as can be determined, Ford was the first pitcher in the history of the game to note the potential of a scuffed baseball. Ford had stumbled upon a way to deliver the most effective breaking pitch in the history of the sport—but he failed to understand the value of his discovery. The pitcher later would say he didn't throw a single scuffed ball in a game that entire season.

Before the following season, Ford caught a break when a teammate caught typhoid malaria. The teammate had been drafted into the majors, but with him now incapacitated, Russ Ford got the promotion instead. Ford became property of the New York Highlanders, who assigned him to the Jersey City Skeeters in the Eastern League. It was there that Ford later claimed he "suddenly remembered the freak pitch" before a batting practice session. He searched around on the ground and found a piece of glass from a broken bottle—fortunately for Ford, there never has been a shortage of broken glass or other refuse in Jersey City—and within minutes he was throwing breaking pitches no one had ever seen before. The ball was both hopping *and* curving, Ford said, an unheard of and virtually unhittable double curve. "[Ford] either was a 'flash' for the day,"

WHEN YOU COME TO A FORK IN THE ROAD, TAKE IT

Dave Keefe might be the unheralded godfather of one of modern baseball's most effective pitches, the split-finger fastball. He's believed to be the first man to throw the forkball, a close cousin of the split-finger in which the first two fingers are spread apart even farther.

Keefe hadn't set out to invent a pitch. The forkball came to him via a fortuitous injury—he'd lost the middle finger on his pitching hand as a child. The missing middle digit created a natural forkball grip. It no doubt also made it difficult to respond non-verbally to fans who took issue with his pitching skills—Keefe compiled only a 9–17 record during five seasons in the majors, ending in 1922. He did, however, remain in baseball for decades as a coach and traveling secretary.

the pitcher said his Jersey City teammates concluded, "or else they were losing their vision."

Ford didn't let them in on his secret. He couldn't. "The success of that experiment gave me the biggest problem of my young life," Ford would later explain. "I had come across a new delivery that without doubt would make me the greatest pitcher in big league baseball—if I kept it to myself! . . . If I told other baseball pitchers about it and they started to throw the [scuffed] ball, it would soon become outlawed because of the advantage it gave a hurler over a batter. Nothing can survive in baseball which impairs the balance of the game."

Ford replaced the piece of broken glass with a more discrete small square of emery paper sewn into his mitt. Anytime he meant to deliver a scuffed ball, he went through the motions of delivering a spitball to throw other pitchers off the trail. By the end of 1909, Ford was in the majors, and for the next two years, scuffing baseballs made Ford one of the biggest stars of the game. He went 26–6 in 1910 for New York, then 22–11 the following season, the only pitcher on the team with a winning record. One sportswriter said Ford "promises to be just as good a pitcher as [Christy] Mathewson." Unfortunately, a sore arm interrupted Ford's run as one of the game's best after just two years, and his record was well below .500 in 1912 and 1913 even with the emeryball on his side. When the team asked him to take a $2,000 pay cut in 1914, he jumped to the new Federal League. For one year Ford was great again, posting a 21–6 record and allowing less than two runs a game. (It's worth noting that the level of play in the Federal League wasn't great that year.) But Ford's sore arm caught up with him in 1915 as his record fell to 5–9.

When the Federal League folded after the 1915 season, Ford was once again property of New York, but by this time his secret was out. According to Ford, one of his infielders with the Highlanders had figured out his trick and sold the information to the Cleveland Indians. Ford didn't identify the infielder, but the most likely suspect would be the brilliant but devious first baseman Hal Chase. Whoever was to blame, Ford believed Cleveland right-hander Cy Falkenberg had appropriated his emeryball in 1913, when the career 69–75 pitcher suddenly went 23–10. Ford confronted Falkenberg, but the Indians' pitcher denied knowing anything about a special pitch. Ford gave him a warning nonetheless: "Keep it mum," he cautioned, "for there won't be any more batting averages if all the [pitchers] start using it."

Once word was out, however, it was just a matter of time. Like Ford, Falkenberg jumped to the Federal League in 1914, and Ford believed this prompted the Indians to share the secret pitch with two more of their hurlers, Ed Klepfer and George Kahler. Neither had much success in the majors, with or without the emeryball, but Ford suspects one or both blabbed, because by the end of 1915, it seemed everyone was scuffing baseballs. After the 1915 season, the pitch was outlawed, just as Ford had feared. (The spitball remained legal for another five years—and even when spitters were finally banned, pitchers who depended on them were allowed to keep throwing the pitch. No such provision was made for Ford, the inventor of the emeryball.) Between the banning of his pitch and his sore arm, Ford "realized [his] bubble had burst." He wrote to new Yankee owner Colonel Ruppert explaining that he couldn't win without the emeryball. New York gave him his release.

Ford drifted through the minors for a few years, then managed a hotel and worked as an assistant cashier in a bank. He later was employed by a North Carolina textile mill. Ford died of a heart attack in 1960 at the age of 76. The pitch he invented might have been the most effective ever conceived. It was too good to last. When the emeryball was removed from the game, Ford's shot at lasting fame departed with it.

LITWHILER'S GUN

Danny Litwhiler, a .281-hitting journeyman outfielder in the 1940s, might have become famous as a baseball player—except for a long string of injuries that sapped his talents. . . . He might have become famous as the first outfielder to play a full season without making an error—except who remembers outfield defense records? . . . He might have become famous as a top college baseball coach—except college baseball isn't popular enough to make anyone famous. . . . But above all else, Danny Litwhiler might have become famous for inventing the JUGS gun. For the past quarter century, the portable radar gun that Litwhiler developed has been the primary tool used to separate future professional pitchers from future Wal-Mart employees. Yet as familiar as the radar gun is on the baseball landscape, few realize that ex-ballplayer Litwhiler was behind it.

In early October 1974, Litwhiler, then head baseball coach at Michigan State University, read an article in the student paper warning that the campus police would henceforth be clocking vehicles' speeds with radar. Most who read that article no doubt called the police a few choice names. Litwhiler instead called the police and convinced officer Adam Zutak to bring the radar gun down to the baseball field. With the police car parked between second base and the mound, two Michigan State pitchers recorded speeds in the mid-80s. Litwhiler realized immediately that he'd seen the future of baseball and fired off a letter to Commissioner Bowie Kuhn informing him of the potential of radar for baseball scouting and training. "I would guess," wrote Litwhiler, "I would be looking for a major league prospect to throw about 90 miles per hour or faster." His initial estimate would become a virtual baseball scouting law. Pitchers who can't hit 90 on the gun—including, apparently, the two Michigan State pitchers who Litwhiler had

FLOAT LIKE A BUTTERFLY

Credit for inventing the knuckleball, the most unusual pitch that remains legal and in use, often is given to Thomas "Toad" Ramsey, a heavy-drinking left-hander said to have first thrown it in 1887. But if Ramsey did indeed throw a ball that knuckled, it likely was because a severed tendon in his middle finger required him to employ some unusual grips. Ramsey drank himself to death at 41, an age at which many modern knuckleballers are still going strong.

Ed Cicotte and Nap Rucker might have been the first major leaguers to intentionally throw knuckleballs. They reportedly started experimenting with the pitch as teammates in the minors. Cicotte, more noted for his spitter than the knuckler, later become infamous as one of the "Black Sox" banned from the game after the 1920 season. He'd spend many of his remaining years working for the Ford Motor Company. Rucker never became particularly famous for anything, his career record a forgettable 134–134. That record would have been better, except Rucker was stuck on some poor-hitting, poor-fielding Brooklyn teams—ten of his 134 losses came on 1–0 scores. In 1908, he pitched a no-hit, no-walk game that wasn't even close to a perfect game—his team made three errors behind him. Rucker did do better than Ramsey and Cicotte in his later years, however, becoming mayor of Roswell, Georgia.

recruited for his initial test—would never again have a legitimate shot at the pros, however impressive their success as amateurs.

Had Litwhiler marketed the product as the Litwhiler Radar Gun, it might have made him famous. Instead he partnered with the makers of the JUGS pitching machine. The radar gun would become known as the JUGS gun, with Litwhiler remaining, as always, on the fringes of baseball fame.

22

THE SPORTING
MUSE

T he right fielder of the St. Louis Wolves had a right to be ticked
off. When comedy team Abbott and Costello bantered about
the fictional Wolves' oddly named players in their famous
"Who's on First?" routine, eight of the nine men on the field were mentioned, their names taking a prominent place in baseball history. Only
the right fielder was left out.

The Wolves and their right fielder were, of course, made up. But
other players—real players—have shared Abbot and Costello's
unnamed outfielder's fate. They narrowly lost their place in one of
those rare intersections of baseball and the arts that doesn't involve a
limited-edition LeRoy Neiman lithograph. Missing such an opportunity often means missing significant fame. After all, Who is one of the
most famous first baseman in the history of the game.

HARRY STEINFELDT, VICTIM OF POETRY
Harry Steinfeldt was denied his chance for lasting fame by a poet. On
July 10, 1910, the *New York Evening Mail* ran a short poem penned by
sportswriter Franklin Pierce Adams. Adams was a second-rate poet
named for a third-rate president, but his diamond doggerel, "Baseball's
Sad Lexicon," nonetheless sent three ballplayers to the Hall of Fame, the
game's Valhalla. In the process, it relegated Harry Steinfeldt to the realm
of barroom trivia, a place far removed from the sport's land of legends.

"These are the saddest of possible words" began Adams' poem.
"'Tinker to Evers to Chance.'
Trio of bear cubs, and fleeter than birds,
Tinker and Evers and Chance.
Ruthlessly pricking our gonfalon bubble,
Making a Giant hit into a double—
Words that are heavy with nothing but trouble:
'Tinker to Evers to Chance.'"

The poem was a homage to the talented infielders of the Chicago Cubs, written from the perspective of a New York Giants fan who'd seen the Cubs turn a few too many potential New York hits into double plays. During that era, Chicago always seemed to come up one play better than the Giants—New York finished second to the Cubs in the National League pennant race four times in five years between 1906 and 1910.

Thanks to Adams' simple verse, Cubs shortstop Joe Tinker, second baseman Johnny Evers, and first baseman Frank Chance would become synonymous with the skill at turning a double play. The poem and the three men it celebrates remain well-known nearly a century later. Back in the 1910s, the Philadelphia A's "$100,000 infield" was considered the equal of the Cubs' trio. But with no poem extolling their virtues, how many fans today could name the then-famous Philadelphia double play combination of Barry-to-Collins-to-McInnis?

In no small part thanks to Adams' verse, Tinker, Evers, and Chance were inducted into the Hall of Fame in 1946. While no one would question that they were fine ballplayers, many will argue that the three are among the dozen or so least-qualified players enshrined in the Hall. Even the Hall of Fame's own web site admits the poem played a large role in "cementing their legend and helping them gain election to the Hall of Fame as a trio 36 years later."

That's all well and good for Tinker, Evers, and Chance. But they formed only three-quarters of the vaunted Cubs infield. The forgotten fourth was Chicago third baseman Harry Steinfeldt. As the third baseman, Steinfeldt didn't quite make the cut in a poem about double plays, and one could argue that his undeniably uneuphonious name might have detracted from the verse as well. But for whatever reason,

Steinfeldt had narrowly missed the cut for lasting poetic name recognition. It's not as though he couldn't have done Tinker's or Evers' job— Steinfeldt was a skilled all-around infielder who could play wherever Chicago needed him. He had been a utility infielder with the Cincinnati Reds early in his career and drew his greatest raves as a shortstop.

With the Cubs, Steinfeldt was considered on par with his fellow infielders. He was a top defensive third baseman and had his moments with the bat, finishing second in the league in hitting and first in RBIs in 1906. "Among the baseball players of the twentieth century, there was no more popular third baseman than Harry Steinfeldt," wrote Pittsburgh columnist John H. Gruber in 1914. "Steinfeldt was a wonderful thrower, accurate fielder, and hard and timely batter."

The 32-year-old Steinfeldt was sold to St. Paul of the American Association before the 1911 season. He refused to return to the minors and was sent to the Boston Nationals instead. Either way, Steinfeldt's departure broke up the famous Cubs infield. The team didn't win another pennant until 1918, and they're still waiting for their next World Series title.

Steinfeldt wouldn't find his way into any poems in Boston either. He didn't play much in 1911 and was cut after the season. It might have been something more than the usual aging player in decline. "Harry Steinfeldt, who is under contract with the Boston Nationals, may never play ball again," read a short article in August, 1911. "He is in a Cincinnati hospital suffering from a complete nervous breakdown and is kept as quiet as possible by the physicians in charge of his case. Even Mrs. Steinfeldt sees him only twice a week. She is very much opposed to him playing ball any more and will urge him to retire permanently as soon as he is out of the hospital."

Steinfeldt apparently didn't follow his wife's advice, since he joined the Cardinals in the spring of 1912. But he was cut before the start of the season, ending his major league playing career. Steinfeldt agreed to manage Cincinnati's entry in an intended third major league known as the United States League, but the circuit folded after just a few games. Steinfeldt returned to the minors, but didn't last long there either and was soon out of professional baseball entirely. It was a precipitous fall for the man who'd been a star only a few years before. He died in 1914 at the age of 38, the cause of death listed as paralysis. Former teammates Tinker and Evers then were still in the majors, and Chance had retired only that year. While those three would enter the Hall of Fame as a group, Steinfeldt never received more than a single Hall of Fame vote in any election.

His legacy could have been very different if only Franklin P. Adams had decided to write about an around-the-horn double play.

DOYLE-TO-EVERS-TO-CHANCE

Harry Steinfeldt was replaced in the Cubs lineup in 1911 by rookie third baseman Jimmy Doyle. Doyle would become "the sensation of the year," according to columnist John H. Gruber, hitting .282 with five homers, very solid numbers for the era. Doyle had his appendix taken out that off-season. He died of a post-op infection on the first day of February.

RAINED OUT

Harry Steinfeldt might have been omitted by a poet, but Bill Voiselle and Vern Bickford were tacitly insulted by one. The pair was the other half of the 1948 Boston Braves rotation that became famous as "Spahn and Sain and pray for rain," a phrase derived from a short poem penned by a *Boston Post* sportswriter that September.

The poem didn't do Voiselle and Bickford justice. The former was 13–13 with a 3.63 ERA, the later 11–5 with a 3.27 ERA—better numbers than Spahn's 15–12, 3.71 that year. "It was no two-man pitching staff," Voiselle said decades later. "They tried to make out like it was."

Voiselle and Bickford wouldn't derive any fame from that year's postseason either. Though both recorded ERAs below 3.00 in the World Series against the Indians, each walked away with 0–1 records in Boston's six-game loss.

Voiselle was out of the majors in 1950 at the age of 31. He would be remembered, if at all, for wearing uniform number 96, a tribute to his hometown of Ninety-Six, South Carolina. The uniform number was the highest in major league history until Mitch Williams wore number 99 four decades later, robbing Voiselle of even that minor numerary recognition.

Vern Bickford improved on his 11–5 1948 rookie record, collecting 16 wins in 1949, then 19 in 1950. But he broke a finger on his pitching hand in 1951 and never had another winning season. Bickford was forced from the majors in 1954 by bone chips in his pitching elbow. Six years later, he was in the hospital with stomach cancer. Still, the ex-pitcher remained optimistic that he could beat cancer and even return to baseball in some capacity. "I believe that because of my experience I could get a coaching job," he said. "[And if not] at least I could teach my three boys something about pitching."

Bickford died a few days later, leaving his wife without a husband and his three young sons without a father and pitching coach. He was just 39. "'Spahn and Sain and pray for rain' just sounded good," Braves pitcher Johnny Antonelli would later say. "But in between there was Bickford."

THE REAL ROY HOBBS

Most departed ballplayers exist only in the record books, a string of numbers all that remains to describe their skills to future generations. But a favored few have extended their big league fame via the big screen. Jackie Robinson was immortalized in *The Jackie Robinson Story*, Babe Ruth in *The Babe Ruth Story*, and Jimmy Piersall in *Fear Strikes Out*, which, in a rare moment of Hollywood creativity, wasn't named *The Jimmy Piersall Story*. Baseball greats Dizzy Dean, Grover Cleveland Alexander, Lou Gehrig, and Ty Cobb also broadened their fame beyond the sporting set by way of the cinema. So, too, have a few

SHE NEVER GOT BACK

Katie Casey is forgotten, even though the words she theoretically spoke remain among the most familiar in baseball history. The *chorus* of Jack Norworth's 1908 song, "Take me Out to the Ballgame," is sung during the 7th-inning stretch at ballparks across the country, yet the *verses* are virtually unknown. Thus few fans realize the tune is about a "baseball-mad" young woman named Katie Casey who is given to utter the lines contained in the famous chorus. (Some versions of the song feature a "Nelly Kelly" in Ms. Casey's place.)

It's safe to say that Ms. Casey herself never seriously regretted losing her spot in baseball history, however, since she was fictional and thus above such pettiness.

lesser lights, such as one-game major leaguer Moonlight Graham, featured in *Field of Dreams.*

A case could be made that Eddie Waitkus should be on this list as well. The first baseman of the 1940s and 1950s is believed to have served as the principal inspiration for writer Bernard Malamud's classic baseball novel *The Natural,* and the subsequent Robert Redford film of the same title. But Waitkus largely missed out on the fame, since his name wasn't used in either book or film, both of which instead featured fictional lead character Roy Hobbs. Today Roy Hobbs is far more famous than Eddie Waitkus, even though Hobbs never went to the trouble of actually existing.

The name change was made with good reason. Waitkus might have served as an inspiration for Hobbs, but real-life events differed substantially from the events in the novel and film. Those familiar with *The Natural* already know the basic plot. A promising young ballplayer is shot by a woman in a hotel room, then must fight his way back into baseball. He makes his return years later and hits a dramatic home run (if you saw the movie) or strikes out (if you read the book). The real-life Waitkus was indeed shot by a woman in a hotel room and like Hobbs fought his way back. But the rest of Waitkus' story has little in common with the plot of *The Natural.*

Waitkus didn't know his assailant, a six-foot-tall, blue-eyed, 19-year-old insurance company typist named Ruth Steinhagen. But Steinhagen knew him. She'd been watching the first baseman intently from the stands since 1947, his second full year with the Chicago Cubs. She'd hung around outside the clubhouse waiting for Waitkus to come out after games. She'd even taught herself to speak Lithuanian to better understand his ethnic background.

It seemed like a harmless crush until the Cubs traded Waitkus to the Phillies after the 1948 season. Unable to see the object of her desire on the playing field, Chicago native Steinhagen wrote Waitkus letters. When he didn't write back she became even more obsessed and reportedly told her friends that if she couldn't have Waitkus, no one could. Her family suggested she see a psychiatrist. Instead, she went to see Waitkus.

On June 14, 1949, Waitkus' Phillies were in Chicago to play the Cubs. According to newspaper reports, Waitkus returned to his Chicago hotel after that afternoon's game to find a note waiting for him. "Mr. Waitkus," the message began. "It's extremely important that I see you as soon as possible. We're not acquainted but I have something of importance to speak to you about. I think it would be to your advantage to let me explain it to you." The note identified its author as "Ruth Anne Burns" and said she was staying in Room 1297-A.

Waitkus talked the matter over with teammates at the hotel bar, and apparently had some misgivings about the situation. But eventually the 29-year-old bachelor did what any 29-year-old bachelor would have done upon receiving an invitation to a woman's hotel room—he went to investigate.

Steinhagen opened the door and invited Waitkus into her room. He took a seat in a chair by the window. "I have a surprise for you," Steinhagen said, reaching into the closet. She drew out a .22 caliber rifle that she'd purchased at a pawn shop, which no doubt wasn't the surprise Waitkus had been hoping for. "What's going on here?" Waitkus asked. "For two years you've been bothering me," Steinhagen reportedly replied, "and now you're going to die."

Steinhagen fired a single shot into Waitkus' chest, piercing his right lung and lodging inches from his spine. "Baby, what did you do that for?" the ballplayer asked, then passed out. Steinhagen knelt beside him for a moment and held his hand. She later would say she intended to kill herself as well. Instead, she called the front desk and said that a man had been shot.

Steinhagen was arrested and, according to newspaper reports, offered a range of sometimes-conflicting explanations for her actions. She said she shot him because of her crush . . . she said she did it just to feel the thrill of murdering him . . . she said she did it for the fame. She also said she'd never been so happy as she was after shooting Waitkus. A jury concluded Steinhagen was insane and sent her to Kankakee State Hospital. She was released three years later, her doctors satisfied that she was cured. Seeing as she didn't shoot any more first basemen, perhaps they were right. Steinhagen returned to a long and otherwise quiet life in Chicago.

The day after the attack, newspapers reported that Waitkus was near death. The ballplayer staged what his doctors would call a near-miraculous recovery, but his 1949 season was over nonetheless. He'd been on

THE OTHER REAL ROY HOBBS?

Eddie Waitkus is the most obvious inspiration for Malamud's Roy Hobbs, but he wasn't the only ballplayer shot by a woman in a Chicago hotel room. Another Cubs infielder, young shortstop Billy Jurges, was shot in his hand and chest by showgirl Violet Valli in 1932. But since Malamud's book was published in 1952—two decades post-Jurges and just three years after the Waitkus incident—and since the mysterious woman in the story appears a better match with Steinhagen than showgirl Valli, it seems reasonable to conclude that Eddie Waitkus was the man who sparked the idea for the writer.

Additional ballplayers served as inspiration for other elements of the Roy Hobbs story. A shot off the bat of Boston Brave outfielder Carvel "Bama" Rowell, for example, shattered the clock above the right-center field wall in Ebbets Field on May 30, 1946, sending shards of glass raining down. The incident is thought to be the inspiration for Roy Hobbs' similar fictional homer.

course for his first .300 season since his rookie year and the second All-Star game appearance of his career. (He'd walked in his only All-Star at-bat back in 1948.) Waitkus, who'd won a Bronze Star for bravery in World War II, would later joke "I was safer in New Guinea."

Waitkus returned to Philadelphia's lineup for their 1950 pennant-winning campaign. He hit a very respectable .284 that year and played five more seasons as well. But he never again hit .300, never played on another All-Star team, and his once great defense seemed to go into decline. Teammate Russ Meyer would later say Waitkus wasn't the same player after the shooting.

Neither, apparently, was he the same person. Previously a friendly, intelligent man popular throughout baseball, Waitkus reportedly became somewhat paranoid about meeting new people. He also developed a serious drinking problem after his playing days, though whether this was related to the 1949 shooting is a matter of conjecture. Waitkus took a job in a Philadelphia department store when his time in baseball ended, but eventually lost both his job and his marriage to alcohol. He'd been considered one of the smartest players in the game, but Waitkus had trouble holding a decent job for most of his remaining years. He did find some happiness working with kids as an instructor at Ted Williams' baseball camp late in life. Waitkus died in 1972 at the age of 53. It was reported that the cause of death was cancer. Meyer had his own opinion. "He died of depression and he died penniless," the old pitcher said.

"The public never let Eddie up from that shooting," Meyer continued. "It destroyed him. He took to drinking pretty hard. The whole thing took its toll.

"You know, the public reaction to something like that—getting shot late at night in a girl's hotel room—is something that will make you feel guilty even if you're not. You can be innocent and say, 'I didn't know her,' and people will say, 'Yeah, yeah, sure.'"

"I don't think Eddie would like to be known as the guy who they modeled 'The Natural' after," Meyer added. "His life was no Hollywood-ending story."

THE MIGHT-BE CASEYS

Could the inspiration for The Mighty Casey, the most famous fictional power hitter in baseball history, have been a man with one career homer? Marginal 1880s Philadelphia pitcher Dan Casey claimed until his death in 1943 that *he* was the largely unrecognized inspiration for the central character in Ernest Lawrence Thayer's legendary baseball poem "Casey at the Bat." Casey's widow was still pressing his claim into the late 1950s.

In truth, it seems extremely unlikely that Dan Casey was the man cheated of a place in history as the real Casey. For starters, Casey had just that one homer in his pro career—hardly a good fit for the heroic Casey mold. And Dan Casey played in Philadelphia, while Thayer lived in Massachusetts and California when he wrote the lines. But if Dan Casey wasn't Casey, who was? Many claimants stepped forward in the decades following "Casey at the Bat's" 1888 publication. So many, in fact, that as the 20th century wore on, one newspaper voiced concern that "Original Caseys" were dying off at an alarming rate.

Thayer himself denied the name Casey had anything to do with any real ballplayer. "The only Casey actually involved, and I am not sure about him, was not a ballplayer," Thayer wrote in 1935. "He was a big, dour Irish lad of my high school days."

Jim Moore and Natalie Vermilyea, authors of the book *Ernest Thayer's 'Casey at the Bat'* identify the Irish lad in question as Daniel

Henry Casey, who in his adult years became not a ballplayer, but a Worcester, Massachusetts school teacher. *This* Casey, apparently, was a rival of Thayer in his youth. Perhaps Thayer derived some private satisfaction out of making his old enemy strike out in a key spot, if only in a poem.

This doesn't, however, rule out the possibility that a real ballplayer served as model for Casey in deed, if not in name. The best candidate for this role is Mike "King" Kelly, the greatest star of his times. Kelly joined the New York Giants on their exhibition swing through the West Coast after the 1887 season, but he did poorly on the tour, much to the disappointment of California's baseball fans. Thayer covered one of these exhibition games for the *San Francisco Daily Examiner* and made particular note of a Kelly strikeout in his article. Only months later, Thayer would famously write about a similar strikeout suffered by the Mighty Casey.

Does King Kelly deserve to be remembered as the inspiration for baseball's best-known fictional character? Perhaps. But perhaps it's appropriate that no ballplayer ever gained lasting fame as the one true Casey. The fictional Casey of Thayer's poem had his chance for glory. He came to the plate, we're told, with the tying run on second and ten thousand eyes upon him. Only the mighty Casey of the poem struck out. This fictional Casey might remain famous for his missed opportunity, but fame requires something more of real-life ballplayers. When you fail to deliver in a big opportunity, your penalty is to be forgotten.

INDEX

Birmingham Black Barons, 69
Bishop, Max, 45, 55
Black Sox scandal, 33, 36, 121, 122, 126, 127, 176
Blackwell, Ewell, 254–256
Blue Jays, Toronto, 21–22
Bluge, Ossie, 84
Boeckel, Norman Doxie "Tony", 173–174
Bogataj, Vinko, 2
Boggs, Tommy, 22
Boggs, Wade, 203
Bonds, Barry, 217, 219–220
Bonds, Bobby, 217
Bonilla, Bobby, 51
Boone, Ike, 61–62, 63–64
Borowy, Hank, 15–18, 47
Bosman, Dick, 240
Bostock, Lyman, Jr., 174, 175–176
Bostock, Lyman, Sr., 174
Boston Braves, 65, 127, 152–153, 270, 298
Boston Globe, 172, 230
Boston Nationals, 297
Boston Post, 173–174, 298
Boston Record American, 154
Boston Red Sox, 36
  1912 World Series, 28, 29
  1915 World Series, 31
  1918 World Series, 18
  1946 World Series, 45–50
  1967 World Series, 262
  1975 World Series, 10–13, 15, 110
  1986 World Series, 14, 26, 35
  trades, 109, 115
Boudreau, Lou, 227
Branca, Ralph, 53, 54
Braves, Boston. see Boston Braves
Brecheen, Harry, 47, 49
bribery. see Black Sox scandal; scandals
Brissie, Lou, 82–84
Britton, Helen, 139
Brooklyn Dodgers, 64, 66, 144–145, 185–186, 283–284
Brooklyn Eagle, 64
Brooklyn Excelsiors, 170
Brown, Bobby, 20

Brown, Mordecai "Three Finger", 91, 92
Brown, Ray, 74–75
Browning, Tom, 235–236
Buckner, Bill, 2, 14, 26, 29, 35
Buffeds, Buffalo, 108
Burg, Pete, 215
Burgess, Smokey, 5, 7

C
Caldwell, Charlie, 89, 90
Cambria, Joe, 100
Campbell, Vin, 194
Canadian-American League, 86
Canadian baseball, 21–22, 75
Candlestick Park, 209–210
Canseco, Jose, 217
Carbo, Bernie, 110
Cardinals, St. Louis. see St. Louis Cardinals
Carlton, Steve, 104
Carman, Don, 243–244
Cartwright, Alexander, 285–286, 287
Carty, Rico, 206
"Casey at the Bat" (Thayer), 303–304
Casey, Katie, 299
Cepeda, Orlando, 226–227
Chance, Frank, 93, 296, 298
changes, in game, 130
Chapman, Ray, 19
Chattanooga Lookouts, 81
Chesbro, Jack, 27, 128, 131
Chicago Cubs, 152
  1907 World Series, 91–92
  1908 World Series, 93
  1918 World Series, 76–77, 162
  1945 World Series, 15–18, 47
  poem, 295–296
Chicago Tribune, 122
Chicago Whales, 75–77
Chicago White Sox, 66, 176–178, 202–203
  1917 World Series, 33–34, 35
  1919 World Series. see Black Sox scandal
  1906 World Series, 91
  1939 World Series, 40–41

Chicago White Stockings, 131
Christian Science Monitor, 87
Cicotte, Eddie, 110, 121, 122, 271
Cincinnati Enquirer, 129
Cincinnati Post, 40
Cincinnati Reds, 89–90, 106
   1919 World Series, 33
   1939 World Series, 39–43, 153
   1940 World Series, 47, 153
   1975 World Series, 11, 12
Clabaugh, Moose, 61–62, 65–66
Clark, Jack, 17, 23
Clarke, Fred, 273, 274–275
Clarke, Horace, 201
Cleveland Forest City, 288
Cleveland Indians, 19, 22, 87, 136
Cleveland Plain Dealer, 70
Clift, Harlond, 102–104
coaches, baseball players as, 29, 30,
   160–161, 189, 205, 220, 221
Coates, Jim, 7, 8
Cobb, Ty, 93, 221, 230
College World Series, 77–78
Collins, Eddie, 34, 36
Colt .45s, Houston, 10, 114
Columbus Citizen, 127
Concepcion, Dave, 46
Conigliaro, Tony, 147–148, 154
Continental League, 75
Cooper, Cecil, 79, 208
Corcoran, Larry, 251
Counsell, Craig, 51, 52
Cowens, Al, 199
Crackers, Atlanta, 289
Cramer, Richard Ben, *Joe DiMaggio:*
   The Hero's Life, 219
Cravath, Gavvy, 132–133
Craver, Bill, 122, 123
Crespi, Frank "Creepy", 187
criminal activity, 125–126
Crosetti, Frankie, 40
Crosley Field, 117, 267–268
Cruz, Jose, 117, 117–118
Cruz, Julio, 118
Cubs, Chicago. *see* Chicago Cubs
Cuccinello, Tony, 202–205
Culberson, Leon, 35, 46

Cummings, William Arthur "Candy",
   286, 287–288
curve ball, first, 287–288
Cuyler, Kiki, 152

D
Darcy, Pat, 15
Dauvray Cup, the, 269–270
Dauvray, Helen, 269–270
Davenport, Jim, 52–53, 54–55
Davis, George, 273, 275–277
Davis, Glenn, 199
deadball era, 131–133
Demaree, Frank, 206–207
Denkinger, Don, 17, 22, 23
Dent, Bucky, 1, 26
designated hitters, 62, 157
Detroit Tigers, 86, 105
   2003 team, 76, 78, 101, 105
   World Series 1934, 43
   World Series 1940, 47
   World Series 1907, 91–92
Devil Rays, Tampa Bay, 61
Devlin, Jim, 121–122, 122–123
Dickson, Murry, 47
DiMaggio, Dom, 46
DiMaggio, Joe, 40–41, 41, 42, 91, 115,
   218–219
Doby, Larry, 87–88
Dodger Stadium, 116
Dodgers, Brooklyn. *see* Brooklyn
   Dodgers
Dodgers, Los Angeles, 258
Dodgers, Montreal, 85–86
Doerr, Bobby, 47, 50
Dolan, Albert J. "Cozy", 283–284
Dolan, Patrick Henry "Cozy", 283–284
Donlin, Mike "Turkey", 190–193
Doubleday, Abner, 285, 287
Douglas, Shufflin' Phil, 36
Doves, Boston, 283
Downing, Al, 112
Doyle, Denny, 12
Doyle, Jack, 206
Doyle, Jimmy, 298
drug and alcohol abuse, 95, 110,
   136, 229

ABOUT THE AUTHOR

Mike Robbins is a freelance writer. His work has appeared in *ESPN: The Magazine*, *MSN/CNBC MoneyCentral*, *Bottom Line/Personal*, the Forbes family of publications, and elsewhere. He's a member of the Society for American Baseball Research, and resides in Brunswick, Maine, and Pensacola, Florida.